What people are saying about Dr. David Eckman, his other books, & *Becoming What God Intended*

"Isolates the issues people have and gives solutions in a way that's fresh and profoundly biblical."

—Josh McDowell, author of over 150 books

"God has given David powerful insights to help people discover who they are in Christ and show them what a huge difference this truth can make in everyday life."

**—Chip Ingram, President,
Walk Thru the Bible Ministries; author of The Invisible War**

"This material has a well deserved reputation for being used by God to bring positive change through the creative application of the Word of God. It has been created by a man, David Eckman, who is not only a committed student of the Word of God, but one who has lived out the principles he presents in the difficult fabric of life and demonstrated the truth of them."

**—Dr. Earl Radmacher, Distinguished Professor of Theology &
President Emeritus of Western Seminary**

"How many Christians really know that their heavenly Father likes them and has a passionate delight in them? That His love is not based on how well they perform? That if they are struggling with addictions, God is not there to punish them but to bless them?" "The beautiful, inspiring message woven throughout Sex, Food, and God is that God is not distant, but close—and wants to be our heavenly Father, even our 'Daddy.'"

—Bob and Geri Boyd, Issues in Education

"David Eckman is a man you can trust. . .His teaching resonates with God's wisdom and compassion."

**—Stu Weber,
author of Tender Warrior & Four Pillars of a Man's Heart**

"I enjoyed reading Becoming Who God Intended and found it both encouraging and helpful to me personally. . .I am a big believer in submitting our imaginations to the Holy Spirit in order to allow him to "reprogram our minds" about who our Abba-Father really is."

—Steve McVey, author of Grace Walk

"Dr. Eckman's wisdom and vision helped me come face-to-face with issues I thought I had addressed long ago. The pain I have lived with for so long is now gone, thanks to being able to give all of my family background over to God."

—Cheryl, Sacramento, California

"I can personally testify that Head to Heart is a powerful discipleship process that can bring spiritual, emotional and relational health. You will also develop some deep friendships along the journey. I recommend every leader and member of our church to participate in this spiritual growth opportunity."

**—Steve Quen, Senior Pastor,
Bay Area Chinese Bible Church**

DEDICATION

to

Roy Low, Ph.D., President, Grace Biblical Seminary

Franco Lo & Staff and Students of Grace Biblical Seminary

MASTERING THE 7 SKILLS OF ROMANS
A PROBLEM-SOLUTION COMMENTARY

By

David Eckman, Ph.D.

Published by Becoming What God Intended Ministries
Celebrating 25 years in ministry

Mastering the 7 Skills of Romans - A Problem-Solution Commentary
Copyright © 2019, 2022 by David J. Eckman
2nd edition.

Published by Becoming What God Intended Ministries
P.O. Box 5246, Pleasanton, California, 94566
Library of Congress Cataloging-in-Publication Data
Eckman, David 1947.
Mastering the 7 Skills of Romans - A Problem-Solution Commentary / David Eckman.
p. 194 cm.

ISBN-13:978-0-9888629-2-0

www.WhatGodIntended.org

ACKNOWLEDGEMENTS

I have had the pleasure of over five decades of conversations on the Book of Romans with pastors Phillip Howard and Frank Griffith. Those conversations were very helpful. I thank them for the stimulating thoughts that resulted.

Without the great efforts of Gayle Encarnacion, Executive Director of Becoming What God Intended Ministries, this work would not have seen the light of day. Her diligence and attention to detail is greatly appreciated. Our Program Manager, Megan Tien, was of significant help in putting the various pieces of this publication together.

Finally, the encouragement of Carol Eckman and her enthusiasm about writing more material and books is so appreciated.

GO DEEPER

Throughout the book you can scan the QR Code to find videos and material on a particular section. You will also find other resources to go even deeper.

Tens of thousands of people around the globe have been impacted by Dr. David Eckman's material.

We invite you to go even deeper through Dr. Eckman's 5-Course Curriculum:

BC101: Becoming What God Intended: Foundations of the Spiritual Life
BC102: Theology of Romans: Mastering the 7 Skills
BC103: Head to Heart: Small Group Discipleship Experience
BC104: Theology of Emotions: How to Minister to Your Emotions
BC105: Skills For Living: A Bridge For the Gospel An Evangelistic Tool

WWW.WHATGODINTENDED.ORG

TABLE OF CONTENTS

INTRODUCTION

TWO OBSERVATIONS & THE APPROACH

CHAPTER SUMMARY: Commentaries on Romans are common, and all of the commentaries create a great wealth of resources. Creating another one, therefore, needs some justification. The justification is based on two observations. First, popularized commentaries on Romans often miss the profundities of what Paul wrote because of the broad sweep of the popular approach. Secondly, what I consider the better commentaries, ones based on the Greek language, often swamp the reader in details and the cumulative argument of Paul is lost in the mass of material. The approach we are embarking on is a **"problem-solution"** commentary based on a close reading of the Greek text. In this way, we can observe the flow of the Apostle's thought, and watch as he presented solutions. With those solutions, we are going to take another step in carefully noting and analyzing how he took the solutions the Trinity provided and turned them into usable skills. Ultimately this is a **"problem-solutions-skills"** commentary.

Romans has an exhausting amount of information in it, and for many it can be exhausting. We must be careful to make the analysis and come away with a conceptual understanding, but finally and most importantly, integrate all of it into the skills needed to live the life God intended. Why?

Christ demanded much of his listeners in the Gospels. Demands were plentiful but how to practice those demands were often not. Here are two examples that could be multiplied many times over:

"Therefore, you are to be mature, as your heavenly Father is mature. (Matthew 5:48)

"He who loves his life loses it; and he who hates his life in this world shall keep it to life eternal. (John 12:25 NAS)

How to do that is the question. In the Gospels (particularly the first three), we have the challenges, but the way of meeting them often was not addressed. That is why Paul's writings are critically important. He told the "how." How do we know this? He wrote his letters, and especially Romans, before the four Gospels which contained the demands of Christ. After the resurrection of Christ, in addition, Paul was personally mentored by Jesus. As you know, he was a most unusual Apostle. He described his relationship to the other Apostles as one who was completely outside the circle of Christ's followers. In fact, he had a murderous rage against them. To describe his circumstance as a "Johnny come lately" or in other words, one who showed up very, very late, he used the Greek term **ἔκτρωμα ektroma**. The word has several meanings: an abortion, a prematurely born child, or a child born dead. Paul probably did not mean a premature baby, but a baby born far, far beyond the expected due date.[1]

> *8 and last of all, as it were to one untimely born , he appeared to me also. (1 Corinthians 15:8)*

His Gospel was not dependent upon the Apostles' experiences or information from them. Christ directly told him what his Gospel to the Gentiles should be. In effect, Christ told Paul the "how" of the Gospel. The "how" was intimately involved with our Union with Christ. In Galatians 1:15 to 2:9, Paul emphatically stated that his Gospel to the Gentiles was directly from Christ and not from the other Apostles.

> *11 For I would have you know, brethren, that the gospel which was preached by me is not according to man. 12 For I neither received it from man, nor was I taught it, but I received it through a revelation of Jesus Christ. (Galatians 1:11-12 NAS)*

Paul himself was very conscious of the fact he was not part of the original twelve. His attitude towards his apostleship though was one of humility.

> *9 For I am the least of the apostles, who am not fit to be called an apostle, because I persecuted the church of God. (1 Corinthians 15:8-9 NAS)*

The Gospel in Romans is uniquely connected to Paul. He was given the Gospel to the Gentiles and Christ made him the Apostle to the Gentiles.[2] It was his position to make sense of the Messiah of Israel to the Gentiles. For these two reasons, we must take very seriously what we find in Paul's writings, particularly Romans: first, Paul's "seven skills" in Romans give the "how to" for the demands of the Gospels, and second, Christ gave the "how to" to Paul to share with the Gentile churches.

As we have said, in his letter Paul presented a series of challenges or problems and progressively through the Book gave solutions or answers to them. As an example, the Book of Romans initially stated that God handed humanity over to its appetites (1:24). An answer was given to this unhealthy domination of the appetites in 6:11-14. Eventually we will see him do that seven different times. To understand Romans, the Book needs to be outlined and examined by this "problem-solution" approach; otherwise, we will become quickly lost in the details, and many details exist. Paul addressed these human weaknesses (the problems) and shared the solutions through the entirety of the work. The end result should be a dynamic outline and clear understanding of its contents. Better than that, we believe it will deepen the Christian's appreciation of grace, and also deepen our appreciation of our Triune God.

The "problem-solution" approach also corresponds to what Romans actually was – a skill training manual.

Paul had seven major skills he wanted the Roman Christians to learn. The letter was not written for the acquisition of knowledge. Instead, the information would create the foundation for the acquisition of skills. This was in harmony with Paul's expressed goal at the beginning and end of the Book.

> *Through whom [Christ] we have received grace and Apostleship unto the obedient hearing of faith among all the nations on behalf of his name. (1:5)*[3]

At the beginning of the Book, Paul's purpose was to proclaim and teach so that the Christian Gentiles would listen obediently. He used the Greek word **ὑπακοη hupakoe** "to hear so as to obey." The same word

---

[1] Johannes Behm, "**ἔκτρωμα**" in <u>Theological Dictionary of the New Testament</u> ed. Gerhard Kittel, tr. and ed. Geoffrey W. Bromiley, Vol. II (Grand Rapids, Michigan: Wm. B. Eerdmans Publishing Company, 1964), pp. 465-467.

[2] Paul mentioned the Gospel that he received from Christ and he proclaimed in Romans ten times: 1:1, 9, 15, 16; 2:16; 11:28; 15:16, 19, 20; 16:25. For Paul the contents of the Gospel was the salvation of Christ apart from the Law.

[3] Unless otherwise stated, all Scripture quotations are Dr. Eckman's own translations. He is a professional translator of both Greek and Hebrew. He was a member of the National Association of Hebrew Professors and was supervised by Professor James Barr at Oxford University. James Barr was widely acknowledged as one of the leading biblical Hebrew scholars of the English speaking world. Dr. Eckman is also an author and contributor to several books one of which is the New King James Study Bible. This observation about Romans 1:5 and 16:26 is from Wendy Choy, M.A..

appeared at the end of the Book.

> *And now being manifested indeed through the writings of the prophets in harmony with the command of the eternal God unto obedient hearing of faith while making it known to all the nations. (16:26)*

Our responsibility is to read, carefully listen, and obey so that we might learn the seven skills Paul described within his Book. The largest problem and question to be answered in Romans is: why is the world of the Gentiles and the Jews morally bankrupt, and what is the way out? As that question is answered, further problems will surface and eventually the answers will be discovered.

You will notice also as you read this book that I have a special love for languages. I believe the best kind of Scriptural meditation is to translate the Hebrew and Aramaic text of the Old Testament, and to translate the Greek text of the Septuagint (Greek Old Testament), and the New Testament. I will frequently quote from two Greek Lexicons (dictionaries):

H.G. Liddell and R. Scott, Greek-English Lexicon.[4]

I like Liddell and Scott's Lexicon because they give a survey of Greek usage outside of the New Testament which is very helpful in understanding the vocabulary of the Greek New Testament.

Joseph Thayer, A Greek-English Lexicon of the New Testament.[5]

Even though it is dated, I enjoy Thayer's because it made judicious comments on the language of the New Testament that border on the devotional.

Further I resort to Brown, Driver, and Briggs, A Hebrew and English Lexicon of the Old Testament[6] because it builds its entries around the Hebrew stems or roots of words. It will never be dated. It is always helpful.

---

[4] H.G. Liddell and R. Scott, Greek-English Lexicon (Oxford: Clarendon Press, 1940, 9th ed.).

[5] Joseph Thayer, A Greek-English Lexicon of the New Testament (New York: American Book Company, 1886).

[6] Brown, Driver, and Briggs, A Hebrew and English Lexicon of the Old Testament (Oxford: Clarendon Press, 1906).

1 | THE COLLAPSE OF IDENTITY

OVERVIEW:

1. Humanity turned over to its desires (1:24)

2. Humanity turned over to its dishonorable moods (1:2)

3. Humanity turned over to a disapproved mind that failed the test (1:28)

4. Humanity experienced a moral and relational collapse (1:29-31)

CHAPTER SUMMARY: Paul wrote Romans so that the Christians in Rome could be spiritually blessed. He told them that two things are presently revealed: the Gospel of God's deliverance of us through faith and God's anger as evidenced through him turning humanity over to its own insides. Since they rejected him and embraced polytheism, he left them with the hearts that made those decisions. Such hearts have led the ancient world into moral chaos.

Paul, a slave of Christ Jesus, a called Apostle, having been set apart for the Gospel of God, 2 which he previously promised through his prophets in the holy writings, 3 concerning his Son, who was born from the seed of David according to the flesh, 4 who was marked off as the Son of God with power by the resurrection from the dead, according to the Spirit of sanctification, Jesus Christ our Lord, (1:1-4)[7]

The resurrection of Christ is God the Father's act of approval for what Jesus had done in his life and ministry and particularly in his death on a cross. Paul in Romans gave the lineage of Jesus, saying that Jesus was predicted in the Old Testament, and he was a descendant of King David. His resurrection from the dead authenticated his position as the Son of God. This resurrection was in harmony with the work of the Holy Spirit, and it was through the power of God the Father. This placed a stamp of approval on Jesus Christ. What must not be forgotten was that Jesus earned and deserved all that he received. He is eternally the Son of God, but His victory over death was won by his ministry and suffering on the Cross.

Paul was a man whose heart was continually open to Heaven. He lived his life in the presence of God so that his will and God's were in harmony.

9 For God, whom I serve in my spirit in the preaching of the Gospel of his Son, is my witness as to how unceasingly I make mention of you, 10 always in my prayers making request, if perhaps now at last by the will of God I may succeed in

---

[7] The translations are my own. If others, such as the New American Standard, are used it will be so noted.

coming to you. 11 For I long to see you in order that I may impart some spiritual gift to you, that you may be established; (1:9-11)

The word that Paul used for God's will emphasized that which God desires. Paul was not praying based on a personal grocery list, but he prayed based upon a personal sense of what God really wanted. Such awareness can only come through taking advantage of access to God's presence and conversing with God the Father through the power of the Holy Spirit and integrating the Scriptures into one's life. Of course, we should take Paul's approach as ours. We should spend enough time in God's presence so that his sympathies and desires should become our sympathies and desires. At that point, it will not only be easy to pray in a healthy way, but it will also be easy to receive effective answers.

Paul wanted to go to Rome and share with them a spiritual gift. The word gift **χάρισμα charisma** "grace or a gift" can refer to grace or a gift or a spiritual gift such as teaching (Romans 12:6-7) or ministering. As an Apostle, Paul would proclaim and teach when he arrived there. Yet before he went, he did in Romans what he would have done anyway – teach. His teaching in Romans is quite a bit different than his other writings. In Philippians, for example, he spoke of his life in Judaism and how that was a loss to him and meant less than nothing in light of participating in Christ's life (Philippians 3:4-9). In Galatians, he wrote of his relationship to the Apostles and particularly Peter (Galatians 2-3). 1 and 2 Corinthians told of his challenges as an Apostle as he addressed specific issues in the church of Corinth. Ephesians and Colossians are magisterial in their sweep of teaching concerning Christ and the Church's relationship to the Trinity. The pastoral epistles deal with the particulars and the challenges of ministry.

PAUL – THE APOSTLE OF TWO WORLDS

Romans was much different. In Romans, he presented himself as a man between two worlds: the world of the Church, and the world of Israel. Strikingly as we look at the 16 chapters in Romans, eight chapters particularly involve the church (5-6, 8, 12-16), and eight involve the Old Testament and Israel's past, present, and future (1-4, 7, 9-11). Indeed the Church was referenced and discussed in Israel's eight chapters, and Israel and the Old Testament were mentioned in the Church's eight chapters. Clearly he presented himself as the Apostle to the Gentiles (1:1, 11:13), and yet in this Book we have a detailed description of the history and role of Israel in God's plan. Paul was the unique man in the middle who could speak of the place of Israel and the place of the Church in the great program of God.

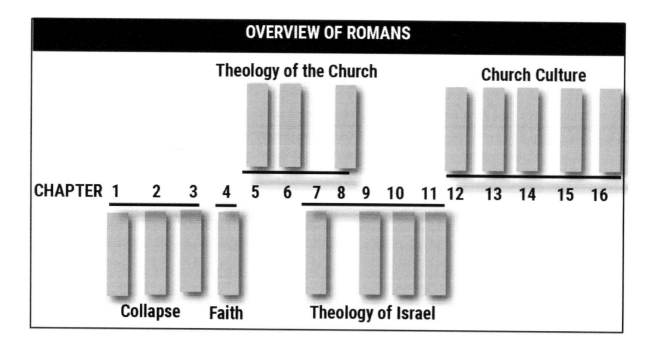

As he wrote of his enthusiasm to go to Rome, he said his eager desire was to give the Gospel in Rome. In this, Paul was not speaking of evangelism. Obviously his recipients had believed the parts of the Gospel leading to salvation. Instead, it appears that he wanted to expand deeply and profoundly on the depths of the Gospel. We can see this because after he mentioned wanting to share the Gospel, he immediately began to speak of that Gospel unashamedly and in detail. One has to appreciate what he just did. It is as if I was on the telephone with someone and I said, "I can't wait to see you so I can tell you a story." Then immediately I launch into the story. The listener on the other end of the line could say, please wait until you get here. But the Roman Christians did not have that option. Paul launched into his description.

As we said, Paul obviously considered giving the Gospel as something more than the outline of truth that would lead to salvation. For him "Gospelizing" was sharing the incredible implications of the Christ Event. This can be seen by his use of the word Gospel.

> And now to him who can establish you in accordance with the gospel that I preach and the proclamation of Jesus Christ, in accordance with that mystery which for endless ages was kept secret. (16:25)

> "Two things were being revealed: first, a righteousness of God was being revealed in the Gospel of deliverance, and secondly, a wrath of God was being revealed on those who were suppressing the truth in unrighteousness."

It is the Gospel that sanctifies, making a person Christ-like. The fruit that Paul intended to have with the Roman Christians was to take them deeper and deeper into Christian truths. This he did in two ways: first, by taking them deeper into the truth of our Union with Christ, and second, by explaining the relationship of the failure of Israel to the emergence of the Church. We can see this in detail in 1:16. Romans 1:16 is a famous verse in the Bible. It is used as a salvation verse, but in actual fact, it is a sanctification verse, a verse that shows us how to grow in our Christian faith.

> 16 For I am continually unashamed of the Gospel, for it is the inherent power of God for deliverance [salvation] to everyone who is believing [note it is a participle], to the Jew first and also to the Greek. (1:16)

In my translation of this verse from Greek, I dropped the word "salvation" and changed it to "deliverance." The reason is that when we hear the word "salvation," we think of being saved from Hell. Not once was Hell mentioned in Romans. Instead, it addressed the "Hell" of life. The Greek word simply means a deliverance of some sort. In the context of Romans, "deliverance" was from God's angry abandonment of the people of this Earth to their own desires. Paul said this deliverance was available to the person who was continually believing. As we continually believe the truth that Paul has given to us in the Book of Romans, we are delivered from the judgment of God's wrath which has enveloped the Earth. We will see what that wrath is shortly. The Gospel of sanctification and deliverance is what the Book of Romans is about.

FAITH TO FAITH

The walk of faith with God was what delivered a Christian from the effects of God's anger towards the Earth. Again, Paul was not talking about faith that brought salvation from hell, he was talking about deliverance by faith from God's present wrath. Notice that verse 17 said that the righteous person shall live by faith.

> 16 For I am continually unashamed of the Gospel, for it is the inherent power of God for deliverance to everyone who is believing, to the Jew first and also to the Greek. 17 For in it a righteousness of God is revealed out of faith unto faith; as it is written, "But the righteous person shall live by faith." (1:16-17)[8]

Verses 16 and 17 are very clearly talking about the walk of faith as opposed to salvation by faith. You can see this by the phrase in verse 17 "out of faith unto faith." Further, Paul stated the righteous person shall live by faith. Our experience with God is based on a daily exercise of faith in what Jesus has done for us and is doing for us, what the Holy Spirit is doing for us, and what God the Father is doing for us daily. As we

---

[8] John M.G. Barclay, Paul and the Gift (Grand Rapids, Michigan: Eerdmans, 2015), p. 461. Barclay points out that the priority of Israel was respected in Paul's statement.

are exercising faith, deliverance occurs. It is a deliverance from God's abandonment of this world to its own insides or heart.

Paul not only described a deliverance from sin within the life of the believer, but he also described deliverance from a wrath of God that is on display on this planet.

> *16 For I am continually unashamed of the Gospel, for it is the inherent power of God for deliverance to everyone who is believing, to the Jew first and also to the Greek. 17 For in it <u>a righteousness of God</u> is being revealed out of faith unto faith; as it is written, "But the righteous person shall live by faith." 18 For <u>a wrath of God</u> is being revealed from heaven against all ungodliness and unrighteousness of men, who are continually suppressing the truth in unrighteousness, (1:16-18)*

Notice that two things were being revealed: first, a righteousness of God was being revealed in the Gospel of deliverance, and secondly, a wrath of God was being revealed on those who were suppressing the truth in unrighteousness. As Christians, you and I must understand both of these revelations to clearly see what God is doing today in this world. On the one hand, the Gospel was being clearly proclaimed by the Bible and the Body of Christ, and on the other hand a wrath of God was very obviously present in this world. As Christians, you and I should be very aware of it.

Revealed Wrath of God: the First Set of Problems (1:18-31)

1. Handed Over to Their Appetites

A wrath of God is very evident in this world today. It is here because humanity has chosen false gods and/or false explanations for reality (such as blind evolutionary chance). To choose such was to go in the direction of cultural and personal destruction.

> *22 Affirming themselves to be wise, they became fools, 23 and changed the glory of the incorruptible God by a likeness, an image in the form of corruptible man and of birds and four-footed animals and crawling creatures. 24 Wherefore God handed them over in the appetites of their hearts to uncleanness, to the dishonoring of their bodies among themselves. (1:22-24)*

Paul described how man had chosen a false explanation for reality. Instead of believing in the one God of the Bible who has created everything, humanity in Old Testament times and Paul's time chose to believe in idols and in many gods. They rejected the creator God. Creation was credited to the false gods. As a result, God became angry and displayed his wrath by turning humanity over to their appetites. Notice that this was a negative act of non-interference. In effect, God was not doing anything but allowing our natures to take their course. He was simply turning humanity over to its own appetites (which was what it wanted anyway).[9] The term Paul used is the common term for appetites or desiring something. For example, it is used of Christ desiring to eat the Passover Meal with his disciples (Luke 22:15). It also appears in the Greek text of the Ten Commandments (Exodus 20:17) as a verb simply meaning "do not desire." Becoming enslaved to our inner life was the worst thing that could happen to us. To understand this, we must understand this peculiar wrath of God.

2. Handed Them Over to their Passions

In Romans 1, Paul said that God handed humanity over to its own insides. God did that three times. First, he handed them over to their appetites. Next he handed them over to their passions. The Greek word for "passions" refers to uncomfortable and unsettling strong emotions or moods.

---

[9] This principle goes all the way back to Adam and Eve in Genesis 3. Eve then Adam became suspicious of God's character and intentions. Further, what attracted Eve about the Tree of the Knowledge of Good and Evil was how it affected her desires: she wanted what it would give her. As a result, God allowed Adam and his offspring to be deeply suspicious of God and believing of Satan, and further, he allowed them to be handed over to their suspicion and their appetites just as he did in Romans 1:24, 26, 28.

25 For these were of such a nature they exchanged the truth of God for the lie [of idolatry], and worshiped and served the creature rather than the Creator, who is blessed unto the ages. Amen. 26 On account of this God handed them over to dishonorable passions; for their women exchanged the natural use for that which is against nature, (1:25-26)

God was not interfering with what humanity was doing on this Earth. Instead of rescuing humanity from its appetites and moods, in a display of his wrath, he turned them over to those very same appetites and moods.

W**hat this tells us was that God wanted humanity to experience the pain of its choices so that the Gospel would be so much more appealing.**

Since they had chosen idols and the many gods, it would have be silly for God to rescue humanity because first of all, humanity may not have wanted to be rescued and second, the credit might have been given to the false gods. As Christians, we must understand that we serve a delivering God who delivers us from our appetites but he does not do the same for the non-Christian.

The word "passions" is an important one to notice. Fourth Maccabees is a document written in Greek that may have been contemporaneous with Paul and Christ. The author's main point was that philosophy and reasonableness should lead to the control of one's emotions. The work did not directly address appetites or desires, but instead emotions.

Notice carefully how the term Paul used in Romans, "passions" or **πάθη pathe** "emotions," is translated in Fourth Maccabees by the New Revised Standard Version.

1 The subject that I am about to discuss is most philosophical, that is, whether devout reason is sovereign over the emotions. So it is right for me to advise you to pay earnest attention to philosophy.

3 If, then, it is evident that reason rules over those emotions that hinder self-control, namely, gluttony and lust, 4 it is also clear that it masters the emotions that hinder one from justice, such as malice, and those that stand in the way of courage, namely, anger, fear, and pain.

20 The two most comprehensive types of the emotions are pleasure and pain; and each of these is by nature concerned with both body and soul.

The term **πάθη pathe** "emotions" is translated "passions" frequently in modern Bibles. The writers such as Paul and the author of Fourth Maccabees would have had to add additional adjectives and change the context for us to derive the meaning of the word "passions." Paul used the adjective "dishonorable" so we would understand he was speaking of unhealthy emotions. Otherwise the word simply referred to our emotional states. That is why Paul had to use the adjective "dishonorable" so that we recognize what type of emotions these were.

3. Handed Over to a Rejected Mind

Paul said that God has turned humanity over to its appetites and its passions or strong negative moods. In the third handing over, God handed humanity over to its limited thinking.

28 And just as they did not see fit to personally know God any longer, God handed them over to a rejected mind, to do those things which are not proper (1:28)

A rejected mind literally meant a mind that failed the test because their mind led them to choose idolatry and the many gods of polytheism. God turned humanity over to the limited, failing functioning of their minds. This was very similar to what the father of the prodigal son did (Luke 15). The prodigal son left the father's house and the father let the son experience the fruit of his poor choices. Like the father in the story, God's love allowed humanity to experience the fruit of its choices. God was leaving humanity to its own insides so that it would flee back to the Gospel and the good Father in Heaven. This type of wrath is the background to the Gospel. We should emphasize this because it explains why God does not continually interfere in this world. Instead he allowed the world to follow the course of what it wanted, what it felt, and what it thought.

The Apostle implied a strong connection between the confusion as to ultimate reality, who God is and who he is not, and who we are as male and female. 1:26 is the strongest statement of the three "handing overs (1:24, 26, 28)" because it directly connected the embracing of a false picture of God with a false picture of what humanity is. The language is very interesting because: first, God handed them over to their appetites because of idolatry, second, he did not interfere when those appetites led in the direction of homosexuality or lesbianism, and third, this activity was against nature. In 1:25 and 1:26 the verb "exchanged" appeared (**μεταλλάσσω metallasso**). Humanity exchanged idols for God so God allowed humanity to exchange (**μεταλλάσσω metallasso**) male for female and vice versa. Twice this transition to lesbianism and homosexuality was called against nature. **φύσις** or nature was used in Greek to describe the basic nature of something be it animal, or plant or tree, or human, or divine. Here is a sample of usage.

- A Christian as a partner of the divine nature (**φύσις phusis** "nature") (2 Peter 1:4)

- Every nature (**φύσις phusis** "nature") of the beasts has been tamed by human nature (**φύσις phusis** "nature") (James 3:7)

- Branches of an olive tree according to their nature (**φύσις phusis** "nature") (Romans 11:21, 24)

> Such a choice of idolatry was totally against the nature of humanity because humanity was made in the image of God.

In the same way, a choice of sexual relations with the same gender was against the very nature of being human. God did not choose this for humanity; it was humanity's choice. God's part of the equation was not to interfere. Uncontrolled appetites had such a force that the most fundamental reality of being human, the difference between men and women was pushed aside. Uncontrolled appetites shoved aside the fundamental realities of being human. In one sense, all sin is a fundamental contradiction of what it means to be human, but homosexuality created a unique example of the basic human contradiction that comes from sin within. To be truly human, a man cannot be alone. He needs to be in a relationship to a female. This essential binary relationship is a reflection of the Image and likeness of God. Idolatry is a fundamental rejection of God's nature, and homosexuality is a fundamental rejection of humanity's nature. Since the first has occurred and God allowed it, so for the second, homosexuality, God permitted that too. Verses 24 and 26 deal with the fundamental change in relationship with God and the genders. Verse 28 dealt with the mind or the **nous (νοῦς). Nous** is the most encompassing Greek term for the mind including the thought processes, the perspective, and how the individual relates to the world and God.

HUMANITY IN REJECTING GOD REJECTS ITSELF

Verse 28 continued the pattern of humanity doing one thing and God responding by not interfering. Humanity's choice has a distinct connection to God's reaction. Humanity did not approve of God (**δοκιμάζω dokimadzo** "approved"), then God turned humanity over to a disapproved (**ἀδόκιμος adokimos** "disapproved") mind. The "a" at the beginning of **ἀδόκιμος adokimos** is a negative meaning "not."

Note the parallel actions:

- Humanity changed the nature of Deity, so God allowed the change in the nature of humanity's appetites (1:24)

- Humanity changed the nature of Deity, so God allowed the change in the nature of humanity's gender attraction (male and female) which was against the nature of humanity (1:26)

- Humanity used its mind to reject a personal relationship with God, so God allowed humanity to use that rejected mind (1:28)

The first two dealt with the nature of God and humanity and the third dealt with the nature of humanity's mind. With the first two, gender attraction became polluted and with the third, the very function of the mind was addressed. That was a strong statement that Paul made. What we have in Romans 1 was the beginning presentation of a series of problems that humanity, Gentile and Jew, created. Paul addressed these problems all the way through chapter 7. Starting at 3:21, he introduced solutions to those problems. As we proceed, we will carefully note, as we have done here, the different problems that humanity created. Also, we will isolate hints of what is to come as to the further problems and the subsequent solutions. Every problem Paul introduced, he also presented a solution in due course.

From a literary perspective, what Paul was doing is quite important to note. He introduced a series of problems within the opening chapters of the Book, and then he systematically gave their solutions. If the reader does not note those difficulties and the solutions, he or she will have a challenge in following Paul's argument and method of presentation. Sometimes his presentation of the problems were more obvious, such as the three "handing overs," or they were more subtle. For example, in Romans 1:25, he used **οἵτινες hoitines** "these." That usage emphasized the quality and the class of the people who changed the truth of God by the lie of idolatry.[10] It could be translated as "they who are of such a nature" that they changed the truth of God. This pronoun "denotes a single object with reference to its kind, its nature, its capacities, its character . . ."[11] The natural question is: why are they of such a nature? The answer awaited in chapter 5 where Paul taught that all humanity participated in the Fall of Adam and we became partakers of the change in his nature.

> **S**o it must be remembered that the best way to understand Romans is to carefully track the problems that Paul introduced, and then to carefully examine the solution that he presented.

After explaining the historical development of man's rebellion and God's response, Paul particularly connected a massive moral collapse to the rejection or disapproval of a relationship and knowledge of God. He then stated God handed them over to a disapproved mind, a mind that failed the test of God's obvious existence. Those who have such a mind were filled with moral failings. The word for "filled" is a perfect participle implying that they have been filled up in the past with these faults and they continue on. It was one thing to have such faults. To be permanently filled with them was far worse. As he listed the failings, he first used four terms with "every" that in such a construction means "every variety of." The first four dealt with what was going on in the heart and the second four dealt with how other people were treated.

Paul then summarized the idolaters by using a significant term, "approving or putting to the test and approving" used earlier in the chapter **δοκιμάζω dokimadzo**.

> *These are of such a nature they are knowing very well the righteous expectation of God that the ones continually practicing such are worthy of death, not only the same they do, but as a group they are <u>approving</u> one another as they are practicing such. (1:32)*

THE SERIES OF TERMS IN ROMANS 1:29-31 CAN BE DIVIDED THIS WAY:	
1. The inner life and what drove it	29 being filled with every variety of unrighteousness, wickedness (Satanic maliciousness), greed, evil;
2. How they acted	29 full to overflowing of envy, murder, strife, deceit, malice;
3. What they became relationally	they are gossips, 30 slanderers, haters of God, insolent, arrogant, boastful, inventors of evil, disobedient to parents,
4. What they were lacking	31 without understanding, without reliability, without family affection, without mercy;

---

[10] A.T. Robertson, <u>A Grammar of the Greek New Testament in the Light of Historical Research</u> (Nashville, Tennessee: Broadman Press, 1934), p. 727.

[11] William Sanday and Arthur C. Headlam, <u>The Epistle to the Romans</u> (Edinburgh: T. & T. Clark, 1902, 5th ed.) p. 46. The term occurs in 1:25, 32; 2:15; 6:2; 9:4; 11:4; and it is particularly touching in chapter 16, see 16:4, 6, 7, 12.

Mastering the 7 Skills of Romans

The three instances of forms of approving were:

1. Not approve of a personal relationship with God (1:28)

2. Disapproved mind (1:28)

3. Approve together (1:32)

As a result, they approved of each other's vicious behavior, even murder, but they did not approve of God. The Apostle gave a completely negative view of the Gentile world. Nothing about it was redemptive or merciful. Paul said that God would deliver or save those who are believing from a series of problems he described in the Book of Romans. We will track those problems so that we will see that Paul's solutions match the difficulties. Here are the first four difficulties.

SUMMARY:
1. Humanity turned over to its desires (1:24)
2. Humanity turned over to its dishonorable moods (1:2)
3. Humanity turned over to a disapproved mind that failed the test (1:28)
4. Humanity experienced a moral and relational collapse (1:29-31)

2 | THE COLLAPSE OF RELIGION

CHAPTER SUMMARY: The intertestamental Jewish writers would completely concur that the Gentile idolaters were murderous and deeply immoral: they were a completely corrupt culture and people. In that sense, Paul was being a typical Jewish thinker and writer. Paul now turned his attention from the world of idolatry to the world of the **"righteous religious."** The religious world, and in particular, Israel, was a complete failure too and practiced the same sins!

This chapter is striking because it began with a wholesale attack on judgmentalism and concluded with the religious failure of Israel. At the beginning, he addressed the judgmental person but when he was done, starting with verse 10, it became clear the Jews were his target.

Throughout the chapter, Paul assumed true spirituality always entailed profound life transformation. Nothing else would suffice. What is critical to understand about this chapter was that Paul was going to use the reality of life change and character as the final arbitrator: did what you believe transform your life so that character change was evidenced? If not, then it was all sham!

Paul started chapter 2 by making a flat and absolute statement about those who continually judge others. It was important to note he used a present active participle meaning "continually presently judging," and he also used the same construction for "practicing," meaning "continually presently practicing." He did not tell us whether these were Jews, Gentiles, or Christians, but shortly we will find out. As we shall see, the Jews were not exempt from God's anger because they did exactly the same things as the Gentiles despite their greater privileges. He had nothing good to say about the Gentiles, but surprisingly he had nothing good to say about Judaism either.

HYPOCRISY OF LEGALISM

In Romans 1, Paul described how humanity had become degenerate, immoral, and law-breaking. This was because they walked away from a true knowledge of God and embraced idolatry. But in chapter 2, Paul transitioned from the idolaters to legalists. Surprisingly, Paul accused the legalists of being as immoral as the idolaters.

1 Therefore you are without excuse, every man who is <u>continually passing judgment</u>, for in that you are judging another of a different sort,[12] you condemn yourself; for you who are <u>judging</u> are <u>practicing</u> the same things. 2 And we know that the judgment of God rightly falls upon those who are continually <u>practicing</u> such things. 3 And do you suppose this, O man, when you are <u>passing judgment</u> upon those who are <u>practicing</u> such things and do the same, that you will escape the judgment of God? (2:1-3)

In 1:32, the verb "practicing" occurred twice, and in 2:1-3, it occurred thrice. The judging person's moral life was on the same level as the idolater. What Paul was essentially saying was that the idolaters and the law keepers were both trapped by sin and the Fall. The law keeper tried to appear moral but could not be, and the idolaters did not care to be moral. Christians must not forget that an overemphasis on rule-keeping and morality from a Christian perspective is a cover-up for hypocrisy. The only hope we have is the work of Christ and the power of the Holy Spirit. We cannot rely on our ability to keep the rules.

Kindness and Repentance

Guilt does not draw us to the God of the Bible. Divine kindness should attract us to him: his kindness and love as illustrated on the cross. Who else but a wonderfully kind Son of God would die for the likes of us?

Or the wealth of his graciousness and forbearance and patience you are looking down on, being continually ignorant that the kindness of God is leading you to a profound change of mind? You yourself, in harmony with your hard and unrepentant heart, are treasuring up anger in a day of anger and righteous revelation of God who shall repay to each according to his activity. (2:4-6)

When people do not respond to God's kindness, they will eventually face the righteous judgment of God. This judgment is based on their reaction as to whether they have responded to the Gospel or not.

W**e must not forget that the greatest deed we can do is trust in Jesus Christ and to live by the fruit of the Spirit so as to love God and others. Accepting God's kindness gives us the ability to do that.**

Wonderfully, God converts by kindness and generosity, not by intimidation and force. When non-Christians reject kindness, they really have condemned themselves. For anyone who does not want to receive kindness can only wait for judgment, not because of their sins, but because they have trampled on kindness.

The Ultimate in Doing Good

The quickest x-ray of the human heart is taken by the Gospel! The Gospel tells us very much about ourselves. When we accept the Gospel, we have done the ultimate in pleasing God. If we reject the Gospel, it is a most terrible crime against kindness and God himself. Love is spurned and spat upon.

And to those who being persuaded out of rivalry and being unpersuaded by the truth and [being persuaded] by unrighteousness, anger and outrage, tribulation and anguish upon every soul of man who produces evil damage, indeed of the Jew and of the Greek. And glory and honor and peace to everyone producing benefit, indeed of the Jew and of the Greek. For there is no favoritism with God. (2:8-11)

Out of the acceptance of the Gospel comes glory and honor and peace because the Gospel changes the human heart.[13] Paul was definitely emphasizing godly character. He also implied as to what the source of that ungodly character was in verse 2:8. Those who will be judged have not obeyed the truth, but obeyed unrighteousness. The word "obey" literally means "to be persuaded." It was a very important word because it

---

[12] ἕτερος Greek: **heteros** consistently refers to something of a different class or category. This could refer to the immoral person or possibly the non-Jewish person.

[13] It is an odd thing that such dishonorable creatures as we should be the recipients of honor by trusting in Christ. To be honored by God in a shame-honor culture was unimaginable. Such practices were reserved for gods, the nobles, and kings.

was often used to describe the Jews who rejected the Gospel. Christ, John, Paul, Peter, and the writer to the Hebrews used the verb "not persuaded" of the Jews.[14]

From living in darkness, we are now living in the light. As we live in the light and in the company of God, our hearts change towards the Father, and towards humanity. The greatest human crime is to reject the God who died on the Cross for us. No greater wrongdoing exists, nor is there any greater act of moral blindness than that, because what more can the Son of God do for anyone than to die in their stead and promise Heaven for free by faith?

You Are Your Secrets

Many of us are massive piles of excuses. Many can justify anything and excuse themselves from everything. Deep within themselves, they keep the truth of who they are hidden, and the decisions they have made about life very well hidden.

> *"The quickest x-ray of the human heart is taken by the Gospel! The Gospel tells us very much about ourselves."*

> *For when Gentiles who do not have Law by nature the things of the Law should do, those not having Law are a Law to themselves. They are of such a nature they are showing the work of the Law written in their hearts while the conscience of them are witnessing, and their reasonings either accusing or defending them, in a day when God will judge the hidden things of men according to my Gospel through Jesus Christ. (2:14-16)*

At the Great White Throne Judgment of the unsaved dead, Jesus will evaluate what unsaved people have done and the secrets of their hearts. In Revelation 20:11-15, we are told that the scrolls of a person's life or the details of their life story will be examined at this judgment. In Romans 2, we are told that the secrets hidden deep within their souls will be brought to the surface so as to be clearly seen. All of this will be done before the face of Jesus who died for everyone and who will be evaluating everyone. That is why it is so important to believe the Gospel so as to avoid such a searching evaluation of our own lives.

The use of "Gentiles" in Romans 2:14 was Paul's term for Gentile Christians (1:13; 9:30; 11:11, 13, 25; 15:9). The whole thrust of this chapter was that God was demanding reality from humanity. Paul maintained that Christian Gentiles could keep the Law by intrinsic nature from the heart (**φύσις phusis** "nature"). Paul's assumption that he developed throughout Romans was that belief in the Gospel resulted in a true intervention in the human heart resulting in righteous living. We must never forget that believing the Gospel is the greatest act of righteousness a human being can perform.

The Jews and the Law (2:17-29)

In the first three verses of chapter 2, Paul flatly stated that the person who was continually judging the other (who was different from them, probably the Gentile idolaters) was practicing the same things as the very people he was judging. He appeared to state that as a universal principle, but then it became obvious in verse 10 that the Jews were implicated in that universal charge, or even possibly the direct recipients of that charge. Then in another block of material in chapter 2, he directly accused the Jews of rampant hypocrisy.

> *17 But if you bear the name "Jew," and rely upon the Law, and boast in God, 18 and personally know his will, and test and approve the things that are essential, being instructed out of the Law, 19 and are confident that you yourself are a guide to the blind, a light to those who are in darkness, 20 a guide of the foolish, a teacher of young, having in the Law the embodiment of knowledge and of the truth, 21 you, therefore, who are continually teaching another [**ἕτερος heteros** "of a different sort"], do you not teach yourself? You who are proclaiming that one should not steal, do you steal? 22 You who are continually saying that one should not commit adultery, do you commit adultery? You who abhor idols, do you rob temples? 23 You who boast in the Law, through your breaking the Law, do you dishonor God? 24 For "the name of God is blasphemed among the Gentiles because of you," just as it is written. (2:17-24)*

---

[14] (John 3:36; Acts 14:2; 17:5; 19:9; Romans 10:21; 11:31; 15:31; Hebrews 3:18; 1 Peter 2:7, 8; 3:1, 20; 4:17) This verb also was the name of the Greek goddess of persuasion, **Peitho**.

Paul gave his answer to this series of questions by quoting the Old Testament Greek Version (LXX) that said Yahweh's Name was blasphemed among the Gentiles. Paul flatly assumed that Israel had failed. The answer to the series of question was "yes," the teachers of Israel were involved in gross hypocrisy. Since Paul was a leading Pharisee at one time, his accusation carried even more power than an accusation from outside that movement.

After the series of accusations, he returned to his argument for true life transformation. The uncircumcised person has a real circumcision of the heart through the Spirit and not the letter of the Law. The uncircumcised person keeps the Law and will judge the Jew who does not. In this context. the uncircumcised man who was spiritual was the Christian.[15] Paul stated flatly that the Jews were engaged in hypocrisy, for they were not keeping the Law, and were under the judgment of God.

As Paul attacked the religiosity of the Jews, we must not forget this was nothing new.

The Old Testament was a long and detailed history of the failure of Israel to keep the Law.

Paul's argument that the Law cannot be kept was not based primarily on a theological or psychological insight, but on the history of Israel. Not only did the Old Testament personalities and prophets speak of the failure of the nation to keep the Law, Paul's contemporary Jewish writers said the same. First of all, the Old Testament recounted the record of Israelite failure. In fact, at the same time Moses received the Law on Mount Sinai, the people had Aaron make a Golden Calf to worship. Both the Northern Kingdom Israel and the Southern Kingdom Judah both went into captivity because they broke the Law and worshipped false gods. As he was in captivity, Daniel recounted the failure of the people in prayer.

> *4 And I prayed to the LORD my God and confessed and said, "Alas, O Lord, the great and awesome God, who keeps his covenant and loving kindness for those who love Him and keep his commandments, 5 we have sinned, committed iniquity, acted wickedly, and rebelled, even turning aside from Thy commandments and ordinances. 6 "Moreover, we have not listened to Thy servants the prophets, who spoke in Thy name to our kings, our princes, our fathers, and all the people of the land. (Daniel 9:4-6 NAS)*

The Book of Malachi, the last Book of the Greek Old Testament and the English Old Testament (the Hebrew Old Testament ends with Chronicles) stated that the Jews were under the curse of God due to their mistreatment of the Temple and the Law (Malachi 2:2; 3:9; also Deuteronomy 27:16 - 29:18). The Qumran community with the Essenes abandoned Judea because they considered the people of Israel accursed, and the Temple an abomination.

Go Deeper:
Scan the QR Code to watch a video on this section or to view more resources

---

[15] In Romans 7:6 Paul contrasted again the Spirit and the letter of the Law. In that context it is readily obvious he was speaking of the Christian.

3 | THE COLLAPSE OF RELATIONSHIPS

THE PROBLEMS:

1. Humanity turned over to its desires (1:24)

2. Humanity turned over to its dishonorable moods (1:26)

3. Humanity turned over to a disapproved mind that failed the test (1:28)

4. Humanity trapped by a chaotic culture exhibiting great immorality (1:18-32)

5. The Jews adopted a performance-based religion resulting in hypocrisy (2-3)

CHAPTER SUMMARY: Both the Jews and Gentiles are trapped under sin, but God has provided a deliverance through Christ that grants righteousness as a gift. God granted the free gift of righteousness through faith.

THE ADVANTAGE OF THE JEW

One of the fascinating things about the Bible was the place of the Jews within it. In both the Old Testament and the New Testament, they were the people of privilege, yet in Romans 2, Paul told us that they had fallen under the judgments of God because they preferred religion to their own Messiah Jesus. Yet, they still had advantages.

Then what advantage has the Jew? Or what is the benefit of circumcision? 2 Great in every respect. First of all, that they were entrusted with the oracles of God. 3 What then? If some did not believe, their unbelief will not nullify the faithfulness of God, will it? (3:1-3)

The great advantage of the Jew was that they had the Word of God. They were the only nation on the face of the Earth to receive the Old Testament and the revelation of Christ in the New Testament. They experienced the ways of God in the Old Testament and the person of Christ in the New. Even with those privileges, some did not believe. Their unbelief did not nullify the faithfulness of God to his own promises. If the Jewish nation did not keep faith, that does not mean that God won't! God is faithful.

Paul's argumentation takes a strange turn. Would the special privileges of the Jews and the grace they have received, place them in the position, oddly enough, in which their hypocrisy, unbelief, and sin would make God's glory even better? The more God forgives, the greater his glory. Especially if the Jews have had a special privilege as the chosen of God, should they not have a special indulgence on God's part when it comes to sins? Since they have so many privileges, may they not have the privilege of sinning more? Unequivocally, the answer is absolutely not. He then summed up his point.

> *What then? Are we [Jews] ahead? Not at all. We previously have charged both Jews and Greeks all are under sin. (3:9)*

Old Testament Condemnation

He used the title "Greeks" as the epitome of the Gentile world and the "Jews" (Judeans) as the epitome of the twelve tribes, and stated that both were under the kingship of sin. This is a fundamental building block of Paul's theology and mission. It is the driving point of the first three chapters. Now, he dramatically underscored his point by a litany of verses from the Old Testament. Paul started the section by using the standard way of introducing an Old Testament quote, "even as it was written that. . . (3:10)"

The opening phrase is, "There is not a righteous person, not even one." This is a paraphrase from LXX Psalm 13:2 (which is Psalm 14:2 in the English Bible) and the rest of the series is largely from that Psalm that found humanity to be hopelessly corrupt. In the Greek Septuagint, the section began with, "There is no one doing gracious good, not even one." As he sometimes did, Paul changed the text by heading it up with the statement, "There is not a righteous person, not even one." That really was the summary statement for verses 11-13.

The section began with Paul stating the three things they were not doing: they were not being righteous, nor understanding, nor continually seeking God (3:10-11). Another way of putting this would be to say, "There is not a righteous one not even one, or an understanding one, nor a seeker of God." Since that was so, they fell into moral turpitude or degeneration. They went aside, and together they had become useless. Sometimes the term "useless" was translated as "worthless." That translation missed the point. We can see how Paul used the term as an adjective in Philemon describing Onesimus.

> *10 I appeal to you for my child, whom I have begotten in my imprisonment, Onesimus, 11 who formerly was useless to you, but now is useful both to you and to me. (Philemon 1:10-11 NAS)*

Just as Onesimus the slave was useless because he abandoned his master, so humanity had become useless, not worthless, because they had abandoned their Master, God. It is important to notice that Paul wrote,

> *Everyone has gone aside. Together they have become useless.*[16] *No one was a doer of gracious goodness, not even one (3:12).*

Note the word "together." Culture is a group exercise. The Greco-Roman world of polytheism took its strength from group belief and practice. Performance-based Judaism had its hypocritical standards enforced by group participation. In the same way, in chapters 12-16, Paul will call for a group participation in the new culture now entering the ancient world, the culture of the church. Following the statement on humanity becoming useless, was the statement that in Hebrew and Septuagint Greek started the section, "Not one was a doer of gracious goodness (3:12)." As we said, Paul changed the beginning of the verses of Psalm 14:1 (Hebrew Bible Psalm 13:1) from "not doing gracious goodness" to "not being righteous."

Paul went on to describe the communication habits of the ancient world. The list was dramatic. The Apostle pieced together various Psalms in his list.

1. Their throat an open tomb (Psalm 5:9)

2. The poison of asps under their lips (Psalm 140:3)

3. Mouth is full of cursing and bitterness (Psalm 10:7)

---

[16] **ἄχρηστος akrestos** "useless" is an adjective from the verb **ἀχρειόω akreriao** "I am useless" in Romans 3:12. This harmonizes with Romans 1:26, 27 where the use according to nature, in this case the Image of God in humanity, became useless also due to lusts and negative emotions.

Then, he described how dangerous they were. He transitioned from verbal abuse to physical abuse.

1. Their feet rush to spill blood (Isaiah 59:7)[17]

2. Their paths are filled with ruin and humiliation (Isaiah 59:7)

3. Personally they have not known a path of peace (Isaiah 59:8)

Paul then returned to where he had started and addressed their relationship to God. No deep respect nor reverence was there for God (3:18). What was at the beginning and end of the section (3:10-11 and 18) explained the viciousness and violence in the middle portion (3:12-17). Paul described the history of the collapse of the Gentile and Jewish cultures in chapters 1 and 2. In chapter 3 though, he used Old Testament quotes to summarize the dismal history of humanity.

Gift of Righteousness

The existence of the moral law as enshrined in the Old Testament leaves everyone without excuse.

19 Now we know that whatever the Law says, it speaks to those who are under the Law, that every mouth may be closed, and all the world may become accountable to God; 20 because by the works of the Law no flesh will be justified in his sight; for through the Law comes the knowledge of sin. (3:19-20)

The Apostle summarized his material from chapters 1-3. No one, Gentile nor Jew, has a defense before God's expressed will in the Old Testament Law. The Law was not a source of help, but a source of insight. The Law supplied the knowledge of sin. After his history of humanity and his use of the Old Testament to describe human failure, Paul then made the great transition to the solution of his problem-solution approach.

21 But now apart from the Law a righteousness of God has been manifested, being witnessed by the Law and the Prophets, (3:21)

A different source of righteousness, inhabiting a different universe than morality or the Law, has come. This other-worldly righteousness has been witnessed to by the Old Testament in the law and the prophets. It was nothing new but it was strangely different. This paradoxical righteousness produced moral people, but not through law-keeping. Indeed, Christianity is more than just keeping rules; it is having the righteousness of God himself. In a sense, a rule keeper is a moral zero. They have done what should have been done. The person believing the Gospel is not morally neutral, but instead, positively has the righteousness of God. Amazingly it has nothing to do with the Law and morality, but it has everything to do with a simple gift of God's righteousness. You have been given the gift of God's righteousness.

Falling Short of Glory

When the Bible says that all have sinned and fallen short of glory of God, it meant something different that what Christians often think. The glory of God was the presence of God in the tabernacle and temple of the Old Testament. It had little to do with the character of God, but much to do with the presence of God.

21 But now apart from the Law a righteousness of God has been manifested, being witnessed by the Law and the Prophets, 22 even a righteousness of God through faith in Jesus Christ for all those who believe; for there is no distinction; 23 for all have sinned and fall short of the glory of God, (3:21-23)

Paul told us what the glory of God was in Romans 9:4 where he said that the covenants and the glory of God were given to Israel. The Book of Ezekiel described how the glory of God left the Temple, never to return. The nation of Israel lost the glory of God. The Gentiles never had the glorious presence of God. In verse 23, Paul said two things: both Jews and Gentiles have sinned and both Jews and Gentiles did not have the glory of God. What we Christians do have is a gift of righteousness through Jesus Christ.

---

[17] The Hebrew text has innocent blood.

The justification or total acceptance that we have in Christ was given as a gift. No strings are attached and no conditions were given except to trust Christ as the Savior.

> *being justified as a gift by his grace through the redemption which is in Christ Jesus; 25 whom God displayed publicly as a propitiation*[18] *in his blood through faith. This was to demonstrate his righteousness, because in the forbearance of God he passed over the sins previously committed; (3:24-25)*

The free gift existed because Christ became a propitiation. A propitiation was an offering that satisfied God and left a sweet smelling aroma in his nostrils as the Old Testament sacrificial system stated. The infinite value of the death of the Son of God was the reason justification was a gift. We cannot add anything to what Christ has done. To do so would be to lessen the value of Christ's work on the Cross. All is of Christ and nothing from us except the exercise of faith in what he did on the Cross. The more we realize who Jesus Christ is and what he means to God the Father, the more we will understand how God can justify us freely as a gift. Further, we will enjoy the gift more.

Righteousness Apart From Law

Paul shortly will point out that Abraham was justified by God before Law existed. In Romans 3, he argued that justification was totally apart from law, but instead was based on the sacrifice of Christ on the Cross.

> *28 For we maintain that a man is justified by faith apart from works of the Law. 29 Or is God the God of Jews only? Is he not the God of Gentiles also? Yes, of Gentiles also, 30 since indeed God who will justify the circumcised by faith and the uncircumcised through faith is one. 31 Do we then nullify the Law through faith? Absolutely not! On the contrary, we establish the Law. (3:28-31)*

Did justification nullify the law? Paul's answer was certainly not. It placed the law in correct relationship to God and to people. In the Law, it described the sacrificial system and how the system addressed the breaking of the Law. But that system was based on animal sacrifices while Christ's justification was based on his position as the Son of God. Who he was as the Son of God and what he did on the Cross infinitely satisfied God the Father. Such was something the sacrificial system never could do. With the coming of Christ, everything was changed from the Old Testament, and the door was opened so that the Gentiles who were non-Jews could become the friends of God.

With these first three chapters, we have the initial challenges that Paul addressed in Romans. At the same, time we have learned about how Paul viewed the Greco-Roman culture and also the religious Jewish culture. As we note these problems, we are laying the ground work for their solutions.

> **N**otice that the first three "turning overs" create the energy that
> produced the polytheistic world and also formed the religious performance-based culture.

The former was marked by unbridled lust and the other by unlimited hypocrisy. The reign of sin was being described and shortly we will begin to see the introduction of the solutions. The first solution appears in Romans 5. The solution is not a skill though. The solution is God's opening of the prison cell we are in. We must learn the skill of walking out of the prison of sin. Following chapter 5 with the first solution, chapter 6 will describe the first three of the seven skills.

THE PROBLEMS:
1. Humanity turned over to its desires (1:24)
2. Humanity turned over to its dishonorable moods (1:26)
3. Humanity turned over to a disapproved mind that failed the test (1:28)
4. Humanity trapped by a chaotic culture exhibiting great immorality (1:18-32)
5. The Jews adopted a performance-based religion resulting in hypocrisy (2-3)

---

[18] Excursus, "Day of Atonement," pp. 160-161.

4 | JUSTIFICATION BY FAITH

CHAPTER SUMMARY: The principle of righteousness through **faith** is exemplified by Abraham and amplified by David's experience so that righteousness by **faith** is nothing new.

Abraham's Justification

Paul transitions in his typical way by asking a question: "What then shall we say Abraham our forefather according to the flesh to have found (4:1)?" He will use Abraham to justify his doctrine of justification by faith. Using Abraham to illustrate our righteousness before God, he shared the story of Abraham, Sarah, and Isaac. Our justification is not based on what we do but on what God has done for us. If we had worked for our justification, then theoretically God would be indebted to us, and he would have to justify us.

> *3 For what does the Scripture say? "And Abraham believed God, and it was reckoned to him as righteousness."*
> *4 Now to the one who works, his wage is not reckoned as a favor, but as what is due. 5 But to the one who*
> *does not work, but believes in him who justifies the ungodly, his faith is reckoned as righteousness, (4:3-5)*

Justification has nothing to do with what we do, so God owes us nothing. Instead, he provided a Son and through that Son, he offered a way for us to be totally acceptable to him. This is based on our trust in the Son. This totally different system negated a legal one or a works-based one. Jesus was the only one who worked, not us! When Abraham was justified, he simply believed what God told him. When we are justified, it is simply because we believe what God told us. That has nothing to do with law or work.

David's Justification

In Romans 4, Paul the Apostle used the example of Abraham and David so as to tell us what justification by faith means.

> *6 just as David also speaks of the blessing upon the man to whom God reckons righteousness apart from*
> *works: 7 "Blessed are those whose lawless deeds have been forgiven, and whose sins have been covered.*
> *"Blessed is the man whose sin the Lord will not take into account." 9 Is this blessing then upon the*
> *circumcised, or upon the uncircumcised also? For we say, "Faith was reckoned to Abraham as righteousness."*
> *10 How then was it reckoned? While he was circumcised, or uncircumcised? Not while circumcised, but while*
> *uncircumcised; (4:6-10)*

With Abraham, justification was stated positively. He was made right with God. With David, it is entirely opposite. Verse 7 told us that lawless deeds have been forgiven and sins have been covered. For Abraham, he was reckoned as being righteous and for David, he spoke of not having sins reckoned or taken into account. The same word "reckoned" was used of both men, one positively and the other negatively, but the result is the same: we are right with God and we are safe from our sins. The term was found in the chapter eleven times: 4:3, 4, 5, 6 (David), 8 (David), 9, 10, 11 (us), 22, 23 (us), 24 (us).

Justification For Gentiles

As Paul argued for justification by faith, he had to answer the question of Jewish privilege. The Law was given to the Jews and Christ came to the Jews as their Messiah. What place do the Gentiles have in all of this?

> *16 For this reason it is by faith, that it might be in accordance with grace, in order that the promise may be certain to all the descendants, not only to those who are of the Law, but also to those who are of the faith of Abraham, who is the Father of us all, 17 (as it is written, "A Father of many nations have I made you") in the sight of him whom he believed, even God, who gives life to the dead and calls into being that which does not exist. (4:16-17)*

Paul went back to the Book of Genesis pointing out that the purpose of the calling of Abraham was to be a blessing to the nations. Further, he would become the Father of many nations. Paul argued, therefore, that the door of faith and justification was thrown completely open to the Gentiles or non-Jews. The purpose of the calling of Abraham was to be a blessing to all the nations of the Earth, and the sending of Jesus Christ was so that Jesus could become the Savior of all humanity.

Christ's Resurrection

Paul argued in Romans 4 that the birth of Isaac was similar to Christ's resurrection from the dead. In order for Sarah to give birth, Abraham had to believe the promises of God that he would have a Son. In order for us to become the children of God, we have to trust in the Son of God. The kind of faith that brought a child from the deadness of the womb of Sarah was the same kind of faith we placed in Christ.

> *And without becoming weak in faith he contemplated his own body, now as good as dead since he was about a hundred years old, and the deadness of Sarah's womb; 20 yet, with respect to the promise of God, he did not waver in unbelief, but grew strong in faith, giving glory to God, 21 and being fully assured that what he had promised, he was able also to perform. 22 Therefore also it was reckoned to him as righteousness. 23 Now not for his sake only was it written, that it was reckoned to him, 24 but for our sake also, to whom it will be reckoned, as those who believe in him who raised Jesus our Lord from the dead, (4:19-24)*

Paul showed again and again that faith was crucial for the life of Abraham and is crucial to our own lives. Paul wanted to connect us to Abraham's faith so that we would imitate it.

Abraham the Father of the Gentiles

With the predominance of the modern church over Judaism, the billion or so people professing Christianity, and the small number of a few million Jews, it seems that Paul's arguments for Christianity as being the legitimate follow-up to Israel are not important. No matter how huge the church may be, there is an essential issue of legitimacy. Paul the Apostle in the Book of Romans made a detailed presentation of his role as the Apostle to the Gentiles (non-Jews). On the one hand, it was a presentation of the relationship of the largely Gentile church to Israel and the Jews, and on the other hand it was a defense and explanation of his ministry. Paul's mission to the Gentiles along with the other Apostles was an astounding success. It changed the history of the Greco-Roman world and eventually the entire path of world history. But a question remained: was this mission to the Gentiles legitimate? Paul answered that question in a unique and powerful way.

The Nation of Israel quite rightly connected itself to the person of Abraham as the father of the Nation. From him came Isaac, and from Isaac came Jacob with his twelve sons. Paul of course knew that, but in

Romans 4, he pointed out something that could be easily overlooked. The purpose of the calling of Abraham went far beyond Israel. In Paul's development of his ministry and its significance, he took it all the way back to that world-changing event of the call of Abraham. Abraham is given credit for the world-changing idea of Monotheism that there is only one God. History underscored Abraham's call as the introduction of Monotheism to the ancient and modern world. In another sense, that was not the most important part.

The important part was given in the purpose of his call. The two-fold purpose was that his seed would become a great nation, and through him all the families or tribes of the Earth would be blessed.

Now the LORD said to Abram, "Go forth from your country, And from your relatives And from your father's house, To the land which I will show you; 2 And I will make you a great nation, And I will bless you, And make your name great; And so you shall be a blessing; 3 And I will bless those who bless you, And the one who curses you I will curse. And in you all the families of the Earth shall be blessed." (Genesis 12:1-3 NAS)

The term for families can refer to tribes or distinct groups. Abraham was told a great nation would descend from him, but he was also told every family on the planet would be blessed through him. Later on, two wonderful truths were connected.

5 And he took him outside and said, "Now look toward the heavens, and count the stars, if you are able to count them." And he said to him, "So shall your descendants be." 6 Then he believed in the LORD; and he reckoned it to him as righteousness. (Genesis 15:5-6 NAS)

The first truth was that of justification by faith. It was uniquely connected to him. He was counted to be righteous because he simply trusted what God had to say. Further, God added the content of what Abraham trusted. He would have a massive number of offspring. What was important to Paul was that this occurred before the foundation of the Nation of Israel and the giving of the Law. The giving of the Law was 400 years later after Abraham. Paul used these truths to show that Abraham was essentially a Gentile (Israel did not exist at the time) who was justified by faith apart from Israel and apart from the Law.

11 and he received the sign of circumcision, a seal of the righteousness of the faith which he had while uncircumcised, that he might be the father of all who believe without being circumcised, that righteousness might be reckoned to them, 12 and the father of circumcision to those who not only are of the circumcision, but who also follow in the steps of the faith of our father Abraham which he had while uncircumcised. (Romans 4:11-12 NAS)

Paul then went on in Romans 4 to underscore the fact that Gentiles had as much of a claim on Abraham as did Israelites. He was not only the father of Israel. He was also the father of all the Gentiles who were justified by faith. Remember, justification by faith occurred when there was no Law.

16 For this reason it is by faith, that it might be in accordance with grace, in order that the promise may be certain to all the descendants, not only to those who are of the Law, but also to those who are of the faith of Abraham, who is the father of us all, 17 (as it is written, "A father of many nations have I made you") in the sight of Him whom he believed, even God, who gives life to the dead and calls into being that which does not exist. (Romans 4:16-17 NAS)

In a sense, the Jews who were criticizing Paul did not notice that the entire world had a claim on Abraham as their father, not just Israel. Paul chose two things to emphasize: first, Abraham was justified apart from circumcision and apart from the Law, and second, he would become the Father of a great Nation, Israel, and the Father of the Gentiles.

Why is this important to us and to you? It means that from the very beginning, God's love embraced the whole world, every family or tribe of the Earth. 4,000 years ago you were in his thoughts at the call of Abraham. One man was introduced to show the principle of justification by faith. According to Paul, Abraham's exercise of faith defined who would become his spiritual children among the Israelites and among the Gentiles. As such, we who have trusted in Christ are now his children. Not only are we his children, but we are also the brethren of Christ.

5 | CHRIST & ADAM

CHAPTER SUMMARY: The benefits of justification by faith are applied to time, problems, and our sins. After speaking of the great benefits of salvation, Paul used Adam and the Fall of **Adam** to contrast him with **Christ** and Christ's Union with Christians.

PEACE WITH GOD

In Romans chapter 5, Paul explained to us the benefits of being justified by faith. In chapter 3, he did not develop those benefits. In chapter 4 however, he illustrated justification by faith and its positive and negative meaning with the life of Abraham and David. Justification means that righteousness is reckoned to us and sin and lawlessness are not. But it means more than that.

> *Therefore having been justified by faith, we continually have peace with God through our Lord Jesus Christ, (5:1)*

Part of the bonanza of grace is that we are continually having peace with God through our Lord Jesus Christ. Whether we feel peaceful or not does not determine our status before God. Whatever our emotional state, whether we are feeling depressed, guilty, or anxious, God is still at peace. He has an adequate answer in the death of his Son to be peaceful about us forever. Our emotions may not reflect his peace, but we should not paint God with our emotions. Instead, we should focus on God's peace with us and as a result, our own hearts may well become quite peaceful.

Past, Present, Future

In chapter 5, Paul told us what the benefits of justification by faith are. In the first verse, he said we have continual peace with God. But there is much more.

> *Therefore having been justified by faith, we have peace with God through our Lord Jesus Christ, 2 through whom also we have obtained our access by faith into this grace in which we stand; and we exult in hope of the glory of God. (5:1-2)*

In verse 2, we were told that we have permanent access in the past, the present, and in the future into the presence of God. Paul used what is called a perfect tense to tell us that our ability to come into God's presence is not determined by time. We also are permanently standing in God's grace. That is also a perfect tense. We have permanent access and permanent standing in grace while we are at peace with God, or more exactly, God is at peace with us. Because of those realities, we can shout about or exult about our future participation in the glory of God. Notice how justification by faith deals with our past, our present, and our future. In the present, we have peace and we have joyful expectation of sharing the presence of God in the future forever.

Exalting in Problems

Paul also developed the meaning of justification by faith relative to the problems that enter into our lives. Everybody has problems. Nobody escapes them. Paul said we can give a happy shout about the way God deals with our problems.

> *3 And not only this, but we also exult in our tribulations, knowing that tribulation brings about perseverance; 4 and perseverance, proven character; and proven character, hope; (5:3-4)*

The problems we have in life are not a proof of our rejection by God, but rather, those problems have become a pathway to Christ-likeness.[19] Our response in a spiritually healthy way to the tribulations or the pressures of life produces perseverance. As we continue to persevere by faith, it develops for us an approved character. As we see problem after problem of life being used to make us like Christ, it also develops within us a sense of hope. We can deal with what happens to us in life. We don't have to be afraid. What we see is that our problems have now become a blessed way to participate in the life and character of Christ. God does not want to waste one problem that we have, but he wants to use it for our spiritual good.

Hope Not Ashamed

Paul already said that problems are the pathway to becoming more like Christ, and this is the hope that we can have in our problems. Paul also recognized that Christianity goes deeper than just the development of character and living on hope.

> *3 And not only this, but we also exult in our tribulations, knowing that tribulation brings about perseverance; 4 and perseverance, proven character; and proven character, hope 5 and hope is not putting us to shame, because the love of God has been poured out within our hearts through the Holy Spirit who was given to us. (5:3-5)*

If Christianity is just character development and hope, it might lead us eventually to embarrassment, shame, and despair. After several decades, hope can be a meager meal! A heart ultimately cannot live on character development and hope. Something much deeper, however, is going on and that is the love relationship between God the Father and his children. Paul stated that God the Father's love was poured into our hearts in the past and it has had a present effect. This love was the ultimate goal and purpose of Christianity.

> To be loved by God and to love him in return ultimately is all there is. Nothing more, nothing less. Love spreads a much better meal than hope or character!

The Great Picture of Love

Paul desperately wants us to understand one thing – we are loved! To illustrate the depth of that love in its intensity, Paul gave a picture or an illustration. This illustration of the intensity of God's love is Christ on a cross.

---

[19] Many Christians may not at first emotionally agree with the thought that problems are the pathway to Christ-likeness. Paul was reflecting the attitude of the believer who has a spiritual perspective (8:5-7) and a transformed mind (12:2). Time and Christian growth may change a Christian's attitude.

6 For while we were still hopelessly morally sick, at the right time Christ died for the ungodly. 7 For one will hardly die for a righteous man; though perhaps for the beneficial man someone would dare even to die. 8 But God is continually recommending his own love toward us, in that while we were yet sinners, Christ died for us. (5:6-8)

While we could not help ourselves or do anything for ourselves, Christ died for us. Paul said that was just the right time or perfect season. We had nothing to offer, nor anything we could do in that season of weakness. Christ's death for us illustrated deeply how much God loves us. Paul then said that God is continually recommending this love towards us. We need that kind of love which loves us in the face of our weakness and failure and helplessness, and we need God's recommendation. His is a good recommendation!

Saved From the Wrath

In Romans chapter 5, Paul developed the applications of the gift of righteousness which he introduced in chapter 3. He told us what it meant. So far, we saw that we have a present peace with God, a permanent relationship with him, as well as a permanent standing in grace. Further, the tribulation and pressures of life will be used to bring character into our lives. The gift of righteousness also means something greater: we are the recipients of God the Father's love. Still more awaits us.

9 Much more then, having now been justified by his blood, we shall be saved from the wrath of God through Him. (5:9)

Justification by faith also has implications for the future. Through the blood of Christ, we shall be saved from the wrath to come. The wrath to come is God's judgment on the Earth when the Antichrist is revealed and the entire Earth worships him. Our fate has been settled by our faith in Christ. Another benefit of justification by faith is future security from God's judgment on this Earth. We have chosen Christ. Other poor souls will choose the Antichrist.

The Three Exaltations

As Paul developed justification by faith in Romans chapter 5, he told us three things we can exult about. First, he said we can exult about the future glory of God. We will participate in God's glory. Then, he said we can exult in our tribulations because God works with them for our good so that we can develop patience and hope. Now, he gives a third reality that we can exult in.

"We must remember that humanity is a profound and deep unity."

10 For if while we were enemies, we were reconciled to God through the death of his Son, much more, having been reconciled, we shall be saved by his life. 11 And not only this, but we also exult or boast in God through our Lord Jesus Christ, through whom we have now received the reconciliation. (5:10-11)

The third is that we have received the reconciliation with God through our Lord Jesus Christ. We are at peace with God. He has offered reconciliation to us; he has removed every obstacle to our full acceptance by him. Happily, we can rejoice about the great grace of our God. As we look at chapter 5, we see the benefits of justification by faith. We can exult about our future; we can exult about our tribulations, but best of all we can exult about becoming the close friends of God through reconciliation.[20]

Our Unity With Adam

These previous benefits exist because of our Union with Christ. This Union became majestically powerful in Christ. Paul in chapter 5 of Romans has stated that much has come to us through justification by faith. It is in the last half of the chapter where he told us of the greatest benefits. Previous to our faith in Christ, we were totally identified with Adam, and our fate had been sealed with him. Now in Christ, we have been liberated

---

[20] **καταλλαγή katallage** "reconciliation" The term can be used of money changing (money is changed from one state to another), or the change from an enemy to a friend, or to a reconciliation of a husband and a wife (1 Cor. 7:11).

from our connection with Adam and we now belong to Christ and are fully identified with him. Before Paul talked about the benefits of being in Christ, he told us what happened to us in Adam.

> *12 Therefore, just as through one man sin entered into the world, and death through sin, and so death spread to all men, because all sinned with him.*[21] *(5:12)*

Sin and death entered the world through Adam. We must remember that humanity is a profound and deep unity. We are totally dependent upon our predecessors for what we have become. It is not only through our DNA that we are connected to our past all the way back to Adam, but it is also spiritually that we are connected to Adam. His choice in the garden has become our day by day reality.

ADAM	
Sin ↓	5:12, 14, 17, 21
Death ↓	5:12, 14, 15, 17, 21
Condemnation ↓	5:16, 18
Condition as Sinners	5:19

To appreciate what Paul meant by sin, we must understand that sin was part and parcel of a system. The system intimately was connected to Adam's choice at the tree. Representing all of humanity, Adam in his unique and unitary role brought sin into the race, resulting in death both spiritual and physical, condemnation, and the status of all of us as sinners.

Sin brought death to all of humanity. Instead of being sustained by the Tree of Life, we became terminal beings. All were condemned by Adam's choice. Through the one man, condemnation resulted for all of humanity (5:16, 18). We entered the condition or status of sinners. **καθίστημι kathistemi** in the passive of the Greek language normally referred to the status or condition a person was placed in. In its use in the LXX (Septuagint) and the Greek New Testament, the form described the status, state, or position a person was placed in. In the bleakest and blackest terms, the sinner was established under the kingship of sin. Romans 5:14 and 17 stated that we were under the kingship of death, and 5:21 said sin reigned as a king in relationship to death. In Genesis 39:4-5 (LXX), the term described Joseph as being placed as an overseer over a household, and in James 4:4, the lover of the world took the condition or status of an enemy of God. The word occurred often in the passive and other forms as a settled condition or status. But the wonderful thing is through the second man, the last Adam, we now are totally identified with Christ. Christ is inseparable from us and we are inseparable from him.

> *"The Infinitely Loved and Lovely Son of God absorbed all the damage and sin of this universe, and through that act, he is ushering in the unheralded beauty of a new, God-centered universe."*

Not to Complain But . . .

I normally don't complain about the ways of God. That always seemed presumptuous to me. If I were to complain, I have one topic where griping would occur. It is the reality of Adam's choice ruining us. Paul's presentation of what Adam did was that one man's choice doomed us all. Notice how often the word "ONE" appears in Romans 5 from verse 12-19.

> *12 Therefore just as through __ONE__ man sin entered into the world, and death through sin, and so death spread to all men, with him **all sinned**—15 For if by the trespass of the **ONE** the **many died** 16 the __ONE__ who sinned; for on the one hand the **judgment** arose from **ONE** transgression resulting in **condemnation**, 17 For if by the trespass of the __ONE__, **death reigned** through the **ONE** 18 So then as through **ONE** transgression there resulted **condemnation** to all men, 19 For as through the **ONE** man's disobedience (refusal to listen) the many **were made sinners**,*

---

[21] Nigel Turner, <u>Grammatical Insights into the New Testament</u> (Edinburgh: T. & T. Clark, 1965), pp. 116-118.

The word "ONE" occurred eight times: five times it referred to Adam and three times it was used of his rebellion. One man and one man's act brought sin into the world, death to humanity, judgment to everyone, the reign of death over all, condemnation to every human, and the constitution of us all as sinners. Under the most basic laws of fairness, that seems ridiculously unfair. Billions and billions of people were doomed as a result. It could not get any worse, but it did. Further, Paul taught that the man's rebellion affected the entire universe.

> *For the eager expectation of creation is awaiting the revelation of the mature sons of God. For the creation was subjected to pointlessness, not willingly but on account of the one who had subjected it based on hope, because also the creation itself shall be liberated from the slavery of corruption unto the liberty of the glory of the offspring of God. For we know that the whole creation suffers together and has childbirth pains together until the present. (Romans 8:19-22)*

The entire creation or universe was subjected to decay and corruption waiting on the deliverance of humanity. What an incredible amount of destruction coming from one man and one choice. What are the implications that we see in this? First, humanity is a composite whole; we are profoundly interrelated. Just as physical DNA creates our physical identity as human beings, so our unity with one another creates our spiritual union and identity; this unity is evil and universal. Second, God determined that Adam's choice and experience of the Fall would become the universal experience of humanity. Lastly, one sinful choice was incredible in its ramifications. It is vastly worse than a human finger pushing a button to set off a nuclear explosion killing millions. The Fall reduced that nuclear explosion to puny dimensions. It is unfair, massively unfair.

THE NEW HUMANITY

One thing may change this: if the same principles that condemned us would be the principles that delivered us. With Christ, that is the case!

> He became human so that the principle of human unity
> would be used for grace instead of condemnation.

What we find is that as Adam was the Head of the Catastrophe, so Christ is more than the conqueror of the Catastrophe and the Head of a New Humanity. Our previous unity with Adam, in a sense, becomes the mechanism for the Christian's present unity with Christ. Adam's previous headship of humanity became the basis for Christ's present headship over regenerated humanity. The most astounding thing of all at least for me, is that one sin was so horrible that it destroyed humanity spiritually, but in stark contrast, Christ took upon himself the almost limitless sins and trespasses of humanity. Not only that, God the Father granted righteousness to those who merely trusted his Son once. At the same time, he promised to usher them into a New Universe wherein the future would be so overwhelmingly wonderful that no one would look back to what they suffered in the Fall! As Paul wrote:

> *For I am reckoning that the sufferings of the present season are not worthy in the face of the about to be revealed glory awaiting us. For the eager expectation of creation is awaiting the revelation of the mature sons of God. (Romans 8:18-19)*

This language of "not worthy to be compared" is astonishing. This amazing reality was based on the difference between the man who caused the damage, and the God-Man who repaired and vastly surpassed the damage with glory. The Infinitely Loved and Lovely Son of God absorbed all the damage and sin of this universe, and through that act, he ushered in the unheralded beauty of a new, God-centered universe. I will cease my complaint because the complaint has been met with an answer beyond any human imagination.

At this point in the problem-solution approach, the original and defining problem was introduced, our Fall with Adam. With the first man, we inherited sin, death, condemnation, and the status as sinners. Without a choice, without being present, we were doomed. Out of those four results, humanity found that the image of God within them was crushed by mismanaged desires, controlling emotions, and ineffective thinking. Religiously, humanity polluted itself. The Greco-Roman world was polluted through idolatry, and the world of Judaism polluted itself through performance-based religiosity. This was the fruit of the tree of the Fall. Humanity was fully identified with Adam and his act in the Garden.

At a different Tree, made out of dead, desiccated, brutalized wood, the only fruit found upon it was a dying man. With this pathetically-appearing dying man, we were given a choice. Choose to trust him, and our status, our condemnation, our death, and the entrance of sin would all be reversed. Notice that in the chart below, only one element is on the solution side. Yet that element of our Union with Christ is crucial for every other solution Paul presented for the problems he isolated in Romans.

PROBLEM	SOLUTION
1. Humanity turned over to its desires (1:24)	
2. Humanity turned over to its dishonorable moods (1:26)	
3. Humanity turned over to a disapproved mind that failed the test (1:28)	
4. Humanity trapped by a chaotic culture exhibiting great immorality (1:18-32)	
5. The Jews adopted a performance based religion resulting in hypocrisy (2-3)	
6. Union with Adam resulting in sin within, death, condemnation, and status as a sinner (5:12-21)	6. Union with Christ resulting in death to sin, life in Christ, justification, and status as a righteous one (5:15-21)

Union with Christ is a solution, but it is not a skill. We have to learn the significance of that in relationship to God the Father, and after learning, we will have the first three skills introduced in chapter 6. Those skills will permit us to integrate the great truth of our Union with Christ into a vital relationship to God the Father, begin the process of liberation from sin within, and introduce us to the indwelling help of the Spirit of God.

OUR UNION WITH THE SON CREATES OUR RELATIONSHIP TO THE TRINITY

Beyond humanity's wildest dreams, beyond the most fevered imagination, the New Testament tells us God the Creator became one of us, so as to rescue us, so as to communicate his Father in terms we can understand, and most incredibly of all to die for us. These are truths that should captivate the Christian's heart every day. Most touching of all, the Son acted out of affection for his creation. Wanting to rescue us, wanting to die for us, wanting to lavish love upon us throughout eternity he did not have his glory in mind; he had us in his heart. How can our minds, our imaginations, and our emotions manage such nobility?

His becoming one of us is the foundation of salvation and the Christian life. Without his union with humanity and his complete union with believers, Christianity would be impossible. The Cross only has meaning because Christ chose to join himself to humanity. The ability to live life in the presence of the Trinity only exists because of our Union with Christ – as he is accepted, we are accepted!

This love was manifested in two ways: Christ identified himself with us, and God identified our sin and ourselves with him. A two-fold identification is presented in the Bible. The Son of God identified with us through birth. He became one of us. Secondly, we became identified with him through the will of God and our immersion into Christ through the Holy Spirit. Both are wonderful. Willingly, the Son of God joined himself to humanity. Willingly, God the Father identified anyone who trusted the Gospel with his Son. When God looks at us, he seems him, and when he looks at him, he sees us. We have become inseparable. This theme of a double-sided identification was developed throughout the Bible. Majestically, it progresses from the beginning of the Old Testament where the woman will bear a male seed who will bruise the head of the serpent (Genesis 3:15) to Revelation 22 where God the Father and the Son are present.[22] On the throne with God, the Son is revealed as the Lamb showing his identification with human sin.

To understand this unity with the Son conceptually is one thing. To understand it emotionally is completely another. With emotional understanding we will enter into the relational and emotional life of the Trinity. Our hearts will feed on the affection, tranquility, and happiness flowing among the Three. As we realize the reality of this double-sided identification, our hearts will sense the acceptance of God, for we are accepted moment by moment as the Son is accepted, and we will not be an observer of the Trinity. Instead, we will participate in the relational life of the Trinity. So let us observe this progression from the Old to the New Testament with believing and adoring hearts.

OLD TESTAMENT PROPHECIES

In the Old Testament prophecies, we have the prediction that the Son will become human (one of us), and will reign over us. In the Book of Isaiah in the Songs of the Servant, it says he will suffer for us and be exalted over the kings of the earth and therefore over us.

The emphasis from the Old Testament texts and the later annunciation to Mary concerned the future of this child, and a future reigning over the nation of Israel. Yet we shall see that this child had a significance going far beyond a throne.

For a child will be born to us, a son will be given to us; And the government will rest on His shoulders; And His name will be called Wonderful Counselor, Mighty God, Eternal Father, Prince of Peace. 7 There will be no end to the increase of His government or of peace, On the throne of David and over his kingdom, To establish it and to uphold it with justice and righteousness From then on and forevermore. The zeal of the LORD of hosts will accomplish this. (Isaiah 9:6-7 NAS) [23]

The Songs of the Servant in Isaiah emphasized the ministry of the suffering servant, but not necessarily his kingship (Isaiah 42:1-4; Isaiah 49:1-6; Isaiah 50:4-7; and Isaiah 52:13-53:12). As we can see from below, the kingship of the Servant was implied, but the title was not given.

"He will not be disheartened or crushed, Until He has established justice in the earth; And the coastlands will wait expectantly for His law." (Isaiah 42:4 NAS)

In the second Song of the Servant, the purpose of the Servant was to regather Israel. Again, no anointing was mentioned nor kingship.

And now says the LORD, who formed Me from the womb to be His Servant, To bring Jacob back to Him, in order that Israel might be gathered to Him (For I am honored in the sight of the LORD, And My God is My strength), (Isaiah 49:5 NAS)

In Isaiah 52-53, the Servant was described as being honored by kings and being exalted above all. As the Songs proceeded, his victory through death is described.

Behold, My servant will prosper, He will be high and lifted up, and greatly exalted. (Isaiah 52:13 NAS)

The beginning of the Song (52:13) and the end of it described his victory through death.

---

[22] In the Hebrew of Genesis, it is clear that the seed is a male. In the Aramaic Targum which is a translation and also often an expansion of the Hebrew text, the translator referred not to the seed of the woman but to the son of the woman, and not to the seed of the serpent but to the son of the serpent!

[23] **καλεῖται τὸ ὄνομα αὐτοῦ μεγάλης βουλῆς ἄγγελος** (Isa. 9:5) The Greek Old Testament (LXX) did not like, for some reason, the implication of the names of this Son, so they interpreted it as, " . . . the name of him is called an angel of great counsel." The Holy Scriptures According to the Masoretic Text, (Philadelphia: The Jewish Publication Society, 1917). It did not translate the divine list of names of this child; it simply transliterated them without offering a translation.

Therefore, I will allot Him a portion with the great, And He will divide the booty with the strong; Because He poured out Himself to death, And was numbered with the transgressors; Yet He Himself bore the sin of many, And interceded for the transgressors. (Isaiah 53:12 NAS)

The twin truths of kingship and suffering appeared in the Old Testament. Obviously, they showed up again in the Gospels. Matthew particularly continued the pattern of the Old Testament and addressed the issues found therein. Something new and important though was brought into the mix by Matthew and the other writers: the first Adam and his failure (Genesis 3) was answered by the last Adam and his victory over sin, death, and the devil.

THE SYNOPTIC GOSPELS

In the Synoptic Gospels (Matthew, Mark, Luke) we have a contrast between Adam and Christ. For example, immediately upon being commissioned as the Messiah with the Spirit coming upon him, Christ was thrust not into Paradise, but into the wilderness.

Then Jesus was led up by the Spirit into the wilderness to be tempted by the devil. 2 And after He had fasted forty days and forty nights, He then became hungry. (Matthew. 4:1-2 NAS)

Instead of seeing the animals created in front of his eyes as with Adam in Paradise, Jesus was out in the wilderness among wild beasts, dangerous animals. Satan, not as a serpent, but in person tempted him not once, but three times. Satan's three temptations echoed the three observations of Eve: that the Tree had food to eat (turn stone to bread), the fruit was beautiful (Christ was shown the glories of the world in one ripple of time), and the fruit would make one wise (Satan gave Jesus seemingly wise advice about falling from the Temple to the crowds below). Jesus succeeded where Adam failed. At a cataclysmic moment, Adam entered into death by eating the fruit of the beautiful tree. With that, any positive benefit or ministry he may have had for humanity ended.

At the end of Christ's three-year ministry, he was nailed to the tree, and the only fruit on the tree was himself.

Christ's death was the mirror opposite of what Adam had and experienced. In the first three Gospels, the Son of God was born as a human baby, predicted as a future king, proclaimed as the sin bearer, and by implication was the Last Adam.

THE GOSPEL OF JOHN

The Gospel of John further develops through discourse and illustration our Union with Christ. The discourses will be illustrated by one example where Christ (John 6:26-58) stated he is the Bread of Heaven. To have life, one has to eat of the Bread of Life.

Jesus therefore said to them, "Truly, truly, I say to you, unless you should have eaten the flesh of the Son of Man and should have drunk His blood, you have no life in yourselves. He who is munching on My flesh and drinking My blood has eternal life, and I will raise him up on the last day. (John 6:53-54) [24]

Not only would he give his life, indeed he would become as Paul explained later, the life source within the believers. Then, Jesus illustrated the union between himself and believers with the wonderful picture of Christ being the vine, we as the branches, and the Father as the keeper of the vine (John 15:1-16). [25]

---

[24] In Greek, verse 53 spoke of the initial eating of Christ's flesh and the initial drinking of Christ's blood. The next verse spoke of the continual munching (**τρώγω trogo** gnaw or munch) on his flesh and continual drinking of his blood. The language was designed to scandalize the crowd.

[25] W. Graham Scroggie, A Guide to the Gospels (Revell, n.d.), pp. 421-422. Scroggie has an excellent summary of the discourses and the illustrations.

"I am the vine, you are the branches; he who abides in Me, and I in him, he bears much fruit; for apart from Me you can do nothing. (John 15:5 NAS)

William Scroggie, a brilliant English Bible teacher, nicely described the difference between Matthew's Gospel and John's Gospel.

It is illuminating to compare the Sermon on the Mount (Matt. v-vii) with the Upper Room Talk (John xii-xvi). The one looks back; the other looks on. The one is the consummation of the past; the other the inauguration of the future. The one is a fulfilment; the other is a prophecy. The one is Jewish in complexion; the other is Christian. The one relates to the Kingdom; the other to the Church. These distinctions help us to understand the difference in the outlook and purpose of these Gospels respectively.[26]

What is fascinating is the truths of the church and its unique relationship to the Trinity are revealed the last night Christ is alive before the crucifixion. The other three Gospels spoke of Christ's life on earth and the consummation of his death. In the teachings of the last night in John's Gospel, Jesus spoke of his future life in and through the church. In John, a metaphor is used to communicate what Paul shared in plain language in Romans 5-6 and his other writings.

ROMANS

In Romans, in particular, Paul merged the implicit comparison of Adam and Christ in the synoptic Gospels with the twin truths of Union with Christ and life through Christ within. Explicitly, Paul made Adam and Christ the source of two humanities: one dead while living, and one living while dying.

For as through the one man's disobedience the many were made sinners, even so through the obedience of the One the many will be made righteous. (Romans 5:19 NAS)

Not only does he teach Union with Christ, but he also takes it a great step forward by stating the believer participated in the great events of the crucifixion, resurrection, and ascension. His history is now the Christian's history before God.

Or do you not know that all of us who have been immersed into Christ Jesus have been immersed into His death? (Romans 6:3) . . . 5 For if we have become united with Him in the likeness of His death, certainly we shall be also in the likeness of His resurrection, 6 knowing this, that our old man [Adam] was crucified with Him, that our body of sin might be done away with, that we should no longer be slaves to sin; (Romans 6:5-6 NAS)

The connection with Adam has been broken through the Last Adam.

So also it is written, "The first man, Adam, became a living soul." The last Adam became a life-giving spirit. (1 Corinthians 15:45 NAS)

HEBREWS

Hebrews is strikingly different. It uniquely applies the ascension of Christ to the problem and challenge of the Jewish believers in Jerusalem. In their continual practice of worship at the temple with its artifacts, sacrifices, high priest, and priests, they were trespassing against the great deliverance of the Messiah Jesus. Great significance has to be applied to what the writer called a trespass. The purpose of Hebrews was to deliver them from a great trespass.

and then have fallen away [after falling into a trespass: **παραπεσόντας parapesontas**][27] *it is impossible*

---

[26] Scroggie, Guide, p. 425.

[27] This is the only verbal usage in the New Testament. The noun trespass occurs a number of times. The verb "to fall into a trespass" is relatively common in Greek. H.G. Liddell and R. Scott, Greek-English Lexicon with a Revised Supplement, (Oxford: Clarendon Press, 1996), p. 1321.

to renew [to be presently renewing] *them again to repentance, since they again crucify* [while they are presently recrucifying] *to themselves the Son of God, and put Him to open shame. (Hebrews. 6:6 NAS)*

In order to break the hold of their cultural background and deliver them from their trespass, the author relegated the priestly system of the Old Testament to unimportance and irrelevance. The Temple became irrelevant through the union of Jesus with humanity and his ascension to Heaven as our Great High Priest. The writer made the argument that Christ was the true high priest and the true sacrifice. Having become one with us through birth as a human, he became the substitutionary sacrifice, and through his resurrection, he became the Great High Priest. Therefore, the priests and practices from the Old Testament have to be left behind. Why? Because he is in union with us.

> T he entire thrust, one might say, of Hebrews was the emphasis on the Great High Priesthood of Christ, the God-Man.[28]

Now the main point in what has been said is this: we have such a high priest, who has taken His seat at the right hand of the throne of the Majesty in the heavens, (Hebrews 8:1 NAS)

In classical Greek (and the writer to the Hebrews is a master of Greek) **κεφάλαιος kephalaios** means "head," and it is used in classical Greek literature as the main point of a discourse "the chief or main point, the sum of the matter."[29] "Head" is used in the same way we would say "key idea." The word "priest" appears 25 times in the 13 chapters of Hebrews. Strikingly in Hebrews, the author said one of the challenges was the Hebrew Christians' lack of maturity to understand the significance of Jesus as the High Priest. This same can be said of believers today: they have become dull of hearing due to being inundated with a mass of disconnected biblical detail. Christ's wondrous union with us and his heavenly protection of us through his session as a Heavenly High priest is largely mere concept at best, or pure ignorance at worst.

Concerning him [Jesus as High Priest] *we have much to say, and it is hard to explain, since you have become dull of hearing. (Hebrews 5:11 NAS)*

Paul presented the ascended Christ not necessarily as a Great High Priest, but as the ascended Head of the Body of Christ (Eph. 1:22; 4:15; 5:23; Col. 1:18; 2:10, 19). In the great description of God's and Christ's love for us in Romans 8, he stated that Christ was continually making intercession for us in Heaven (Romans 8:34) without mentioning a priestly title. The Gospel of John emphasized that Jesus will remain faithful and keep the believer secure through time. Even though John did not mention a high priestly title, he did teach that Christ would function as a priest for us in Heaven.

"And this is the will of Him who sent Me, that of all that He has given Me I lose nothing, but raise it up on the last day. (John 6:39 NAS)

As we scan the Old Testament, the Synoptic Gospels, the Gospel of John, Romans, and Hebrews, we see a developing picture of the double-sided union. Christ has become one with us, and we are one with him. Now we are inseparable throughout eternity.

These five different sources were observing the same truth that the Son of God became one of us. As sources, they share the same commonality of Christ as the God-Man, yet they progressively develop different ways of looking at the same reality.

---

[28] It is disconcerting to read the Greek Old Testament text (LXX), and come across the phrase "the anointed priest." In Greek it is written **ὁ ἱερεὺς ὁ χριστὸς** (Lev. 4:16), or literally translated into English, "the Priest, the Christ" because Christ means "anointed" in Greek.

[29] Liddell and Scott, Lexicon, p. 944.

SUMMARY	
1. Old Testament	The child was born to be king, and the man was born to die
2. Synoptic Gospels	The child was born to be victorious through death, and the last Adam
3. Gospel of John	The child was born to be the life of humanity, and the Christocentric identity of the New Humanity
4. Paul	The child born was to be not only our life within, but also our history in our crucifixion, resurrection, and ascension with him
5. Hebrews	The child born will become the sympathetic High Priest in Heaven and the sacrificial substitute on earth. With him, the shadow of the Old Testament laws fades away.

With the table above, we have a marvelous illustration of progressive revelation. In the passage of time, the ultimate seed of Eve born through Mary is developed as the one who will meet all of our needs. As the Bible unfolds, it takes the birth of the God-Man and through the progression of Scripture, we see him finally in Heaven as our Great High priest and the Head of the Body of Christ.

His becoming one of us is the foundation of salvation and the Christian life. Without his union with humanity and his complete union with believers, Christianity would be impossible. The Cross only has meaning because Christ chose to join himself to humanity. The ability to live life in the presence of the Trinity only exists because of our Union with Christ – as he is accepted, we are accepted!

6 | UNION WITH CHRIST

CHAPTER SUMMARY: The same **Union with Christ** becomes the basis of a living relationship with the Father and the means to deal with the presence of sinful behavior in a person's life.

Probably it would have been more helpful if the chapter divisions for Romans 5 and 6 were different.[30] Romans 5:1-11 defines what the significance of the gift of righteousness is. It unpacks what was introduced in Romans 3:21-31. Then, Romans 5:12 started with **Διὰ τοῦτο dia touto** literally "on account of this." The phrase was sometimes translated as "therefore" but that is not as strong, nor does "therefore" carry the fuller implications of "on account of this."

<u>On account of what?</u> In 5:6-11, our justification and deliverance were all connected to Christ. Christ drew all of believing humanity into his death and resurrection. On account of the previously described connection to Christ, Paul then connected this mechanism of justifying union to another union - a condemning union with Adam. This is very important because it speaks to the very essence of being human. To be human means that our fate was determined by a Headship, by an ultimate decision maker. The first time it was Adam, and the second and last time it was Christ. The way chapter 6 was placed, it appeared to start a new subject, that being, how to deal with sin within. But 6:1 was just a natural continuation of 5:12 on.

On the one hand, it was a natural continuation, and on the other hand, it introduced two new connections to that Union with Christ. First, we are joined to him in his experience on the Cross and his subsequent resurrection. Second, those truths were the basis of our living relationship to God.

TOTAL LIBERATION AND UNION WITH CHRIST

Paul was wonderfully straightforward as to the nature of Christianity. At its core, it was not a legal system. A legal system not only gave rules, but punishments were also part of the system. In Romans 6 however, Paul told believers that instead of a legal system, they were joined to Christ. In their Union with Christ, they have suffered with Christ, died with Christ, and been resurrected with Christ. In their suffering with Christ, they

---

[30] The chapter divisions were developed by Stephen Langton, an Archbishop of Canterbury, around A.D. 1227.

have paid the penalty for sin. Yet Christ was the one who had done the suffering and not them. In the death of Christ, they have suffered the ultimate penalty for wrongdoing. Yet Christ tasted death for us so that we did not have to swallow a morsel of doom. In Christ's resurrection, in fact, we have been freely granted a living relationship with God the Father.

> *What then are we saying? Should we remain in sin in order that grace should increase? Never! We who are of such a nature that we have died to sin, how yet shall we live in it? Or are you ignorant that as many of us who were immersed into Christ Jesus, into his death we were immersed? (6:1-3)*

Paul began this section with four questions. Typically with Paul, a transition to a major new thought would be introduced by a question. Here, we have four questions. Obviously, something important was to follow.

"What then are we saying?" is asking what our response to the Union described in chapter 5 should be. What has to be noticed about chapter 5 is that these were things that were done for believers. All the believer did was believe. In 5:1-11, the Christian was the **passive** recipient of justification. Christ justified them through the passage of time. God was now working with their tribulations for their good. While they were weak, ungodly sinners, and hating God, Christ died for them. Finally, believers can exult because they have received a new status as reconciled ones. In all of this we are passive. In chapter 6, we go from being passive to being participants, to being active in our relationship to God.

The next question opened the door to participation with Christ and to being active in our relationship to God the Father. "Are we to continue in sin [under the kingship of sin, and relational death] in order that grace might increase?" (6:1). Again, we are the **passive** recipients of what God and Christ did for us. Romans 5:20 stated where sin abounded, grace abounded all the more. Shall we continue to help sin abound more? Shall we continue in passivity? The obvious answer is, no. Then, he

> "*Typically with Paul a transition to a new thought or a major new thought would be introduced by a question.*"

connected us back to a statement in Romans 5:12 which described how sin entered the world through the one man Adam, and as a result, constituted us as sinners (Romans 5:19). Then, he asked the critical question: "We who are of such a nature have died to sin, how yet shall we live in it?" (6:2). A statement like this has to be connected directly to its source in chapter 5. The common mistake in reading Romans was to **not** recognize that Paul created building blocks as he wrote. Every chapter built on the previous. This should be obvious, but often because the reader or commentator was not noticing the building blocks, Paul's book was treated like disparate or disconnected parts. What is Paul's point? He wants the listener or reader to recognize that a doom occurred with Adam and a deliverance from that doom occurred with Christ. With Adam, we were constituted sinners and inherited sin; we were under its dominion, its death, and its condemnation. We had no choice but to live as sinners. Now Paul wanted to emphasize that we have a choice because a true deliverance has occurred.

Then, he asked the truly critical question. "Or are you ignorant that as many of us who were immersed into Christ Jesus, into his death we were immersed?"(6:3). In chapter 5, we have learned about the benefits we receive from what Christ has done on the Cross and who he is. In chapter 6, a whole new application was introduced and that is not only in Union with him as to Headship, but Union with him in the central events of his ministry, his death, burial, and resurrection.

Baptism (Immersion)

This aspect of Union with Christ was expressed through the use of the word "baptism." The word "baptism" and the verb "to baptize" are in actual fact, transliterated words; they came from the Greek verb **βαπτίζω baptidzo**. This transliteration occurred for other words in our English Bible, for example "Amen." That is a Hebrew verb and it means "I believe." That may seem like a scholarly or academic piece of information, but in reality, it is of great personal importance in understanding what Paul was actually saying. That was because the word **βαπτίζω baptidzo** in ancient Greek as it appeared in the New Testament means "to dip, immerse sink."[31] That is the definition found in a fine and standard Greek dictionary of the New

---

[31] G. Abbott-Smith, <u>A Manual Greek Lexicon of the New Testament</u> (Edinburgh: T. & T. Clark, 1937, 3rd ed.), p. 74.

Testament that deals with only the language of the New Testament. We should look at how the same word was used in Classical Greek (5th to 4th centuries BC) and in that language before and after that time period. We are excluding the texts of the Bible. The great Greek-English Lexicon of Liddell and Scott gave as its definition, "dip, plunge." Some of the usages were interesting such as Jerusalem being flooded with people, or being drowned in debt, or a cup plunged into a vat of wine, or dying cloth, or swimming or bathing.[32] It is obvious that the term was not particularly religious until the New Testament period. Another way of gaining insight into the use of the verb is to look at other writings in Koine Greek (common Greek) that were not included in the work of Liddell and Scott, that were contained usually in letters written before, during, and after New Testament times. This would give us the common understanding of the term. In Moulton and Milligan, a lexicon (dictionary) that specialized in such letters, the word was used for a submerged boat or being submerged in calamities (Mark 10:38 shows such usage where Christ spoke of being submerged in the calamity of the Cross).[33] These three dictionaries give us a full spectrum of the meaning of the word in the Greco-Roman world.

What is very important to realize is that this term was not used in a religious context to denote a rite before the time of Christ. It had no religious baggage. In the modern world, it has immense religious baggage. John the Baptist and Christ took a term and used it afresh for a new rite. Of importance and also in the Greek Old Testament, **βαπτίζω baptidzo** was not used for the Israelite practice of plunging into water for ritual cleansing.

The reason why not was probably because the ritual washing was done by the individual, but in John's Baptism and Christian Baptism, it is done by one person for another. "I am submerging someone else" is the thought. Therefore, to appreciate the power of what Paul wrote, we must "wash" out any religious baggage we bring to the text. If we completely push aside any thought of the Christian rite of baptism and instead use the term in its native meaning of "dipping or plunging" something or someone into another thing or reality, we may well discover a wondrous truth afresh. We will use the word "immersion" instead of "baptism" to avoid confusion. An immersion demands three things: an "immerser," a person to be immersed, and a substance or something to be immersed into. It is absolutely not a Jewish Mikveh or place of washing oneself because the element of the 'immerser' is missing. The ministry of John the "immerser" illustrated the three. He immersed. A repentant Jew was immersed. The element the person was plunged into was water (Matthew 3:6-11). To answer the question of what happened in an immersion, one must describe who was acting, who was being acted upon, and what was the element used to plunge the person into.[34]

Here is a list of the three things as found in the New Testament.

	IMMERSER	RECIPIENT	ELEMENT
1	John	The Jews	Water (Matthew 3:6)
2	Jesus	The Jews	Holy Spirit and fire (Matthew 3:11)
3	John	Jesus	Water (Matthew 3:16)
4	Disciples	The Nations	Water (presumed) (Matthew 28:19)
5	Pharisees	Pots and Pans	Water (Mark 7:4) In the previous verse, the Pharisees wash themselves (**νίπτω nipto** wash a part of the body, verse 3 and John 13:5)

---

[32] Liddell and Scott, Lexicon, pp. 305-306.

[33] J.H. Moulton and G. Milligan, The Vocabulary of the Greek Testament (London: Hodder & Stoughton Ltd., 1914-1929), p.102.

[34] The word in the Greek Old Testament (LXX) meant "to wash or bathe" **λούω louo**. This was not used by Christ for baptism although the verb did occur in the New Testament (John 13:10). Abbott-Smith, Lexicon, p. 272. **βαπτίζω baptidzo** "I immerse myself" was used for Naaman in the Greek middle to describe Naaman immersing himself seven times. The second instance was in Isaiah where lawlessness overwhelmed or immersed him (Isaiah 21:4). Only two uses were in the LXX of the texts from our Old Testament.

	IMMERSER	RECIPIENT	ELEMENT
6	God the Father (presumed)	Jesus	Crucifixion and Death (Mark 10:39)
7	Jesus	Wash	Arms and Hands (presumed) (Luke 11:38)
8	Jesus	Disciples	Holy Spirit (John 1:33; Acts 1:5) in direct contrast to immersion in water
9	Peter and Disciples	Converting Jews	Water (Acts 2:38-41)
10	Holy Spirit (presumed)	Christians	Death of Christ (Romans 6:3)
11	By Cloud and the Sea	Israelites	Moses (1 Corinthians 10:2)
12	Holy Spirit	Believers	Body of Christ (1 Corinthians 12:13)
13	Holy Spirit (presumed)	Believers	Christ (Galatians 3:27)

As we look at this table, an obvious difference appears. When water was involved, it made a statement about the condition of the person's heart. This statement appeared to have permanent implications, either a statement of repentance or a statement of commitment to Christianity. What is of great significance is that whenever the word "to immerse" appeared, it needed to have the element defined. Other realities were listed that were not water and did not depend upon water. Note that they were the Holy Spirit and fire (Matthew 3:11), crucifixion and death (Mark 10:39), the Holy Spirit (John 1:33), death of Christ (Romans 6:3), Moses (1 Cor. 10:2), Body of Christ (1 Cor. 12:13), and Christ (Galatians 3:27). The conclusion is that for the native speaker of the common Greek of Christ's and Paul's time, when the word "immerse" βαπτίζω **baptidzo** was used, the natural question would be, "Into what?" One should not presume water. The most blatant example was the "immersion" into Moses. The fact that the Israelites were untouched by the water of the Red Sea was the basis of their "immersion" into Moses!

Let us take a look at what it meant to be immersed into Christ's death in Romans 6:3.

COMMENTATORS HAVE THREE WAYS OF UNDERSTANDING PAUL'S USE OF IMMERSION	
1. Referring to the rite but with a further connection to Christ's suffering, death, and resurrection.	A common way of dealing with Paul's question about knowing that we were immersed into Christ's death was to first refer to the rite of water immersion and then talk about being joined to Christ and his death. A commentator that I admire, a man of uncommon insight, did just that. He wrote: "Here the Apostle turns them back to their baptism, that initial step in public confession of the Lord upon whom they had believed. . . We must first of all receive the statement of our death unto sin with Christ (verses 2 and 11) as a revealed federal fact, and then allow the Apostle to press the symbolical setting forth of that federal death by the figure of water-baptism."[35]
2. Referring to the rite	This one assumes that it is the rite which truly immerses the person into Christ. This would be inherent in Catholic theology and doctrine. The rite caused the Union with Christ. The rite was not a symbol of our Union with Christ.
3. Referring to simply immersed or fully connected and covered with Christ (no direct reference to the rite).	The English transliteration of "baptize" obscures the point of what Paul was asking in Romans 6:3. If its literal meaning was used in translation, the greatness of what the Trinity has done for us will be shown forth in all of its power. *Or are you personally ignorant that we who are of such a nature as to have been plunged, immersed, fully identified with Christ Jesus, into his death, we were fully plunged, immersed, and identified? (6:3)*

---

[35] William R. Newell, <u>Romans Verse by Verse</u> (Chicago: Moody Press, 1938), p. 204.

The native speaker of Greek **would not** have first thought of water baptism. The native speaker would sense the power of the imagery. For a bowl to be plunged into water or a piece of cloth to be plunged into dye, or for a person to be plunged into catastrophic circumstances (all used with the word **βαπτίζω baptidzo**), it has to be completely surrounded by this new element. This new element would change the reality of the thing or person being so plunged. What Paul implied by this question in 6:3 was that trusting in Christ was more than just having a Savior provided. <u>A fundamental change has occurred in who we actually are.</u> Our human existence has been redefined. We have not only been given a Savior, we have been given a new valid life changing history that is effectual on the deepest levels of our person. The entire verse is filled with meaning. The beginning started with a negative, "Do you not know by your experience," based upon a verb that referred to personal knowledge.[36] Paul was asking if the experiential reality had escaped them of their death with Christ. He wanted to take them from the mentality that they had been merely saved by Christ to the mindset that they were united to Christ in his person and further united with his death, burial, and resurrection. Such now was their own. Not only have they been rescued from Adam's choice and death, they have been granted an entirely new intrinsic history in Union with Christ. This history was the central event of Christ's life and it became the central defining event of ours.

> *Therefore we have been buried with him through this plunging, immersion, this act of full identification unto that death, with the result just as Christ was raised out from among the corpses through the displayed glory of the Father, thus also we ourselves should live in a brand new way of life. (6:4)*

What we have here was not a call to a moral life but an entirely new way of looking at our lives.

The moral implications come later in 6:11, but here was an orientation to a totally new way of looking at ourselves. Romans 5 told us that we were in union with Adam with his history being our history. In union with him, we inherited sin, death, condemnation, and our establishment as a sinner. What we did after that was somewhat meaningless because our only real choice was how evil we chose to be. That reality was essential to understand who we were and the human condition. Chapter 5 told us that through Christ we have been justified. Now in chapter 6 what was true of us with Adam was completely reversed by Christ who provided a death to our union with Adam and a new quality of life with him.

The word translated "we should live" was **περιπατέω perpateo.** The word is often translated "walk," but as it appeared in context, it can refer to physically walking around or walking according to a principle or energy. In Romans, it referred to walking by the flesh or walking decently, or walking in love (Romans 8:4; 13:13; 14:15). It reflected the organizing principles of a person's life. This organizing principle is our indivisible Union with Christ and his history on the cross. Previously we had an indivisible union with Adam, and the union was so immensely powerful only the death of the God-Man could break it. Now that we are in this new Union, Paul insisted that Christians should learn the reality of it and live accordingly. This Union is innate.

> *For if (and it is true) we have come to be grafted (or joined so as to be become one) in the likeness of his death, but in strong contrast to that death we shall also be in the likeness of the resurrection. (6:5)*

Verse 5 reinforced the emphasis on death from the previous verse and took it a bit further. The word "grafted" when it referred to plants meant plants planted together in groups, but when it referred to just two things of differing natures, the emphasis was upon a united indivisible joining. Paul wanted the Roman Christians to clearly understand a true death had occurred in the Adamic union with its entrance of sin, death, condemnation, and our establishment as sinners.[37] A true death occurred in Union with Christ but

---

[36] The same word, meaning knowing personally, occurred in 7:1 where it spoke of the personal experience of the Jewish Christian with the Law.

[37] Moulton and Milligan, <u>Vocabulary</u>, p.598. Liddell and Scott, <u>Lexicon</u> p. 1689. The emphasis on grafting or union is entirely striking in Liddell and Scott. One illustration was the coming together of a wound to heal.

it was a likeness for us of what happened on the cross because we did not suffer and die. But this three-fold emphasis in verses 3, 4, and 5 was to make sure the Christian recognized that a true death to Adam's world and ways had occurred. It was expressed through an immersion into death, an immersion that involved a true burial, and a grafting together in that death. Verses 4 and 5 add the element of Christ's resurrection, but the initial emphasis was upon the death to the Adamic realities. Paul was determined to make the point as strongly as possible that we are to live a new life.

Verse 4 stated that we should walk in a new kind of life, and this life shall be in the likeness of his resurrection. Eventually, we too will be resurrected or raptured while living, but now we are called to a resurrection kind of life. In verse 5, we share in the likeness of the resurrection but verse 4 emphasizes that we are free to live an entirely new kind of life.

> *Continually knowing this personally that our old man* [Adam and our union with him] *was crucified with him, in order that the body of sin should be nullified so that no longer we should be slaving for sin. (6:6)*

It is fundamentally important to note in verse 6 that what Paul assumed, was personal experience on his part and the Roman Christians. **γινώσκοντες ginoskontes** is a verb emphasizing personal knowledge and experience. It is in contrast with the beginning of verse 9 **εἰδότες eidotes** which means knowing information or truth. In verse 9, Paul stated the realities of Christ's death and resurrection. But in verse 6, he was stating the experiential reality.

The goal of this crucifixion of the old man, to whom we belonged and were liberated from by this death with Christ, was to nullify the body containing sin. The word I translated "nullify" is an interesting combination of three elements: the basic element was the verb "to work," the next element was a negative changing the meaning to "not work," lastly a preposition was added to the front meaning "thoroughly." The end result would be "completely not work." Several versions like the King James or the New Jerusalem Bible translate it as "destroy," but the difficulty with that translation was it implied destruction resulting in non-existence. That was not supported by the way Paul described the body of the Christian, so the idea of nullifying the functioning of that body as a goal and result probably fits much better.

> *For the one having died is completely justified from sin. (6:7)*

Contextually, this statement was incredible because the sin he referred to was the death dealing sin of 5:12-21. That sin brought death (spiritual and physical), condemnation, and our status as sinner. As Paul reiterated that we had died to Adam's union with our death in Christ, he also made the point that we were justified from the sin with its condemnation. The Greek word is **κατάκριμα katakrima** "a state of being condemned."[38] The complete opposite of that is **δεδικαίωται dedikaiotai** "a state of complete justification" in 6:7. I translate it as "complete justification" for this reason: it is a Greek perfect tense that means we are justified in the past, present, and into the future.[39] By every means possible, Paul stated that we have escaped our Adamic union by death with Christ and we have been justified from that union. Then, he proceeded to build on that.

> *And since it is true we have died with Christ, we believe that we shall live with him. (6:8)*

---

[38] **κατάκριμα katakrima** also occurred in Romans 8:1. That was very important because in Romans 7, Paul described the incredible confusion that occurred in believers when they added moralism to the Spirit's work in Christ and how that unleashed sin's power in a believer's life. But in the transition to the solution of walking by the Spirit in chapter 8, he made the prefacing comment in the same way he made the summary comment in 6:8 that the condemnation no longer existed but justification reigned instead.

[39] Sometimes the verb was translated as "freed" which is true but it misses the forensic force of the Greek verb. The better commentators who work with the Greek text translate it as "justify" and not "freed". Archibald Thomas Robertson, Word Pictures in the New Testament (Broadman Press: Nashville, 1931), Vol. IV, p. 362. Sanday and Headlam, Romans, p. 159. This second commentary stated, "The sense . . . is still forensic: 'is declared righteous, acquitted from guilt." The person was free because they were acquitted.

So we have six statements of death:

1. Immersed into **death** (6:3)

2. Buried with him through the immersion into **death** (6:4)

3. Grafted into the likeness of his **death** (6:5)

4. Our union with Adam was **crucified** with him (6:6)

5. We have **died** (6:7)

6. We have **died** with him (6:8)

Those six repetitions must shake our soul. For they say explicitly we have entered a new world of reality and experience with our conversion to Christianity. We are dead but what are we dead to? We are dead to the Adamic realities of the fifth chapter: sin (5:12, 13, 20, 21), death (5:12, 14, 15, 17, 21), condemnation (5:16, 18), and the condition or status of being sinners (5:19). The last three stem from the first entrance of sin into the world through Satan.

ADAM	CHRIST
Sin	Died to sin (6x)
↓	↓
Death	Alive with Christ
↓	↓
Condemnation	Justified from sin
↓	↓
Condition as sinners	Condition as righteous ones (5:19, 6:4, 8)

The purpose of this death was to liberate the Christian to a new kind of life: "we should walk in a new kind of life (6:4)," "in strong contrast to that death we shall also be in the likeness of the resurrection (6:5)," and "we shall live with him (6:8)." To put these thoughts together: we shall live with him a new kind of resurrection life similar to Christ's.

But the critical thought is by death with Christ, we have died to Adam's death!
Sin, death, condemnation, and our status or condition as sinners
has been ended by our death with Christ.

After speaking of our death to our Adamic union through our death with Christ for the sixth time, Paul prepared for a transition. At the end of Romans 6:8 he said, ". . . we believe that we shall live with him." Paul slightly changed the subject to emphasize Christ's experience, not ours. That phrase is important because it was not referring to a future resurrection, but it continued the theme of "walking" in a new kind of life emphasized in 6:4-5. To solidify that, Paul spoke of Christ's present life after his death and resurrection. His goal was to link Christ's present condition in Heaven with our Heavenly privilege of being accepted with the Father as he is.

Knowing the fact that Christ having been raised out of the dead no longer dies, death is no longer ruling over him. For that he died, he died to sin once-for-all, and that he lives, he lives to God. (6:9-10)[40]

Verses 9 and 10 state what we have to understand about our present "with him" status. Not only does that

---

[40] ἐφάπαξ **ephapax** "once for all" is critically important to appreciate. The sacrificial system of the Old Testament endlessly repeated the animal sacrifices. The once-for-all nature of Christ's sacrifice shows the supreme importance of the God-Man. His sacrifice addressed immeasurable guilt past, present, and future thereby bringing peace. ἐφάπαξ **ephapax** "once for all" is very important, if not crucial, in the Book of Hebrews (7:27; 9:12; 10:10). It strongly contrasted the once-for-all nature of Christ's sacrifice and Heavenly priesthood with the Old Testament system.

status connect to what happened on the Cross and resurrection, it continues on to Christ's life in Heaven. Our Union with him continues into Heaven itself. Our status with God is the Heavenly presence of Christ; we are with him. Of course, this links back to justification being a reality in the past, present, and future as described in Romans 5:1-2. But the justification flows out of our Union with Christ.

The Great Transition

With Adam, our freedom of choice disappeared. His choice at the Tree in the Garden doomed us all. The marvelous reality of Christ's coming was that choice was restored. At the dead and ugly tree on which the God-Man was stretched out before God, angels, and humanity, we were given the choice of the Gospel. At the beautiful Tree in the Garden we had no choice because sin never granted choice. At our conception and birth, its tentacles gripped our hearts. But now our choice of the Gospel has set us free.

In Romans 5:19, we had the status or condition of a sinner while being under the kingship of death and sin (5:14 death, 17 death, 21 sin). In contrast to that, Paul wrote that we have been granted the status or condition of righteous ones. With that new status, we have freedom to participate in the life of God. After six chapters and ten verses, Paul finally told the Roman Christians what they must do. This is critical to understand. Paul assumed that with Adamic union came the entrance of sin, death, condemnation and the status as sinners. Freedom to respond to God was lost under the kingship of death and sin. Thanks to our Union with Christ, we are now dead to that combination of factors. Paul's six-fold repetition that we have died to the Adamic union brought Christians to the point where they could respond in freedom to a relationship with God the Father. Finally, Paul issued a command to believers. Prior to this, he simply informed Christians of the truth and implications of Christ's deliverance. With having status of righteous ones, we are now free to obey.

FIRST COMMAND IN THE BOOK OF ROMANS

This command that he gave certainly was the most important command in Romans. In fact, I will argue that it was the most important command in the New Testament. In fact, I will say that it was the most important command in the Bible.

Even so you yourselves should be assuming yourselves to be corpses on the one hand to sin, and on the other hand, continually living to God in Christ Jesus. (6:11)

The "even so" connects to the life Christ is living in relationship to God, and we are involved because ". . . we shall also be *in the likeness* of the resurrection (6:5)." The Greek word I translated as "even so" is **οὕτως houtos** "thus or even so."[41] "It was used in reference to what precedes absolutely," and "Pointing [to] the moral after figures of speech, parables, and examples."[42] Paul took the example of the resurrected Christ, and made that the basis of the moral in 6:11: as he is alive to God so we should assume ourselves to be!

The use of the word "corpses" fits right into what we have been told previously that we have been:

1. Immersed into death (6:3)

2. Buried with him through the immersion into death (6:4)

3. Grafted into the likeness of his death (6:5)

4. Our union with Adam was crucified with him (6:6)

5. We have died (6:7)

6. We have died with him (6:8)

---

[41] William F. Arndt and F. Wilbur Gingrich, A Greek-English Lexicon of the New Testament and Other Early Christian Literature (Chicago: The University of Chicago Press, 1957), p.602, 1b.

[42] Arndt and Gingrich, Lexicon, p. 602, 1b.

> There is no stronger metaphor in life than death, to be a corpse.
> That absolutely illustrated the complete change in status between being in Adam
> (with sin, death, condemnation, and our status as sinners), and being in Christ.

The next important word he used was **λογίζομαι logidzomai** "to assume or reckon." Ardnt and Gingrich's <u>Lexicon</u> defined this word " . . . as a result of calculation *evaluate, estimate, look upon as, consider.*"[43] This term occurred an unusual number of times in Romans, 19 times, far more than any other New Testament writing. The rest of the New Testament has 20 usages. His usage is important to observe. It has to be contrasted with faith. With faith, we are called to believe something to be true that was not true for us heretofore, as Paul said in Romans, it involved hoping for a future reality as stated in 8:24.

> *For in hope we have been saved [by faith], and hope being seen is not hope, for who hopes for what he sees?* (Romans 8:24)

With **λογίζομαι logidzomai** "to assume or reckon" we are to presume it is presently true. It is an assumption. Note the interconnection between "reckon" and "faith."

> *For we are reckoning* [present tense] *a person to be justified apart from works of the Law. (Romans 3:28)*

Note that reckoning assumes a present reality to be true. Reckoning does not make it true as faith would. It is valid and true whether we believe or not. Another example.

> *For what is the Scripture saying: And Abraham believed God and it was reckoned to him for righteousness.* (Romans 4:3)

Notice "reckoning" stated the righteousness was now a present reality. Paul was saying in Romans 6:11 that as Christ was alive to the Father, so are we and we are to assume that because we have been delivered from our Adamic union to Union with Christ. We are continually granted his acceptance and righteousness. We are now ordered to assume that to be so. Assuming does not make it so, but assuming actualizes the truth of it.

Each word in 6:11 is important. The next word is **νεκροὺς nekrous** "corpses." Why are we to assume we are corpses? It was because of the six-fold statement (6:3-8) of our death with Christ to our previous death with Adam.[44] Christ's death nullified our spiritual and relational death with Adam and will eventually nullify physical death by our resurrection. Obviously "corpses" was a metaphor. We are not physically dead, but we are to assume ourselves dead (corpses) to a set of realities. We should not simplistically assume that just deals with temptation. In 5:12 - 6:10, "corpses" was also used to describe what happened to us through Adam and the deliverance through Christ. It began with sin's entrance into the world and the concomitant circumstances, death (spiritual and physical), condemnation, and status as sinners that came with it. All of those realities we have died to through Christ. Now our responsibility is to assume it by completely ignoring those realities. Instead we are to build upon the relationship in Christ we have with God the Father. Our union with Adam has ended and we have left condemnation behind and death. We do have the presence of sin within but we have been granted a new status as righteous ones. In that new status we are to deal with the chaos that sin within can bring.

We have to make an important point: a metaphor does not create a relationship, but a metaphor can define a relationship. The metaphor is to be a corpse to sin and to be continually alive to God. We have to actualize that by abandoning the darkness of unbelief and entering boldly into a relationship with God. We are not to allow ourselves to stay within the status of sinners, but embrace the full force of being righteous ones with God, our new status. It is similar to the metaphor of the vines and branches (John 15:1-8). Metaphorically, we are branches but relationally we are called to assume the truth of our Union with Christ and the care of the Father as the vinedresser.

---

[43] Arndt and Gingrich, <u>Lexicon</u>, p. 477, b.

[44] Paul did not use Adam's name but the word "man." On the one hand, that was exactly what Adam meant in Hebrew. On the other hand, using "man" instead, he distanced his statement from an individual to the representative man as Christ was the representative man.

WHAT ARE THE ASSUMPTIONS OF ROMANS 6:11?
1. We are to assume we are completely dead to union with Adam; it is gone
2. We are to assume the relational and spiritual death that came with sin is over
3. We are to assume condemnation is gone and we are permanently justified
4. We are to assume we are not to stay within the status of sinners because that is nullified
5. Equally we are to assume we must abandon ourselves to a living relationship to the Father and ignore completely the call of sin within by focusing on the Father

That is what we come to now.

> *. . . and on the other hand, continually living to God in Christ Jesus. (6:11)*

Two things we are to reckon: that we are non-participants in the kinship with Adam and the kingship of sin and death, and we are to continually assume we are alive to God as Christ is presently in Heaven. ζῶντας **zontas** "continually living ones" is a present active participle meaning this reality is continually true. This assumption does not create the reality but it allows it to become a relational reality and it is actualized by our new status as righteous ones through the presence of the Spirit of God in our lives. Our new status has us in Union with Christ, with a new Father in Heaven, and a new and true Helper, the Holy Spirit. We are called to radically ignore our past with Adam and fully embrace our new realities.

The state of being continually alive to the Father is the gift of the Trinity to us. With Christ we have died, been buried, raised, and ascended to Heaven with him. We have been declared righteous, or using other Pauline language, we have the righteousness of God in him (2 Corinthians 5:21). Instead of having to struggle with the flesh, we have the Holy Spirit to help us experience Heavenly wisdom from the Father and the impartation of Christ's life as the fruit of the Spirit. All of this is based on what we are ordered to assume.

The entire Christian life as presented by Paul flowed out of the twin truths: we have died to our union with Adam and we are alive to God in our Union with Christ. Our ability to deal with the appetites of sin within comes from the truth of 6:11. Our ability to operate apart from the Law as empowered by the Holy Spirit came from that (Romans 7:5-6). Then, in Romans 8 the privilege of walking by means of the Spirit is hinged to being separated from the Law of sin and death (developed in 5:12-21 and chapter 7) so that we might live by the Law (the Torah) of the Spirit of life in Christ Jesus (8:1-2; 6:11). Walking by means of the Spirit created the opportunity for the essential ingredient of having a spiritual perspective while leaving behind the perspective of the flesh (8:5-7). After chapters 9-11 addressing the life and history of Israel, Paul then connected the truths of chapters 5-8 to say that the goal was to have a transformed mind that was other centered (7:25; 12:2). This other centeredness would be the foundation of the Christian community described in chapters 12-16. Romans 6:11 then stated the conclusion of our Union with Christ: we are to assume that we are alive to God the way Jesus is alive to God. Sin is paid for, death had been conquered, and as he is accepted by the Father, so are we.

This assumption of being alive to God the Father begins a synergistic process in Paul's Romans wherein we as redeemed persons participate with the Trinity in learning how to use our liberation in Christ. Based on the contents of Romans, seven skills exist and we are examining the first three. In chapter 17, all the seven skills are presented, and detailed instruction given on how to integrate them into our lives.

SKILLS OF ROMANS

07

BEING ALIVE TO GOD THE FATHER BEGINS A SYNERGISTIC PROCESS OF FOLLOWING THESE STEPS:
1. Mastering the skill of focusing on the Father and staying in his presence (6:11-13)
2. Mastering the skill of assuming our Union with Christ (6:11)
3. Mastering the skill of not "listening to our appetites" (6:12)

But it all starts with assuming that we are continually alive to the Father as Christ is alive and we have been delivered from the reign of sin. Mastery of all 7 Skills will result, over time, in a profound process of change within us. But the two-fold assumption or reckoning is that we are corpses to sin and its system and we are continually alive to God the Father.

Doing this is a seven-fold challenge because the seven steps above all imply the challenges we have.

1. Previously we have never assumed we are alive continuously to the Father

2. Previously we had never assumed our Union with Christ

3. Previously we always listened to our appetites

4. Previously we have never built our life around Holy Spirit prompting

5. Previously our perspective has been Earthly and sensual

6. Previously our mind has been a slave to the flesh

7. Previously we have lived for ourselves and not others

This is a very steep learning curve. With that learning curve as the challenge, Paul immediately reminded the Roman Christians not to be pulled back to the dark kingdom from which they have been delivered.

Do not let sin be reigning as a king in your mortal body so that you listen to its appetites. (6:12)

Paul has stated flatly that we have been delivered from the reign of sin and death, but with the seven challenges above, we could easily feel and live like we have not. Even though we have been dramatically severed from union with Adam, we can still continue to orient ourselves to our appetites through which the flesh gives it orders, and orient ourselves to a fleshly perspective (based on the Fall, culture and our family background).[45] We can voluntarily return to the land of death (even though we are not citizens of that land) and serve a king from whom we have been truly rescued. Without learning the management of emotions and appetites, we may find ourselves drawn back to the kingdom of death. Through them, we can be drawn back to our identity with the past and live on their illusions.

In 6:11, Paul started by telling us what to do regarding sin, and in 6:12, he returned to that to say what he meant by being a corpse. We were not to "listen." The word **ὑπακούω hupakuo** means "to listen as to obey." **Hupo** means to be "under" and **akuo** means "I hear" (acoustic comes from this word). We are to respond like a corpse to the voice of sin. What is the voice of sin? It is unhealthy and immoral desires.

> **W**e have to learn to recognize what is going on in our desires and as we recognize unhealthy ones, we turn our attention to the Father so as to obtain health and self-control.

With that learning curve in mind, I believe we have a definition of "presenting ourselves to God" that Paul now spoke about in 6:12-13. After stating the principle of counting ourselves alive to God, Paul applied it to the appetites of the flesh.

And do not be presenting your members as weapons of unrighteousness to sin, but you immediately present yourselves to God like a living one out of the dead and your members as weapons of righteousness to God. (6:13)

The critical word in the text is **παρίστημι paristemi** "to stand around or near." The word can simply mean to be around someone or it can have the additional idea, depending on context, of being under someone's

---

[45] David Eckman, Head to Heart: Experiencing the Father's Affection (Pleasanton, California: BWGI Publishing, 2020, 4th ed.), Sessions 2-4.

influence or command.[46] With sin, we would be under the influence of painful emotions and desires. With God, we would be under the influence of the Holy Spirit with the fruit of the Spirit and Heavenly wisdom. To present ourselves to God is to enter into a synergistic relationship wherein we cooperate so as to grow spiritually and to experience the leading of the Holy Spirit as he leads us with dynamic spiritual power. The force of sin is beguiling and powerful, but the influence of the Spirit is winsome and more powerful. The challenge we face is like a well-developed "muscle memory" where over time our mind and emotions have become habituated to wrongdoing. I developed a bad habit in swimming freestyle of only turning my head to the right side to breathe as I swam. After time, it seemed impossible to change because "muscle memory" had taken over. It was only with great concentration and practice that I changed to breathing on both the right and the left. When we first start dealing with the chaos of sin within, many of us assume that it is impossible to change. As we start practicing the skills, we will be in for a pleasant surprise.

Sin leads us to lose our dignity in wrongdoing, God the Father treats us with profound dignity and gives us true freedom in the process of spiritual growth.

For sin shall not lord over you, for you are not under Law but under grace. (6:14)

Paul made the flat statement that even though the Christian walk is synergistic (we have to participate), sin will not dominate us. Interestingly, he used the term **κυριεύω kurieuo** "to be a lord or master" and not **βασιλεύω basileuo** "to reign as king." The reason is because we are under grace and not law. The first law in the Garden, "do not eat lest you die" really was illustrative of the legal system. It was primarily negative (as are nine of the Ten Commandments), and fiercely punitive, "you sin and you die." Thankfully, we are not under that system, so we can find help in time of need. What we have here is simply the reiteration of statements in Romans 5: the primary one being that where sin reigned as king, now it is God's purpose that grace should more excessively reign through righteousness unto eternal life through Christ (5:20-21). A whole series of statements in chapter 5 made it clear that grace is now the supreme "law" of God (5:2, 15, 17, 20-21). We are under grace and as we respond to grace, we can be confident that the lordship of sin will be abrogated.

Presenting Ourselves

The next section began with a question just as 6:1 began with a series of questions.

What then? Should we sin because we are not under Law but under grace? Absolutely not! (6:15)

This question was a bit different than 6:1-3 with its four questions. The key question asked whether we shall continue in sin. 6:1 was a noun, "sin," while 6:15 was a verb, "should we sin." The first described a relationship to sin as a slave to a master (again notice "reign as a king" in 6:12 and "reign as a lord" in verse 14). But the issue in verse 6:15 was perpetrating one act of sin. He answered that question with another question about what they knew. He was asking them if they knew the "stand around principle."

*Do you not know [47] that when you are presenting yourselves [**παρίστημι paristemi** "to stand around or near"] to someone as slaves to listen to, you are slaves of the one whom you listen to, either of sin resulting in death, or of obedient listening resulting in righteousness? 17 But thanks be to God that though you were slaves of sin, you listened from the heart to that form of teaching to which you were committed, 18 and having been liberated from sin you were enslaved to righteousness. (6:16-18)*

The word Paul the Apostle used in verses 16 and 17 means **ὑπακούω hupakuo** "to listen as to obey." It implies that the master who is speaking can speak with such force that it bends the will of the recipient. That is certainly true for both sin and God the Father. Our status before God is that of free daughters and sons and not of slaves. Paul always used the word slaves in the sense of those who are powerless before their master. If

---

[46] In John 18:21 used of servants standing around to serve or of kings waiting to serve (Isaiah 60:10 LXX), or of a worshipper standing before God and watching carefully (Psalm 5:3 LXX).

[47] The "know" of verse 16 was **οἶδα oida** "to know information or learn by analysis" as opposed to 6:5 **γινώσκοντες ginoskontes** "knowing by experience." Paul assumed that Christian truth only has value when it is known experientially.

the master is God, we are controlled by him. If the master is sin, we are controlled by sin. Of course, this is bad and good news. It is bad news if the master is sin; wonderful news if the master is God. Paul commended the Roman Christians for listening so as to make God their heavenly master. The listening that Paul referred to was the listening of the heart. As we assume a living relationship to God through Christ, we will find the mind and the emotions can focus on what God is saying and respond.

Paul then said that he was "humanly speaking" (6:19) and A.T. Robertson commented on this: "He begs pardon for using "slaving" in connection for righteousness."[48] The analogy of slavery did not completely fit because the Christian response of obedience is predicated upon kindness and gracious empowerment. Paul then commended the Roman Christian for having already presented themselves to God so that they have entered the process of sanctification.[49] In verses 20 and 21, Paul emphasized that the Roman Christians had no benefit nor fruit from their previous life with its slavery to sin. That life was a life of death, spiritually and eventually physically.

In verses 22-23, Paul gave a summary of what he described earlier in the chapter before he entered the incredible teaching on the Law and the believer in chapter 7.

> *But now having been freed from sin and enslaved to God, you derive your fruit, for the process of sanctification, and the outcome, eternal life. (6:22)*

God's way of changing our lives is through an intelligent and predictable process.

1. The process starts with Romans 6:11 where Paul tells us to count ourselves alive to God the Father. At that point we are freed from the power of sin.

2. As the process works, it introduces the fruit of the Spirit (Galatians 5:22). The fruit of the Spirit changes our internal characteristics to qualities such as love, joy and peace. As these qualities become the atmosphere of the heart, it leads the person to do things that are pleasing to God and helpful to others.

3. And then these qualities and actions become the energy for the process of sanctification. The word for sanctification refers to the process and not the final result.

4. We are supposed to take the fruit of the Spirit and use those powerful qualities to do God's will. As we do the Father's will, we discover the experience of eternal life. Eternal life is not referring to being in heaven, but it refers to the heavenly experience a Christian can have on the Earth. We can be participating in the life of heaven now. In the context, it was in contrast to the reign of death and sin in this life.

Notice that in this process, we work together with the triune God. We focus on the Father, based on our Union with Christ, and we are empowered by the Holy Spirit. We are participants in a relationship and not cogs in a process.

What makes this process effective is that it is based on grace and not Law, for the wage under the legal system is death.

> *For the pay wage of sin is death, but the free gift of God is eternal life in Christ Jesus our Lord. (6:23)*

ὀψώνιον **opsonion** "a soldier's wage or wages generally."[50] This was a remarkably forthright statement of principle by Paul. Sin and death were well deserved wages for being a slave to unrighteousness, but in contrast, grace gave the experience of eternal life as a gift. Romans 6:23 has a contrast between wages and gift. In the Greco-Roman world of Paul's time, wages were paid to only free men and women. They were not paid to

---

[48] Robertson, <u>Word Pictures</u>, Vol. IV, p. 364. Robertson pointed out that Paul used similar language in Romans 3:5 and Galatians 3:15. Paul used slavery as his illustration but he obviously felt it was inadequate for the true liberty and grace of Christ. See also 1 Corinthians 3:2 where Paul spoke of feeding the Corinthians spiritual milk and not meat.

[49] Arndt and Gingrich, <u>Lexicon</u>, p. 9. "(LXX) *holiness, consecration, sanctification*; the use in a moral sense for a process or, more often, its result (the state of <u>being made</u> holy) is peculiar to our literature . . ." [emphasis mine].

[50] Arndt and Gingrich, <u>Lexicon</u>, p. 606-607.

slaves. A distinct contrast was made between working for something and, therefore, receiving something that was totally deserved. Wages were not given to slaves but to those who hired themselves out. The Greek word was frequently used of soldiers who volunteered to serve. They worked hard for what they earned. In the same way, we have worked hard for what we deserve – death. We can rejoice that Paul said that our salvation has come as an undeserved gift in the face of a very, well deserved judgment to outer darkness and Hell.

Traditional Chinese culture is based on reciprocal relationships. If you give a gift to a person, the assumption is that you will be given back a different gift of equal value. The idea of a gift with no strings attached hardly exists at all in traditional Chinese culture. In one sense, a gift in that culture is actually a bill. It is also sometimes hard for an American Caucasian Christian to understand what a free gift really is. The text of the New Testament may help us: the word "free gift" is always used of being given an undeserved gift. For example, the word for "gift" in Greek was used also of being insulted or being mistreated when it was not deserved. Christ was beaten and he did not deserve it and that was called a gift in Greek and translated "without cause" (John 15:25)! [51] This word for "gift" was used in Greek for undeserved mistreatment or an undeserved present.

In chapter 6, we have seen another solution added, the capacity to control and manage desires. That is the solution God provided through his Son and the Holy Spirit. Our part is to integrate the truth so that the knowledge of that capacity becomes actualized by our relationship to God and integrated as a spiritual habit into our life. As we proceed, we will be given other solutions, but each solution is the springboard for learning and mastering the 7 skills of Romans.

PROBLEM	SOLUTION
1. Humanity turned over to its desires (1:24)	Believers given the capacity to manage desires and control them (6:11-13)
2. Humanity turned over to its dishonorable moods (1:26)	
3. Humanity turned over to a disapproved mind that failed the test (1:28)	
4. Humanity trapped by a chaotic culture exhibiting great immorality (1:18-32)	
5. The Jews adopted a performance based religion resulting in hypocrisy (2-3)	
6. Union with Adam resulting in sin within, death, condemnation, and status as a sinner (5:12-21)	Union with Christ resulting in death to sin, life in Christ, justification, and status as a righteous one (5:15-21; 6)

Romans 6 described an incredible series of gracious realities Christ has brought into our lives. Now Paul was going to describe the greatest threat to those gifts. Amazingly it was the Old Testament Law itself!

---

[51] See also Galatians 2:21 where it can be translated " . . . then Christ died for no reason [as a gift or gift-wise]." Liddell and Scott, Lexicon, p.404. **δωρεά**, Ion. -**εή, ἡ,** a gift, present, esp. *a free gift*, bounty, Lat. beneficium, Hdt., Aesch., etc. II. acc. **δωρεάν** as Adv., as a free gift, freely, Lat. gratis, Hdt.

7 | THE COLLAPSE OF THE LAW

CHAPTER SUMMARY: Paul explicitly illustrated that we are not under the **Law**. From that, he proceeded to describe the danger of the **Law** and its use by sin: first, in the past it led to his spiritual death, and second, it led him to describe the present powerlessness of the believer without the aid of the Holy Spirit. As the most powerful illustration possible, Paul used his own slavery to the flesh as a Christian. At the same time, it implicitly argued for the necessary help of the Holy Spirit in chapter 8.

What You Need to Know About Old Testament Law

The typical Evangelical and Catholic has two major misunderstandings about the Old Testament. The first is that the Law was simply a moralistic system when instead it was an entire legal system addressing nearly all aspects of Israelite life. The second is that the God of the Old Testament was mean and a "score-keeper," very different from the nice God of the New Testament. Both the belief about the Law and the belief about God are false.

The Law contained 613 laws addressing worship, uncleanness, the kingship, community property, marriage, and numerous other subjects.[52] The legal system was punitive and not restorative. Yahweh was restorative, and under his gracious reign sins were forgiven, punishments were lifted, and the people and nation were blessed. What made the Law work was God giving life to the system of rules. In a faith relationship with Yahweh, the Israelite would be blessed.

> *How blessed are those whose way is blameless, Who walk in the law of the LORD. 2 How blessed are those who observe His testimonies, <u>Who seek Him with all their heart</u>. (Psalm 119:1-2 NAS)*

In that sense the Law of Israel was intended to be a synergistic system wherein a living relationship to Yahweh would result in the Law being kept.

T**he Law would not work without a gracious God at its center.
Enablement was found with him.**

Yahweh had to be the one who made the Law effective as confessed by the Psalmists in particular.

---

[52] Excursus I will address the nature of the Law in detail.

Blessed art Thou, O LORD; Teach me Thy statutes. (Psalm 119:12 NAS)

Through this trusting love affair between Yahweh and the individual Israelite abundant life and preservation of life was given. Notice how the implementation of the Law and the gift of blessing was from God. The blessing was found in a faith relationship with the God in the Tabernacle and later the Temple. The God of the Temple brought life to the nation and empowerment to the believing Israelite.

For a day in Thy courts is better than a thousand outside. I would rather stand at the threshold of the house of my God, Than dwell in the tents of wickedness. (Psalm 84:10 NAS)

Thou wilt make known to me the path of life; In Thy presence is fulness of joy; In Thy right hand there are pleasures forever. (Psalm 16:11 NAS)

Psalm 119, the longest Psalm in the Old Testament, is the embodiment of the synergistic principle that God had to give life to the Law with its ordinances and rules.

Deal bountifully with Thy servant, That I may live and keep Thy word. (Psalm 119:17 NAS)

Turn away my eyes from looking at vanity, And revive me in Thy ways. (Psalm 119:37 NAS)

This theme was repeated over and over: as Yahweh gave abundant life the Law would be kept (Psalm 119:17, 25, 37, 40, 50, 77, 88, 93, 107, 116, 144, 149, 154, 156, 159, 175). Obviously Psalm 119 emphasized the connection between the keeping of the Law and the enablement of Yahweh. In other Psalms it was recognized that life, and abundant life, and the capacity to obey came from the presence of God (Psalm 41:2; 69:32; 80:18; 85:6; 138:7; 143:11).

Then we shall not turn back from Thee; Revive us [make us alive], and we will call upon Thy name. (Psalm 80:18 NAS)

In the eyes of the Old Testament the Law was majestic. One of the most positive statements concerning the Law is from Psalm 19.

7 The law of the LORD is perfect, restoring the soul; The testimony of the LORD is sure, making wise the simple. 8 The precepts of the LORD are right, rejoicing the heart; The commandment of the LORD is pure, enlightening the eyes. 9 The fear of the LORD is clean, enduring forever; The judgments of the LORD are true; they are righteous altogether. (Psalm 19:7-9 NAS)

What we have in the Old Testament is a wonderful Law (Psalm 119:18, 129), a wonderful God, and a wonderful Holy Spirit who was in the midst of Israel (Isaiah 63:11). How then could Paul say something like this?

9 And I was once alive apart from the Law; but when the commandment came, sin became alive again, and I died;10 and this commandment, which was to result in life, <u>proved to result in death for me</u>; (Romans 7:9-10)

How did this commandment, the tenth one saying, " . . . do not covet," which was meant to bring life through its content, with the tutelage and empowerment of Yahweh, and the presence and power of the Holy Spirit result in death? Our examination of Romans 7 will answer that in detail. In the meantime, let me answer that in the broadest terms.

The wondrous Law was accompanied by the enablement of God, and by the presence of the Holy Spirit. What changed? The change agent was God in the person of Jesus.

The name of Jesus meant in Hebrew "Yahweh has Saved!" In the New Testament, he was the living presence of the Old Testament Yahweh. To reject him was to reject the Father who was exactly like him. The Messiah came to Israel and what he found was that the Law and a real relationship with Yahweh was set aside for a hypocritical and prideful practice of a thoroughly watered-down version of the Law. In fact, this watered-down version completely undercut the role of the Law in Israel. The implicit goal of the Pharisees was to ignore a faith relationship to God and to earn the blessings of Yahweh through their own fleshly efforts. Jesus confronted them.

> 19 "Did not Moses give you the Law, and yet none of you carries out the Law? Why do you seek to kill Me?" (John 7:18 NAS)

Rejecting him, the Pharisees participated in a judicial murder of God. Before his death on the cross Jesus said this.

> 38 "Behold, your house is being left to you desolate! 39 "For I say to you, from now on you shall not see Me until you say, 'Blessed is He who comes in the name of the Lord!'" (Matthew 23:38-39 NAS)

With the rejection of Christ, the Temple was left empty of any divine presence and of any blessing. With the rejection and murder of Israel's Messiah, Jesus arose from the dead and became the Head of the Body of Christ. In the Old Testament the Holy Spirit, as we know, left Saul and alighted upon David (1 Samuel 16:13-14). What happened on the Day of Pentecost the nation of Israel was left behind, as with Saul so with Israel, and the Spirit came in flaming tongues of fire to the Church, the Body of Christ (the Body of David's greater Son).

Without empowerment the Law is just words on paper. Christians are called to ". . . serve in **newness of the Spirit**" and not in oldness of the letter (Romans 7:6). They become dangerous words when Christians use the morality from the Old Testament Law as a guide to spirituality instead of relying on the relationship to our Father, our Union with Christ, and the fruit and wisdom from the Spirit. As Paul pointed out in Romans 7 the Law's purpose now is to tell us what is wrong and to be avoided. The Trinity does not need a rule book to help them to make us holy.

Putting this in simplest terms: with the appearance of the Christ, a vastly greater privilege was granted to those who exercise faith than was given to Israel.

> **C**hristians can live life in the presence of the Trinity
> needing only the Law to tell them what is sin.

The Christian life is like driving a car down a lane of the highway and the Law is simply the rumble strips on the road that vibrate the car to tell the driver she is drifting off the road.. We are to wake up to those alerts and stay within the guardrails of the Trinity. The positive Christian life is totally dependent upon the Three, and we do not need a rule back in our back pocket. We will now enter Romans 7 and see how Paul the Apostle to the Gentiles expressed these truths.

Romans 7, from my perspective, is one of the most unique and interesting chapters in the Bible. Isaiah 52-53 gives a fascinating picture of the Servant of Yahweh dying for the children of God. It is astonishing in its material and scope. Romans 7 also is astonishing in its material, scope, and insight. From my perspective, Isaiah gave a marvelous picture of God and Romans 7 gave a marvelously disquieting picture of humanity. At the same time, it gave amazing insights into the nature of being human. To understand Romans 7 is to understand ourselves.

THREE ISSUES WITH THE HUMAN CONDITION

To appreciate what Paul has to say about the human condition, the contextual issues behind Romans 7 and its examination of the Law are important to understand. Three different issues need to be borne in mind.

Issue #1

The first issue was that even though believers had been given a wonderful deliverance in Christ as described in Romans 5-6:14, starting with 6:15, Paul presented a challenge where he emphasized that believers could become enslaved again to sin.

> *Do you not realize that when you present yourselves to someone as slaves for obedient listening, <u>you are slaves of the one to whom you listen and obey</u>, either of <u>sin resulting in death</u>, or of obedient listening resulting in righteousness? But thanks be to God that though you were slaves of sin, you became obedient listeners from the heart to that outline of teaching which you were handed,(6:16-17)*

This possibility of entering the sphere of death again was based on 6:11 where Paul commanded that believers reckon themselves continually alive to God the Father and dead to sin. The synergistic relationship that the Trinity created for us with them was not without the possibility of failure. In fact, Paul stated that we needed to be careful with even one sin because that could open the door to failure and slavery.

Issue #2

Paul said five times before chapter 7 that we were not under the Law. In the whole Book of Romans he said that ten times. Other than the fact that Gentile Christians were not under the Law, what were the further implications of that positively and negatively? An explanation would help. It was one thing to say that Israel failed to keep the Law, which he did indeed say in Romans 2-3, but the reason for that failure was not addressed. Hypocrisy was the criticism that Paul leveled at the Jews, but what were the deeper reasons? Shortly, we shall see that the deeper explanation was the second thing Romans 7 addressed.

Paul reiterated ten times that Gentiles and Christians were not under Law.

1. For when Gentiles who <u>do not have the Law</u> do instinctively perform the requirements of the <u>Law</u>, (Romans 2:14 NAS)

2. But now <u>apart from the Law</u> the righteousness of God has been manifested. (Romans 3:21 NAS)

3. For we maintain that a man is justified by faith <u>apart from works of the Law</u>. (Romans 3:28 NAS)

4. For sin shall not be master over you, for you are <u>not under law</u>, but under grace. (Romans 6:14 NAS)

5. What then? Shall we sin because we are not under law but under grace? May it never be! (Romans 6:15 NAS)

6. Therefore, my brethren, you also were made to <u>die to the Law</u> through the body of Christ, (Romans 7:4 NAS)

7. But now we have been <u>released from the Law</u>, (Romans 7:6 NAS)

8. And I was once alive <u>apart from the Law</u>; (Romans 7:9 NAS)

9. For the law of the Spirit of life in Christ Jesus has set you <u>free from the law</u> of sin and of death. (Romans 8:2 NAS)

10. For Christ is the <u>end of the law</u> for righteousness to everyone who believes. (Romans 10:4 NAS)

So why was it necessary to avoid participating in the Law? That will be answered in detail by Paul in chapter 7.

Issue #3

A third reason was based on the absence of a critically important subject, the person of the Holy Spirit. The word "Spirit" occurred once in Romans 7, and 14 times in Romans 8 which has 39 verses. Chapter 7 was really about <u>the absence</u> of the Spirit, and the explanation of why the gift of the Spirit was so critically important. Romans 8 was about <u>the presence</u> of the Spirit and his ministries. Chapter 7 looked backward and forward, backward to why the Law was ineffective, and forward to the ministry of the Trinity with special emphasis on the Holy Spirit. The purpose was to lay the foundation for the fundamentally important ministry of the Spirit. The reason for why we need the Holy Spirit in our lives was spelled out in Romans 7. One must remember that Paul assumed that a living relationship to the Trinity was all that a believer needed. Yet the Law became a subtle and powerful trap when that was part of the equation of sanctification as opposed to relying on a vibrant relationship to the Trinity.

Our approach to Romans 7 is based on a careful analysis of the opening illustration and Paul's outline of his text in that chapter. Paul has a very helpful outline in his use of three questions. Further, he gave an illustration (one of the only three true illustrations in the Book of Romans) to bridge chapters 1-6 to chapter 8. Often commentators seem to treat the three questions and the illustration as disconnected, disparate parts. Yet Paul gave us a quite clear outline and a simple illustration to follow and understand.

As was said, Romans 7 is a challenge to many Bible teachers and commentators. We can help our understanding by noting three questions and the opening illustration.

Outline of Romans 7

1. <u>First Question</u>: "Do You Not Personally Know?" to those who Personally Know the Law (1)

    a. Opening Illustration (2-3)

    b. The Illustration Explained (4-6)

3. <u>Second Question</u>: Is the Law Sin? (7-12)

4. <u>Third Question</u>: Did the Law Become Death (spiritual death)? 13-25

<u>First Question</u>: Do You Not Personally Know? Liberation Through the Spirit (7:1-6)

The opening illustration of chapter 7 stated two times (7:4, 6) that we were no longer under the Law. We were freed from the Law.

> *Or do you not personally know, brethren (for I am speaking to those who personally know the Law), that the Law lords it over a person as long as he lives? 2 For the married woman was bound like a slave by Law to her husband while he was living; but if the man should die, she was released from the Law concerning the husband. 3 So then if, while her husband was living, she was joined to a different kind of man, she shall be called an adulteress; but if her husband died, <u>she was free from the Law</u>, so that she was not an adulteress, though she was joined to a different kind of man. 4 Therefore, my brethren, you also were made to <u>die to the Law through the body of Christ</u>, that you might be joined to another of a different kind, to him who was raised from the dead, that we might bear fruit for God. (7:1-4)*

Even though it would be a mistake, the Law was the only moral option other than complete reliance on the Trinitarian relationships that Christians could accept. Since it was God derived, no other alternative system to Christianity would suffice. With the Law being abrogated, every other moral system was abrogated. Why? Because the change agent that wants us to leave the Law behind is the Holy Spirit. The Old Testament Law was God given, but without the Holy Spirit, no empowerment existed.

With the coming of Christ, we are given a relationship to God the Father through our Union with Christ so that we experience the deliverance and fruit from the Spirit of God.

The second husband who was of a different sort was Christ and with our union with him, we could bear fruit to the Father. The Book of Romans clearly taught that we are not under the Law, but under the rule of the Spirit. That was the positive statement. The next verse was the negative statement describing the torture the Law produced within the unsaved.

> *For while we were in the flesh, the moods of sins, which were being energized by the Law, were continually at work in the members of our body to bear fruit for death. 6 But now we have been released from the Law, having died to that by which we were bound, so that we serve in newness of the Spirit and not in oldness of the letter. (7:5-6)*

Verse 5 with the phrase "in the flesh" was explained as to its meaning in Romans 8:9.

But you yourselves are not in the flesh but in the Spirit, since indeed the Spirit of God dwells in you. But if anyone does not have the Spirit of Christ, this one is not of him. (8:9)

Paul was describing how the Law worked with those who did not have the Spirit of God within (the unsaved). Moods **τὰ παθήματα ta pathemata** "strong uncomfortable emotions" were being continually energized by the Law, and the end result was the very natural overflow of wrongdoing (like fruit) into the life, and the end result of that, spiritual death. Paul described these sins as being driven by uncomfortable emotions. With each sin, a subsurface amount of pain was driving the sin. Such a combination would create the natural growth of death-dealing fruit. The point he was making was that Law created an unhealthy emotional atmosphere within. This atmosphere was so powerful that it drove the person into the clutches of death.

In the first place in his illustration, the Law and Christ were the different husbands. This implied that our choice of the Law would be the rejection of the Christ. Then, Paul introduced the Holy Spirit as the alternative to the written Law and with that, it was the only mention of him in chapter 7. Paul's approach to the spiritual life was a complete dependence on the Trinity. To underscore that, he repeatedly emphasized how ineffectual the Law was. He pointed out that the Law produced painful emotions or moods. These moods were actually brought forth by the Law as naturally as fruit was produced by a tree. But this fruit produced death. This should bring to mind the Tree of the Knowledge of Good and Evil. These emotions produced a murderous fruit.

Now he said what he has said repeatedly, we were not under the legal system of the Old Testament. In fact, we can include any rules-based system with that. The reason was that Paul had only one true method for the spiritual life and that was a living relationship to each member of the Trinity where we would relate to God as Father based on our unity with Christ as we were empowered by the Holy Spirit. We can say any rules-based system will lead to emotional pain and the same type of death that Adam and Eve experienced. A Trinitarian approach will lead to participating in the life of the Trinity!

Typically with Christ and Paul, they first presented an illustration and then gave an explanation of the illustration.[53] The illustration using marriage and death and remarriage was the strongest possible way of stating we were not under the Law. The chapter began with an illustration that stated as firmly as possible that the Law's reign was over. This would naturally lead to a speculation as to why the Law was set aside. The two questions following the illustration and its explanation could have been asked by a Rabbinic critic of Paul who wanted to refute and condemn him, or they could have just been asked by a new Christian or any Christian who found the whole thing confusing.

These two questions echoed chapter 5 where through Adam sin entered, and then death followed (spiritual and physical): sin (5:12, 13, 20, 21), death (5:12, 14, 15, 17, 21). Further, Christ's death and resurrection addressed the issues of sin and death. The two words were not randomly chosen by Paul but the two words were the immediate result of Adam's Fall. Since Paul presented the Law as energizing strong painful emotions, the natural question was how bad was the Law really? How could a good God give an evil, pain-inducing Law? Paul had the questioner directly link the Law to the result of the Fall, sin and death (particularly spiritual death). With that linkage, Paul proceeded to give this astonishing description of the connection between the Law and sin.

Second Question: Is the Law sin? (7:7-12)

Paul began by giving the purpose of the law.

What then are we saying? Is the Law sin? Absolutely not! But sin I did not personally recognize except

---

[53] There were only three true illustrations in the Book of Romans: the first was the widowed woman who remarried (7:1-3), the second was the clay pot (9:20-23), and the third was the Olive Tree of chapter 11:17-24, with verse 17 and 24 being the only verses that actually mentioned the Olive Tree. In the first two illustrations the explanation of them followed the illustration. In the third the explanation was woven into the illustration. For the widow illustration the explanatory comment in verses 4-6 then led to the two crucial questions of the chapter (7:7, 13).

through Law, for indeed [sinful] *appetite I did not recognize except the Law was saying – you shall not desire* [sinfully]. *(7:7)*

$\mathbf{L}$aw has a magnificent purpose. Its purpose was to tell us what is wrong.[54]

It surprises us that such is the whole purpose. But we must remember it is profoundly difficult for human beings to recognize their own wrongdoing. In parts of the world that have not been influenced by Christianity, absolutely barbaric practices exist and are not condemned. For example, the poor are allowed to die in the streets of India and the population walks by without noticing. If you asked them if they are bothered by the dying people directly under their feet, they would be surprised by the question. Many people from around the world have been amazed by the efforts our emergency workers would make to save sick and dying people. The reason they work so hard can be traced back to the Old and the New Testament with its emphasis on the infinite value of a human being. In the Old and New Testament were laws and rules protecting the value of persons. Without those laws, Western culture would have no conscience whatsoever. The Law performs an extremely valuable service for us both personally and culturally. But what the Law cannot do is change our character. Only grace can do that.

Paul made the interesting point that it would not have initially occurred to him that coveting was wrong. The Law needed to tell him that. The Greek text in Romans simply has "don't you desire." In Exodus 20:7, the desiring was connected to wanting that which was not our own and that was why the word "covet" was used. Due to the Law, unnoticed desire became observed, and then it stirred up a frenzy of coveting.

Then, Paul shared a truly incredible psychological insight.

> *But sin, finding a base through the commandment, effectively produced in me coveting of every kind of unhealthy desire for apart from the Law sin is dead. (7:8)*

Sin is like the invisible man who needs clothes for us to know he is there. In the same way, sin needs the Law so that we know sin exists. This is the difference between a reaction and an eruption. An eruption spontaneously happens like a volcano. But a reaction needs an agent to cause the reaction. This is a very strange thing to understand. How can a rule change our emotional life? Yet it does. In some strange way a rule produces a strengthening of our desires so much so that we become enslaved to them. Further, it produces a deep seated sense of failure and oddly, a deeper sense of obligation. This becomes part of the **τὰ παθήματα ta pathemata** or emotional pain from Law or sin. But it is striking that Paul says that sin is a corpse without the Law or a rule. Sin is like Frankenstein which needs empowerment to come alive. Paul was saying that Law plus sin created uncontrolled fleshly living. That is stunning. This should be an encouragement to us to pursue life within the Trinity. It doesn't matter if it is a little Law or a lot of the Law, such does not bring spiritual life. It brings death. We are forced to the only alternative, a spiritual life completely dependent on the Spirit of God.

To explain what he just said, Paul then gave the example of his own life experience.

> *And I was for a time alive apart from the Law;[55] but when the commandment came, sin became alive again, and I died; 10 and this commandment, which was to result in life, proved to result in death for me; 11 for sin, taking opportunity through the commandment, deceived me, and through it killed me. (7:9-11)*

Paul was alive apart from the Law for a length of time. "Length of time" is **ποτέ pote** "an indefinite length of time." It was used of the man born blind (John 9:13). It could easily be a lengthy period of time. English translations often translated **pote** with "once." That is an ambiguous translation because it could imply "just once and it was over quickly." I do not believe that was what he was saying here. Paul was once

---

[54] Romans 3:20, " . . . for through Law is a personal knowledge of sin."

[55] There is what I consider an embarrassing theory that this "being alive" referred to Paul before the time of moral accountability when he was a child, embarrassing because Rabbinic Judaism considered every Jew under the Law particularly after circumcision. Sanday and Headlam, Romans, p. 180. This commentary is very good but this silly error still crept in.

spiritually alive and then he spiritually died (since he obviously wrote Romans, he did not physically die!); sin was dead and it came to life **again**. The Greek word is **ἀναζάω anazao** "to live again." Occurring twice in the Greek New Testament, it was also found when the father said to the elder brother in Luke 15:24, ". . . your brother was dead and now he is alive **again!**" This comment by the father was an excellent illustration of what Paul meant by death. If sin was ignored because the believer was in a living relationship with God the Father, then sin is dead (relationally). It has not ceased to exist but it is not in a determinative place in the person's life. When we ignore God and listen to the lusts of sin, neither does God cease to exist, but we are dead to him.

This tells us that Paul practiced the truths of Romans 6 and lived a spiritual life. But something happened. How could he have been alive and then die? Yet it is necessary and important to notice the consistency that Paul exercised in his use of the sin and death vocabulary. To listen to the commands of sin was also simultaneously to enter the realm of death and be "killed."

Judaism has only two ways to get out from beneath the Law: one is by death, and the other is by conversion to Christianity since Orthodox Jews assumed that no Gentile nor Christian was under the Law. At the very beginning of Romans 7, Paul stated the legal principle.

> *. . . the Law rules over the man for the entire time he lives. . . (7:1)*

The same was said by Paul in Galatians 4:4.

> *. . . God sent forth his son, begotten out of a woman, having become under the Law,*

In a sense, Paul qualified for both conditions: first, he became a Christian, and second he died with Christ to the Law that he might be joined to another, Christ. In Romans 7, Paul assumed that life was spiritual life with God; he was living the abundant life that Christ promised. Because he was living the abundant life: sin was dead and he did not have a master-slave relationship to it. Then, the content of the commandment focused his attention and as he tried to perform that commandment by his own will and not by the empowerment of the Holy Spirit, he found that his relationship to God died – and a relationship to sin became very much alive. The language was very dramatic. We are either alive to God or alive to sin. Our life source is dependent upon what we relate to. If we relate to God, we are spiritually alive. If we relate to desire and Law, we are killed and are dead to God.[56]

To truly understand what Paul said, we must master the thinking of Romans 5, 6, and 7. All of Romans 5-7 was based on how Paul viewed the temptation and Fall of Genesis 3. Eve and Adam were faced with a choice, either obey God and maintain a living relationship with him, or succumb to their growing desire to eat of the fruit of the Tree of the Knowledge of Good and Evil.[57] They were faced with the choice of the lure of desire, or their relationship with God. When they ate, God did what he did in Romans 1:24, he handed them over to the Kingship of appetites or sin. On the other side of that choice was death, spiritual or relational death. Physical death would come later. On the day Adam ate of it, he truly died. His death was a spiritual one, a relational one.

---

[56] An excellent summary of the different views concerning whether Paul was describing himself as a Christian in Romans 7 is found in C.E.B. Cranfield, <u>The Epistle to the Romans</u> (Edinburgh: T. & T. Clark, 1975), pp. 342-347. His conclusion was "(i) that it is autobiographical, the reference being to Paul's present experience as a Christian; and (vii) that it represents the experience of Christians generally, including the very best and most mature."

[57] I would translate the Hebrew of Genesis 3 "The Tree of the Experience of Benefit and Wretchedness." The Tree was not emphasizing a choice but a process. If the fruit was eaten which appeared to be an obvious good, it would be followed by the wretched experience of the Fall.

In Romans 5-7, Paul made this a consistent principle: to choose desire over God was to enter death, to die, to be killed. When the commandment "You shall not covet" came, sin came alive again, and in choosing coveting, Paul entered the realm of death. He died relationally or spiritually. Notice his language.

- Sin became alive again, and I myself <u>died</u>; **ἐγὼ δὲ ἀπέθανον** (7:9)

- And it was found for me, the commandment unto life, that one was unto <u>death</u> **καὶ εὑρέθη μοι ἡ ἐντολὴ ἡ εἰς ζωήν, αὕτη εἰς θάνατον** (7:10)

- Sin. . . through the commandment completely deceived me and through it killed **ἁμαρτία . . . διὰ τῆς ἐντολῆς ἐξηπάτησέν** [58] **με καὶ δι᾽ αὐτῆς ἀπέκτεινεν** (7:11)

- . . . but sin, in order that sin should be manifested through the good [Law] for me was working <u>death</u> **ἀλλὰ ἡ ἁμαρτία, ἵνα φανῇ ἁμαρτία, διὰ τοῦ ἀγαθοῦ μοι κατεργαζομένη θάνατον** (7:13)

To understand Romans we must keep reminding ourselves of the building block nature of the book. Chapter 7 builds off of chapters 5 and 6. In those two chapters, sin died in relationship to us and we became alive in relationship to God. The Apostle described entering life through Christ (1:17; 5:17; 6:4, 13, 22), and sin dying (6:2, 6, 7, 11, 13, 14, 16, 18, 22). Nevertheless, we have to actualize our relationship to God by assuming ourselves alive to him in Christ.

I am quite confident that serious Christians find this language of Paul tension-creating. The immediate question would be, do we lose our salvation when we enter the realm of death by choosing desire over God? I believe that question should be answered two ways. First, we do not have the appreciation of the power of appetite apart from God. When we chose appetite over God, we do not enter a mild Spring warm rain. When we choose sin, we enter a hurricane, not a drizzle.

> **I**n a sense, in Christ we live in the eye of a hurricane. Our hearts are peaceful because the Holy Spirit gives us the fruit of the Spirit, love, joy, and peace. But outside of the eye is the turbulence and danger of the hurricane.

Paul viewed the presence of sin within and the flesh as quite powerful and dangerous and with them, they bring relational death.

Second, because these truths about us falling into relational death certainly are disturbing, we find that Scripture goes out of its way to encourage us concerning God's faithfulness, and our security with him. Paul told us that we are joined to Christ in Heaven, that we have the Holy Spirit as a permanent deposit to give us confidence about our salvation (Ephesians 1:13-14), and that we were chosen of the Father before the foundation of the Earth (Ephesians 1:1-4).

Paul's explanation about relational death occurring when we count ourselves alive to sin and listen to its appetites leads to his next question. He powerfully affirmed the fact that the Law is positive.

> *So that, the Law is holy, and the commandment is holy and righteous and beneficial. Therefore did that beneficial thing become a state of death for me? Absolutely not! Rather it was sin, in order that it might be shown to be sin by effectively causing death to me through that which is beneficial, that through the commandment sin might become excessively sinful. (7:12-13)*

Since Paul wrote this text, it is crystal clear that Paul did not die physically, but he died in his relationship with God through sin as it used the Law and the commandment. Twice in verse 13, Paul said, "that beneficial thing become a state of death for me," and "that it might be shown to be sin by effectively causing death." Notice that Paul said repeatedly that the Law was good or beneficial and righteous and holy. It was not the Law that was the difficulty. Law showed clearly how dangerously devious sin was. First, the Law told us what sin is, and then tragically it empowered sin so that we could not avoid seeing its strength. In fact, sin is so strong that it renders ineffective our relationship to God when we take our eyes off of our Father in heaven

---

[58] "Completely deceived" **ἐξηπάτησέν** was the same word (without the prefixed preposition **ἐξ**) used in the LXX when Eve explained to God why she ate the fruit (Genesis 3; 2 Cor. 11:3). Paul certainly knew that word usage and Romans 5-7 was really a broad recapitulation of Genesis 3 and the Fall.

and focus on the commandment instead. This tells us that our heart really has only one center.[59] When the center of our heart is God the Father, we are spiritually alive and healthy. When the center of our heart is a rule, sin is inflamed, our emotions are corrupted, and our relationship to God dissolves. Over and over again Paul told us our spiritual life has to be totally dependent on the Trinity.

The Power of the Flesh

We need verses 7:9-12 as background to the staggering realities of 7:13-25. How did Paul discover the profound weakness of the Christian without the aid of the Holy Spirit? He did it by embracing the practice of a good moral principle without resorting to the empowerment of the Holy Spirit. When he attempted that, he died relationally to God the Father and discovered the power of the flesh within. Note the outline below.

- The past discovery of the power of the flesh through the commandment (7:9-12)

- The present power of the flesh within (7:13-25)

- The deliverance of the Law of the Spirit of life in Christ Jesus (8:1-13)

Within the description of his own relational death, Paul posed the question: did the Law by some strange alchemy become death? His answer was that the problem was not within the Law. The problem was within us. We have the source of death within.

Third Question: Did the Law become Death? (7:13-25)

In this amazing section, Paul described how the Christian apart from the present work of the Holy Spirit was hopeless in the face of sin within. Paul proceeded to answer that question by describing the "hurricane within," the relational death when the Christian listened to and obeyed sin. This section is all in the present tense (which is quite important) showing that this was a present reality.

> For we understand that the Law is spiritual; but I am fleshly, having been sold unto sin. For that which I am effectively working out, I do not personally recognize; for what I am not desiring I am practicing, but what I am hating, I am doing. (7:14-15)

Two words are important to understand: one is "carnal" and the other is "sold unto sin." σάρκινός **sarkinos** "fleshly" was used by Paul to describe the Corinthian Christians (1 Corinthians 3:1; he also called them "babes"). The **-ινός -inos** ending in the word emphasized the evident source or what the thing was made of, as opposed to what its characteristics were as indicated by the **-ikos** ending.[60] πεπραμένος **pepramenos** "having been and remaining sold" underscored that without spiritual intervention by the Holy Spirit, the Christian was in a state of slavery to sin and was in the realm of death. Without the Holy Spirit, the life of the Christian was a life of massive contradiction.

"Human beings including Christians have a naive belief that we can be virtuous without the direct intervention of God. Without God's help, the only real choice we have is do we want to sin blandly or outrageously."

Paul described something odd. Basically, his activity was going in the opposite direction to his emotions or desires. One of the things we need to remember is how hopelessly we are turned against ourselves because of the Fall and sin. One of the realities of our lives is that we are an inherent contradiction. Emotionally, relationally, psychologically, spiritually, we sometimes feel and think in ways that are a complete contradiction to our sincerely held beliefs.

This was one of Paul's critically important points in his comments on the problem with the Law. If we

---

[59] Christ said that very clearly in the Sermon on the Mount. First, he said where our treasure is that is where our heart shall be. Secondly no one can serve two masters, he will either love the one or despise the other (Matthew 6:22, 24). In 6:23 he also said the darkness within those who choose another lord than the Father was great darkness. Great darkness appeared to be a metaphor for death!

[60] Richard Trench, Synonyms of the New Testament (Marshalltown, The National Foundation for Christian Education: n.d.), p. 256. See also Robertson, Grammar, pp. 158-159. Bruce M. Metzger, Lexical Aids for Students of New Testament Greek (Princeton: Theological Book Agency, 1969), pp. 43-44. What Paul appeared to be saying by using this ending was that the basic quality of the Christian without the intervention of the Spirit was fleshly.

focus on the rules, we do not have supernatural help because we are not focusing on God the Father through our identity with Christ as empowered by the Holy Spirit. We are not making ourselves available to the source of spiritual power, but instead we are relying on ourselves to keep the commandments and the rules.

To avoid being a hopeless contradiction in our lives and relationships,
we must pursue a healthy relationship with God the Father.
The source of this contradiction is the presence of indwelling sin.

And I myself am no longer effectually producing this, but the indwelling sin in me [is]. *(7:17)*

What this powerfully underscored was that in salvation and regeneration, we have not received the "resurrection, transformed" body. Instead, we were left with the inherent problem of indwelling sin. This inherent problem was to be solved as we synergistically worked within our life with the Trinity. Based on this, he made an observation about the flesh. In Paul's progression of building blocks, he now introduced the flesh in chapter 7 and will give the solution to the flesh in chapter 8.

For I recognize that there does not dwell, that is presently in my flesh, a beneficial thing. For the desiring [to do good] is immediately present, but effectively working out the good is not. (7:18)

In detail, Paul went on to describe the inherent contradiction between what his heart wanted to do and what actually happened. This reality was so repetitive that he reduced it to a law or a principle, the principle of the other law.

For I joyfully agree with the Law of God in the inner person, 23 but I am seeing a different kind of law in the members of my body, continually warring against the law of my mind, and leading me as a prisoner of the law of sin which is in my members. (7:22-23)

Paul used the word law to refer to an overarching system that addressed the entirety of our inner life. In these verses he was referring to the law of sin in our members that takes us captive. In our mind, we can appreciate God's Law and expectations. But such appreciation does not control our will, or our desires, or our actions. Instead, those realities should be spiritually controlled by a living relationship to God the Father.

We should note of great importance that Paul reintroduced the word **νοός nous** "mind." This anticipated the building blocks of chapter 8 and 12. In 1:28, Paul stated that God handed humanity over to a rejected mind. With this reintroduction of **νοός nous** in chapter 7:23, we have a strong indication that something profound had happened within in our minds as believers that gave us the ability to see reality anew. Shortly, Paul will state the tremendous importance of the **nous** in the spiritual life.

This was very similar to what Paul said in Romans 5. According to him, because of Adam, sin has come into our lives and we have become constituted or established as sinners.

Human beings including Christians have a naive belief that
we can be virtuous without the direct intervention of God. Without God's help,
the only real choice we have is deciding whether we want to sin blandly or outrageously.

We may not choose to do something awful, but that does not mean we are compassionate, loving, and forgiving. Selfishness, bitterness, and indifference may pass unnoticed in our hearts and in our actions. The more honestly we look, the more appalled we may be. Paul would say that was because we have the law of sin in our members, and another law of being captured by sin within.

The way out is referred to at the end of Romans 7 and developed in Romans 8 and 12 (after the three chapters, 9-11, about Israel).

Distressed and miserable man I am! Who shall rescue me from the body of this <u>death</u>? And thanks be to God through Jesus Christ our Lord. Therefore then, I myself, on the one hand, by the mind I am serving the Law of God, and on the other hand, with the flesh the Law of sin. (7:24-25)

Note carefully that Paul again connected death to the power of sin within. To obey sin was to enter the realm of non-relationship, death. Note also how the negative use of the word "flesh" appeared first in 7:6, and chapter 7 became a building block for the solution to the challenge of the flesh as it was developed in chapter 8. The verse in 7:6 spoke of us serving in a newness from the Spirit that will be further defined in chapter 8 which introduces skill numbers 4 and 5.

On the surface, the solution to this difficulty seemed odd. What appeared to be impossible to solve, Paul presented it as being solved through the mind. If we take the building block approach where he introduced the problems in chapter 1, and carefully observe how he put building blocks together to show the solutions to those problems, sense will be made out of what the Apostle was saying.

Note how Paul sequentially dealt with the three "handing overs" of chapter 1.

PROBLEM	SOLUTION
1. Humanity turned over to its desires (1:2)	Believers given the capacity to manage desires and control them (6:11-13)
2. Humanity turned over to its dishonorable moods (1:26)	Believers given the capacity to deal with moods through the Holy Spirit (7:5-6)
3. Humanity turned over to a disapproved mind that failed the test (1:28)	The Solution is 7:23, 25. Believers have an approved mind that approves God's ways (12:1-2)

The challenge of the flesh, introduced in 7:6, 18, 25 and the word "fleshly" used in 7:14, is addressed in chapter 8.

Chapter 7 is easily the most shocking chapter in the entire book. On a conceptual level, what Paul shared was powerfully forceful. His expression of those truths is breathtaking.

Paul underscored four things in chapter 7:

1. When Law is without enablement, it is useless and dangerous. Sin reduced Law to an abject handmaiden.

2. Death (spiritual and relational) always accompanied sin, even one act of sin. As it was in the Garden, one act of sin brought immediate spiritual death with physical death to follow, so it was with Paul. <u>Sin and death were inseparable.</u>

3. The Christian presently is completely unable to deal with sin and the flesh without enablement. Our intentions and our actions are in complete contradiction. God has so chosen to reduce us to a complete level of dependency so that we might learn the life of the Spirit.

4. In one sense, we are forced to reacquaint ourselves with our own humanity through the Triune relationships. We discover the proper use of our emotions, appetites, and mind not through rules. Instead, a growing dependency and relationship to each unique member of the Trinity not only introduces us to them, but also introduces us to a proper use of our own inner life. We are like babies or children in having to learn the simplest things.

Our dependency cannot be on our obedience to the Law. Instead the dependency is upon the life of God within. A way out exists. The way out is within us. It is the spiritual and proper use of the mind. This we will see in chapters 8 and 12.

8 | SPIRITUALITY

CHAPTER SUMMARY: The role of the Holy **Spirit** and his ministry was presented by Paul. This ministry sustained believers in the suffering of this world. In the midst of life's pain and threats, we must remember we are profoundly loved by the Father and the Son.

Two things were obvious in chapter 7, no hope exists for us with the Law, and no hope exists for us within ourselves, our flesh. This sets up the entrance of the Holy Spirit in chapter 8. Very little mention was made of the Spirit in the first seven chapters of Romans (five times). In chapter 8 he was mentioned 18 times. Previously the roles of the Son and the Father were developed, but it was in this chapter where the Spirit takes prominence. The Person of the Holy Spirit liberates the believer from sin and the Law and gives support through the sufferings of this life. In the face of the discouraging news he shared in chapter 7, Paul shared very good news indeed in chapter 8.

Liberation Through the Spirit (8:1-11)

> *Now not one condemnation therefore for those in Christ Jesus. For the Law of the Spirit of life in Christ Jesus has set you free from the Law of sin and of death. (8:1-2)*

κατάκριμα katakrima "condemnation" occurred three times in Romans. Once here and twice in chapter 5. After the choice of Adam, sin entered the world, then death, and then the third element came, condemnation for every descendant of Adam. A natural question would arise from chapter 7. Since sin and death occurred when a Christian sinned, did condemnation also occur? After this unsettling description of Christian failure in 7:14-24, naturally one would wonder how secure the failing Christian might be before God. In 8:1, Paul gave the definitive answer, not any condemnation whatsoever in Christ Jesus existed. Our Union with Christ is our security.

"The Law cannot be kept through human effort. Human effort only piles on more sin to be condemned."

Paul described the Law of sin and death in Romans 7. Because of the reality of sin, a preoccupation with the Law can produce spiritual death. Because of the reality of sin within, we are continually being captured by sin and death always came with it. That, Paul called the (Old Testament) Law of sin and death. Based on an entirely different system or law opposed to the Law of the Old Testament, we have been liberated. This new Torah or law is connected to the Holy Spirit. The Holy Spirit brings us life-changing fruit that makes us free to live, free to be joyful, free to be loving, and free to be peaceful. This law is also in connection with Jesus Christ. In our Union with Christ, we are safe from legal condemnation. With the presence of the Spirit of God, we are safe from the control of sin. The solid foundation for this is no condemnation in Christ Jesus.

The Old Testament Torah or Law dominated the life of the Israelite. It was a complete system of politics, religion, and the law. In the same way, the new Torah or law of the Spirit is to thoroughly dominate our lives. The life giving reality of the Holy Spirit is the new law's foundation. Paul then went on to explain this lack of condemnation. God did not condemn us. Instead he condemned sin in the flesh.

> *For the powerlessness of the Law in which it was weak on account of the flesh, God sending his own Son in the likeness of sinful flesh and for sin, he condemned[61] sin in the flesh, 4 in order that the righteous requirement of the Law might be fulfilled among us, in the ones not walking according to the flesh, but according to Spirit. (8:3-4)*

The legalists and the Christian agree on the same thing. The Law of the Old Testament is significant and its rules must be kept. But the issue is how it should be kept. For the legalists, it is through an act of the human will. The legalist supposed that if he kept the expectations of the Law, then God was obligated to bless him. But the Christian starts out at a different place. The Christian assumes that she already is completely blessed in Christ Jesus. Further, the keeping of the Law has to occur through the power of the Holy Spirit. The Law cannot be kept through human effort. Human effort only piles on more sin to be condemned. So human fallenness created two problems: one is guilt, and the other is weakness. Paul was saying that he has found a solution to the dilemma of the Old Testament. That solution was found in Christ in the power of the Holy Spirit. Again, the legalist and the Christian agree on the importance of rules or morality, but it is how those rules are kept that matters. It is not human power that will succeed. What matters is the power of the Spirit of the Father.

> *For those who are according to the flesh are setting their perspectives on the things of the flesh, but those who are according to the Spirit, the things of the Spirit. For the perspective set on the flesh is **death**, but the perspective set on Spirit is life and peace, (8:5-6)*

Paul, at this point, introduced four critically important terms, "walking," "setting perspective," "perspective," and "according to Spirit." All were related to the ministry of the Holy Spirit. The four terms were introduced in an interrelated pattern.

περιπατέω peripateo "to walk or arrange the way we live." There is a literal use of this term and a figurative use. As a literal term it meant to walk around. It could be used of a long journey or walking around in some type of clothing. In its figurative use it can be used of living a worthy life (Ephesians 4:1), walking or living in the light (John 12:35), and living or walking in harmony with a number of ethical and spiritual values. In effect, it emphasizes by what values or influences we organize our lives.[62] It is the larger term used by Paul for organizing one's life around the Spirit.

The next two words deal with thought and perspective. We will translate these as "having a perspective" or "perspective." This is quite important to notice the difference between the word perspective and the word **νοός nous** "mind." Our English translations make a mistake when they casually translate **φρονέω phroneo** "to have a perspective" and **φρόνημα phronema** "perspective" as "mind." For example, the King James Version, the New American Standard Version, and the New Jerusalem Bible all used "mind" for their term. This obscured an important distinction that Paul made between perspective (8:5-6) and mind (12:2). Simply put, a perspective is a settled way of thinking while mind is the instrument of thinking and relating. One is the product (perspective) and one is the machine (mind) so to speak.[63]

---

[61] **κατακρίνω katakrino** "condemned" is the verbal form of **κατάκριμα katakrima** "condemnation." We should note that by use of this verb Paul was stating, not us, but sin within us was condemned.

[62] Arndt and Gingrich, pp. 654-655.

[63] W. E. Vine, <u>An Expository Dictionary of New Testament Words</u> (Old Tappan, New Jersey: Fleming H. Revell Company, 1940), Vol. III, p. 69. Vine has a clear and helpful set of distinctions between mind and perspective.

φρονέω **phroneo** "to have a perspective" This term means to 1) "think, form or hold an opinion," 2) "set one's mind on," and 3) "have thoughts or (an) attitude(s), be minded or disposed." Note that the emphasis is on the conclusion of the thought process, the attitude that results.[64]

φρόνημα **phronema** "perspective" Arndt and Gingrich define this as, "way of thinking, mind(-set)."[65] The -μα on the end of the word is important to note because that ending was used with verbs to form a noun from the verb and the ending referred to the completed process, the settled perspective.[66]

κατὰ πνεῦμα **kata pneuma** "according to Spirit." We should organize our life and have a perspective in harmony with the Spirit of God. This is critically important. It shows that the Law of the Spirit of Life in Christ Jesus produces fruit within the life. κατὰ πνεῦμα **kata pneuma** will influence what we do in the world around us, περιπατέω **peripateo** "to walk or arrange the way we live," and will influence our mental processes φρόνημα **phronema** "perspective." Further, this is a complete contrast to "sin and death" wherein this new law is <u>life</u>. Also, this perspective as it is influenced by the Spirit of God, brings peace, a tranquility that is a world apart from the turmoil Paul described within himself in 7:14-24 and the absolute chaos of 1:24-32. We have three components mentioned as being under the influence of the Spirit, physical "walk," mental "perspective," and emotional "peace."[67]

Paul is taking us on a remarkable journey. He had mercilessly described the tragedy of the human condition wherein idolatry nor religion offered deliverance, but simply two different types of slavery. In the midst of the description of the development of the process of deliverance, he presented the most shocking description of all, his own fleshly corruption. At the same time, he continued to progressively introduce the steps out of that disaster as each member of the Trinity was related to us in a distinctly helpful way.

Now, we should examine where we are on Paul's path of deliverance. Paul's material is so dense and challenging, it is easy to get confused and lost in its thickets. We have now observed five of the skills that will lead to deliverance, and two remain left to examine. Those skills will be found in chapters 12-16. We must keep reminding ourselves that knowing the solutions to the problems Paul has isolated in the Book of Romans does not mean we are practicing the solutions. To do that we must know how to apply the skills. The presentation of the skills in detail will be in chapter 17.

07

SKILLS OF ROMANS

THESE ARE THE FIRST FIVE SKILLS PAUL WANTED THE CHRISTIANS IN ROME TO MASTER:	
1.	Mastering the skill of focusing on the Father and staying in his presence (6:11-13)
2.	Mastering the skill of assuming our Union with Christ (6:11)
3.	Mastering the skill of not "listening to our appetites" (6:12)
4.	Mastering the skill of following the prompting (walking by) of the Spirit (7:6, 8:4)
5.	Mastering the skill of having a Heavenly perspective (8:5-6)

Chapter 6 of the book of Romans started a process of spiritual development. In Romans 6:11, the believer was to establish a relationship with God the Father based upon his or her identity in Christ. In chapter 8, we were told that this living relationship was to be augmented by a heavenly perspective. This perspective was set on the things which are important to the Spirit of God. Those important things were our identity in Christ, our total crucifixion with him, our resurrection with him, and our living relationship with the Father like Christ has. A perspective set on the flesh was preoccupied with the emotions, painful ones, and desires, strong ones, coming from the flesh. Following the flesh led to a relational death with God the Father. This contrast showed the importance of having a heavenly perspective. If we have a heavenly perspective, our lives will be

---

[64] Arndt and Gingrich, <u>Lexicon</u>, p. 874.

[65] Arndt and Gingrich, <u>Lexicon</u>, p. 874.

[66] Metzger, <u>Lexical Aids</u>, p. 43.

[67] For other resources teaching these truths, see: Eckman, <u>Head to Heart</u>, Session 15. David Eckman, <u>Becoming What God Intended</u> (Pleasanton, California: BWGI Publishing, 2021), pp. 110-120. The second book closely examined Galatians 5 and "walking by means of the Spirit."

in harmony with the Holy Spirit. If we have a fleshly perspective, our relationship with God the Father is powerless. What is the right perspective? It is taking seriously what the Holy Spirit takes seriously. Part of the perspective of the Spirit was a calm acceptance of the truths of God and the expectations of God. Those same truths and expectations generate hatred and hostility from the perspective of the flesh.

> *Wherefore the perspective of the flesh* [is] *hostility towards God, for it cannot be under obedience to the Law of God, for not is it possible. You yourselves, however, are not in the flesh but in the Spirit, if indeed [and it is true] the Spirit of God dwells in you. But if anyone does not have the Spirit of Christ, this one does not belong to him. (8:7-9)*

Even though we have a choice as to whether we should set our perspective according to the Spirit or according to the flesh, we can have confidence that we belong to Christ because the Spirit of God is in us. When Paul says we are in the Spirit, he means that we are under the influence of the Spirit of God so that we have the possibility of living spiritual lives. Those who are in the flesh do not have the possibility of living spiritual lives. Everywhere they turn, the flesh surrounds them.

Notice that the Spirit was called the Spirit of God and the Spirit of Christ. This was very interesting because Christ was never called Christ of the Spirit nor was the Father called the God of the Spirit. It is the consistent pattern in Scripture that the Father and the Son possessed the Spirit but they are not presented as possessed by him. This means that in some way, the Spirit was dependent on the Father and Son and the Father and Son were not dependent in some way (unknown to us) upon him. In this set of Trinitarian truths, we were also indwelt by Christ.[68]

> *And if* [and it is true] *Christ is in all of you, on the one hand, the body is a corpse* [dead] *on account of sin, and the Spirit life on account of righteousness (8:10)*

Notice how consistent Paul was. Paul's stunning description of his own corruption in Romans 7 was in harmony with the statement about the status of the Roman Christians. For them, their bodies were dead and for himself, Paul said that he died (7:9). He was in death (7:10, 13 two times, 24), and he was killed (7:11). This was remarkable. Ending that unique section, he stated flatly that he bore the body of death and his flesh was serving sin (7:24-25). Paul was saying we carry about with us a spiritually dead body, and yet with the Spirit's presence within we can have the life of Heaven inside and a vibrant relationship with the Father. Left to our own devices, the Christian life would be a disaster, but with the Spirit's help, we are more than conquerors in this life.

> *And if* [and it is true] *the Spirit of the who had raised Jesus out of the dead is dwelling in all of you, the one having raised Christ out of the dead shall make alive your mortal bodies through his indwelling Spirit in all of you. (8:11)*

Verse 11 can be taken two ways. It can be reinforcing the point of verse 10 that the body is spiritually dead and therefore now needs life from the Spirit, or it was making the added point that our mortal bodies (bodies that are going to die) will be raised from the dead. Both were true. 6:11-13 said the mortal body and its members should be used as weapons of righteousness. Obviously this only would be true by the Spirit's power. We need to be dependent on him as we relate to the Father through our unity with Christ. I would understand based on the context, Paul was referring to the Spirit's ability to bring spiritual life into us.

> *Therefore then, brothers, we are not debtors to the flesh to live according to the flesh. For if you are living according to the flesh, **you are about to die**. And if you put to death the practices of the body, you shall live. (8:12-13)*

Death was the natural environment for sin. Sin's throne was in the land of death. All of the inhabitants were spiritually dead before they ever physically died. The death motif has been throughout Romans from

---

[68] Of great importance to realize is that all three persons of the Trinity inhabit the believer, but it is the Spirit of God who mediates their presence to us. The Spirit brings us assurance of the Father's love, and the Spirit brings the character of Christ into our lives in the fruit of the Spirit.

chapter 5:12 on to this point (8:13). The preponderance of the references were to spiritual death, or, as we have been saying, relational death. Since the significant majority of references were to spiritual death especially starting with Paul's soliloquy or personal meditation on his spiritual death from 7:14-25, we can presume he was referring to spiritual or relational death in 8:13. It was an absolute principle of Paul's theology that in sinning, entry was made into the reign of death (spiritual).

From 5:12 to 8:13, Paul referenced death, dying, and being killed nineteen times.

- Death (physical and spiritual): 5:12 (2 times), 14, 19

- Spiritual Death: 5:17, 21; 6:16, 21; 7:5, then Paul's self-meditation on spiritual death 7:9, 10, 11, 13 (2 times), 24 (very important defining reference); 8:2, 6, 10, 13[69]

In this portion of chapter 8, he addressed the problem of the flesh, so again let us note how Paul sequentially dealt with the challenges of sin within.

PROBLEM	SOLUTION
1. Humanity turned over to its desires (1:2)	Believers given the capacity to manage desires and control them (6:11-13)
2. Humanity turned over to its dishonorable moods (1:26)	Believers given the capacity to deal with moods through the Holy Spirit (7:5-6)
3. Humanity turned over to a disapproved mind that failed the test (1:28)	The Solution is 7:23, 25. Believers have an approved mind that approves God's ways (12:1-2)
4. Humanity trapped by a chaotic culture exhibiting gross immorality (1:18-32)	The Solution is 8:3-13. Believers practicing the culture of Heaven (14:1, 4: 15:7)

The Privileges of Sonship

After dealing with the unique experience of 7:14-26, and the necessity of walking by the Spirit, the Apostle underscored the privileges of those who believe in Christ. At this point, Paul transitioned to what Christian maturity was and what the privileges of believers were. Leaving the struggles of the spiritual life behind, he stated the privileges of the Christian life.

For those who are of such a character that they are being led by the Spirit of God, these are the mature sons of God. For you have not received a spirit of slavery leading to fear again, but you have received a spirit of adult son adoption[70] by which we continually shout and proclaim, "Abba! Father!" The Spirit himself witnesses along with our spirit that we are the offspring of God, (8:14-16)

Paul told us that if we are brought along by the Spirit of God that we are the mature sons of God. He used the Greek word for a mature son to indicate the relationship that the believer has when he is responding to the Spirit. This leading was a marvelous gift of freedom because we were not being treated as slaves but as beloved children of God. This aspect of maturity was indicated by the phrase Spirit of adult adoption. **υιοθεσίας huiothesias** "adult son adoption." In the ancient world, normally only adult males were adopted.[71] They were adopted because they were loved and trusted and so were given significant responsibility in the home. This is important truth that the Spirit wants to drive home into our hearts. God loves us and has

---

[69] Certainly Paul then understood that spiritual death started with the first man's eating of the fruit, and physical death followed much later. Of the two it would appear obvious that spiritual death was the more important.

[70] Trevor J. Burke, Adopted in God's Family (Downer's Grove, Illinois: InterVarsity Press, 2006), pp. 22, 133. This is an important book on the significance of Adult Son Adoption.

[71] Eduard Schweizer, "**υιοθεσίας**," in Theological Dictionary of the New Testament (Grand Rapids: Wm. B. Eerdmans, 1972), pp. 397-398. This article has an excellent description of how seriously **υιοθεσίας huiothesias** was taken in Greek culture and how it involved a young man and not a baby.

entrusted his work to us. Therefore, the Spirit bears witness with our spirit that we are the offspring of God. Our spontaneous response to all this should be the declaration that God is our Abba Father.[72] This is something we continually shout because of the Spirit's ministry in our lives. We are not slaves but we are sons who are granted great significance by God. Paul continued to emphasize the significance of the children of God.

> If [and it is true] we are offspring, also we are heirs. On the one hand, heirs of God, and fellow heirs with Christ, if indeed we suffer with him in order that also we will be glorified with him. (8:17)

Present Suffering and Spirituality

The very end of verse 8:17 transitioned Paul to the key topic for the rest of the chapter. The issue of suffering will be addressed throughout. Immediately Paul stated his assumption about that suffering.

> For I am assuming that the emotional and physical sufferings of the present season are not worthy relative to the about to be revealed glory for us. (8:18) [73]

That assumption was a basic part of Paul's eschatological justification for enduring the present tribulations. It was not as strong as his statement in 2 Corinthians 4:17 where he stated that an eternal weight of glory will be given "beyond excess unto excess [literally]" for the momentary light affliction of this life. In fact, this future glory involved the universe itself.

> For the eager expectation of creation is awaiting enthusiastically the revelation of the mature sons of God. For to futility the creation was made obedient, not willingly but on account of the one making it obedient in hope, because also the creation shall be liberated from the slavery of the corruption into the freedom of the glory of the offspring of God. (8:19-21)[74]

Humanity has tremendous significance in the program of God. Humanity was created not only to experience the love of God but to be an illustration to the universe as to how God would treat a rebellious creation.

Humanity and Christians are used as an illustration to angels of God's multi-faceted grace. Humanity's relationship to the universe even has a physical component to it, meaning that when the rapture occurs and believers are transformed to the image of Christ, then the universe will end its slavery to corruption and futility, and enter into the freedom of the children of God. This shows the tremendous importance of humanity to the program of God. Who you are has massive significance to the universe and to the Trinity. God the Father gave his Son for you, underscoring your importance to him. Further, the transformation of the Church at the Rapture acts as a time piece for the universe. As you go through the boring moments of your day, remember the universe in a sense is waiting with bated breath for what will happen to you next.

This also has great implications for what happened in the Garden of Eden. If Adam had rejected the offer of Satan, based on what we see here in Romans 8, the access to the Tree of Life would have been unhindered, meaning he would physically live forever. In addition, with the glorification of humanity, the Universe will then fulfill its purpose of being the home of glorified humanity. Heaven will be our home, and the Universe will be our front and backyard.

Paul then linked together three realities, the universe, ourselves, and the Holy Spirit by the term "groaning," στενάζω stenadzo "to sigh or groan," and στεναγμός stenagmos "sighing or groaning."

---

[72] κράζω kradzo "to cry out" This can be used of a loud proclamation (Matt. 21:9, 15; Luke 19:40; John 1:15; 7:20, 37; 12:44).

[73] "I am assuming" was translated from λογίζομαι logidzomai a key word in Romans occurring in 6:11 for assuming that we are dead to sin and continually alive to God.

[74] This restoration of the universe appears to be the introduction of the eternal state. Note the dispensational outline of Romans contained in the Excursus.

1. The whole creation **groans** together and suffers the pain of childbirth (8:22)

2. We ourselves within ourselves are **groaning**, eagerly awaiting the adult adoption, the redemption of our body (8:23)[75]

3. The Spirit itself intercedes for us with **voiceless groanings** (8:26)[76]

This was a tremendous picture of the incompleteness of creation. Everything awaits a magnificent liberating change. The creation and the Spirit understand the incompleteness of life, and we should too. The more we understand the more we will sigh. The universe is draped in sadness that also enters our own hearts and even within the heart of the Trinity the sadness exists![77]

The Spirit's Intercession

And likewise also the Spirit helps us with our particular weakness, we do not understand how it is necessary to pray, but the Spirit itself intercedes [for us] *with voiceless groanings. And the one continually searching the hearts understands what the perspective of the Spirit is because he intercedes on behalf of the holy ones* [the saints]. *(8:26-27)*

Probably the most embarrassing part of our spiritual life is our prayer life. Often prayer life is repetitious, or boring to ourselves. And it can be spiritually silly. Often believers confuse the members of the Trinity, and basically use prayer to express their unbelief. Thankfully we are not left alone with our prayers. Instead, the Holy Spirit is also helping us. The Spirit's concern runs so deep that he cannot express his requests in words. Instead they come out as voiceless groanings. This means that God the Father who is continually searching the hearts has to read what is the perspective of the Spirit. The beauty of this is that the Holy Spirit's concerns and intercession is always in harmony with what God desires for us. In our day to day life, the Spirit and God the Father are in continual interaction about what is spiritually best for us.[78] It is like a mother and father who continually talk over their plans for their child and discuss what is the best thing that they can do **today** for their child.

WE WHO ARE THE LOVERS OF GOD

And we all are understanding that God is causing all things to work together for benefit to those who love or passionately delight in God, to those who are called according to his purpose (8:28).

In the previous verse, that is 27, Paul described how the Spirit of God interceded for Christians. This intercession was received by God the Father and as result he caused all things to work together for good. Notice that it was the work of the Spirit of God and the love of God the Father that combined so that we receive a spiritual benefit. In the verse following 8:28, it described the entire pattern of God's love towards us from the beginning of creation to our future in heaven.

29 Because whom he established a relationship beforehand, he also predestined to be inwardly and outwardly conformed ones to the image of his Son, that he might be the first-born among many brothers; (8:29)

---

[75] Part of the Greek custom of adult adoption was the presentation of the new son to the community. That may be what Paul was referring to. Paul alluded to that also in Colossians 3:3-4 with the great revelation of the glory of God's children. In Colossians 3 the community was the watching universe of angels. This was also true in the Roman legal context where witnesses had to see the adoption and view the documents involved. Burke, Adopted, pp. 68-70.

[76] To make this equivalent to "tongue speaking" is to completely misunderstand what Paul wrote. The term was **ἀλάλητος alaletos** "unspoken, voiceless" meaning the Spirit was in such pain he could not give voice to it!

[77] This groaning goes all the way back to Genesis 6:6 וַיִּתְעַצֵּב **wayyithatseb** "then he [Yahweh] felt grief upon his heart." To extend grace apparently meant the Trinity had to experience sorrow. For after the grief of Genesis 6:6, Yahweh extended grace to Noah (Genesis 6:8). In future extensions of grace in the Old and New Testament, this sense of God's grief goes unmentioned.

[78] This interaction between the Spirit and God which also involves God the Son creates a dynamic reality that is profoundly different than a philosophic approach to understanding the sovereignty of God. This intercession seems like a day to day dynamic that also includes our synergistic involvement.

These monumental realities created a divine pattern for our lives (starting before the foundation of the world and extending into endless time) that eternally brings good.

Verse 8:28 I would call a "spiritual Rorschach test." The psychological test evaluates what is going on in the subconscious of an individual. This verse works the same way. Some Christians read it and immediately feel guilty that they may not be loving God at the moment or have only fleeting moments of affection for God the Father. Other Christians read it and feel encouraged by God's care. What is in their subconscious controls how they understand the verse. For one, it generates guilt for another gratitude. How should we understand this verse?

In the construction of the sentence in 8:28, the terms "who love or passionately delight in God," and "those who are called according to his purpose" are synonymous.[79] What was Paul's assumption here? Paul assumed that this plan stretching from before time to eternity future would result in a Trinitarian romance between believers and God. Who are the elect? They are the lovers of God. Who are Christians? They are the lovers of God. What is the great proof that they are the lovers of God? John the Apostle told us. The lovers of God are those who believe the Gospel and love Christ, rather than the darkness (John 3:19-21). The haters of God have a passionate love (Agape) for darkness and do not come to the light who is Christ. We indeed who believed the Gospel are the lovers of Christ and God. Our trust in Christ has stupendous significance to God the Father. Those who believe in the Son are loved of God and their faith expressed their love for God. It is inconceivable to Paul that those who have been elected from the foundation of the world will not become lovers of God. When we believed the Gospel, our romance with God began.

To ask the question we have asked a number of times before: Is the pattern of God's plan based upon our love or is love the natural result of that eternal life planned by God? Paul affirmed, to be known by God always results in loving God (1 Cor. 8:3). Through the truths of Romans, the practice of the 7 skills, and the inevitable transformation brought by God's plan, we are the lovers of God. It is unthinkable that God's love for us is dependent upon us and his plan for us is dependent upon our love. Paul already described in detail that in our fallen state while we were hating God, God loved us (Roman 5:8 and particularly verse 10). John affirmed not that we loved God first but he loved us (1 John 4:19).

We have examined what is in verse 8:28, but it is worth noting what is not. Something is strikingly absent from verse 28 that would be noticed by those familiar with the Old Testament. It is this phrase where God spoke:

> . . . *to the ones loving me and to the ones guarding my statutes (Exodus 20:6; Deut. 5:10)*[80]

Anyone who expected the New Testament to be a continuation of the Old would assume loving God would be expressed by guarding his statutes and ordinances.[81] With Paul, not only did he not guard the statutes and ordinances, he rejected them! He rejected them as a part of the spiritual life. Participating in the life of the Trinity was far better and truly the only alternative. He assumed that those who are involved in the grand scheme of God's redemption would fall in love with God. Again, strikingly this is the only place in Romans where Paul mentioned believers loving God. As was his habit, he spoke much more of us loving one another than of loving God.

This may come as a shock, but Paul never directly commanded Christians to love God.

In contrast, four times he demanded and commanded husbands to love their wives. Certainly, we would

---

[79] Harvey, Romans, p. 209. Harvey correctly comments that those loving God are defined appositionally by those being called and further clarifies who they are. In the diagramming of this verse by the BibleWorks diagramming module the two phrases are placed as being directly equivalent in meaning.

[80] τοῖς ἀγαπῶσίν με καὶ τοῖς φυλάσσουσιν τὰ προστάγματά μου (Exod. 20:6 and Deut. 5:10)

[81] Commentators have noticed that omission. Cranfield gave an Old Testament list where love was connected to guarding the Law and serving Yahweh. Cranfield, Romans, Vol. I, p. 424, fn. 4. Dunn commented on the expectation that a person familiar with the Old Testament would have had about love being joined to the keeping of the commands. He recognized that it was significant (and I would say extremely significant) that Paul did not join love to Law keeping. Dunn, Romans, Vol. I, p. 481.

think that God is more significant than a wife, and therefore, Paul should be endlessly demanding we should love God. He did not! Note this chart.

COMMAND TO LOVE GOD IN PAUL	LOVE FOR GOD AND CHRIST	LOVE FOR THE BRETHREN	COMMAND TO LOVE WIFE
None	**Six times**	**At least 26 times**	**Four times**
Indeed, Paul nor John did not have "Love the Lord your God with all your heart . . ." as Mat. 28:37; Mark 12:30; Luke 10:27 did.	• Rom. 8:28 • 1 Cor. 2:9, 8:3 • Eph.6:24; 2 • Thes. 3:5; 2 • Tim. 4:8	Examples: • Rom. 12:9, 13:8-10 • 1 Cor. 14:1 • Gal. 5:13-14 • Eph. 4:2, 5:2 • Phil. 2:2 • Col. 3:14 • 1 Thes. 4:9, 5:8, 13; 1 • Tim. 1:5; 2:15, 4:12, 6:11; etc.	• Eph. 5:25, 28, 33 • Col. 3:19

When we deal with Romans 12, we will go into great detail explaining why Paul did not have a direct demand, an imperative in Greek, to love God and Christ.[82] Suffice to say that for Paul, love for God develops out of the discovery of God's and Christ's love for us and the practice of the 7 skills. In Paul's second earliest epistle, 2 Thessalonians, we see that for the Apostle love for God was an interactive growth process.

And may the Lord lead your hearts directly into the love of God and into the steadfast patience of Christ. (2 Thessalonians. 3:5)

The word for leading is **κατευθύνω kateuthuno** meaning to guide a person or to make a person's way straight.[83]

> **N**ote very carefully that the process of falling in love with
> the Father and Son is dependent upon the Trinity.
> We are in a reciprocal love relationship with the divine as initiated by the Trinity.

At the present time, many Christians are like the Apostle Peter who when asked by Christ if he had Agape love for him (John 21:15-17), he could not comfortably answer in the affirmative. Essentially he said, "You know I like you a lot." What happened over time with Peter was that as he discovered Christ's Agape love for him was unwavering, his heart developed unwavering love for Christ. Immediately following John 21:15-17 to show how Peter's love would grow, Jesus looked to the end of Peter's life when Peter died a martyr (John 21:18-19). At the end of his life out of Agape love for Christ, he died on behalf of Christ! We are involved in such a divine love affair that it is inevitable that we too will become more and more the lovers of God.

Romans 8:29 stated that we were to be conformed to the image of his Son. The word conformed means to be like him from the inside out. The word was always used of a thorough change throughout the entirety of something. We are in the process of reflecting the character of Jesus Christ through our entire personality. And notice that this makes us sisters and brothers of Christ who is the firstborn of God. He is firstborn because he is eternally generated by the Father. We are the Father's offspring because we are born again through the Spirit. The Father's purpose is to enjoy you as his offspring and for you to enjoy him as your Father.

God's ultimate plan is that he should have many children like his Son the Lord Jesus Christ. This is the ultimate goal of all reality. If someone were to ask you what is the purpose of your existence, you should respond and say, my purpose is to be loved by God the Father and to love him in return; in fact, in the same way Jesus is loved by God the Father and is loving him back. When Paul explained why all things work for

---

82   See page 104.
83   Thayer, Lexicon, p. 339.

the benefit of those who were called, he based that on the intercession of the Holy Spirit which deals with our day by day life with God. Then, secondly he based it on the grandeur of the overall plan of God the Father. Everything existing is working for our benefit. Truly we are the lovers of God.

The Central Truth of Romans

In the context of a suffering creation, suffering believers, and a suffering Holy Spirit, we have presented to us the greatest statement of God's love probably in the Bible. In the face of great suffering, Paul dramatically affirmed the determined love of the Father and Son for his own.

> *What then shall we say to these things? If* [and it is true] *God is on our behalf, who is against us? 32 He indeed did not spare his own Son, but handed him over for us all, how will he not with him also everything graciously grant to us? (8:31-32)*

Classical rabbinic argument was usually from the greater to the lesser or the lesser to greater. Paul, the former Rabbi, used the rabbinic way of arguing from the greater to the lesser. The greater reality he referred to was that God gave his own Son for us. Since he cannot give anything greater, it follows that with him, everything else will be given to us freely. He freely gave us his Son, so that being the case, would he not freely give us everything else that pertains to godliness?

Our sense of security and being loved by God is directly dependent upon the value that we place on Jesus Christ.

If we realize that Jesus is infinitely valued and loved by the Father, and that the Father gave this infinitely valuable Son for us, we should relax in the confidence of the Father's love. Christian confidence comes from a sense of knowing who Jesus Christ is, the Son of God, and how much the Father loves him. Every Christian value flows out of the relationships within the Trinity. The more we understand those relationships, the more confident we will be. In a sense, the Father gave a trillion dollars for us, so we should never worry about the small change.

The Son's Intercession

> *Who will bring a legal charge against God's elect? God is the continually justifying one; who is the one condemning? Christ Jesus is the one who died, rather he who was raised, who is at the right hand of God, who also is continually interceding for us (8:33-34)*

God is incredibly prejudiced on our behalf. From the beginning he has chosen us and in the present time he is continually justifying us. Not only is God the Father prejudiced towards us, but his Son is too. This is illustrated by the fact that Jesus is continually interceding for us. What we find in Romans 8 is that the Holy Spirit and the Son are both speaking to God on our behalf. This double intercession leads to Paul's conclusion that all things work together for our good. But do you realize how dynamic this is? Two divine persons are continually talking to God the Father and making suggestions to him about what would spiritually benefit us as we go through our day. This is astonishing. More than that, the Father listens to what they have to say and then he thinks about and ultimately decides what will benefit us. What we have here is an incredibly dynamic process.

On the one hand, God has an overarching plan that involves all of the time of eternity. On the other hand, the three members of the Trinity are in a continual dialogue about what will benefit us the most in the moment of this day. This reflects the highly personal nature of our relationship to the Trinity.

The Central Theme

> *Who shall separate us from the deep passion (love) of Christ? Tribulation, or tightened circumstances, or persecution, or famine, or nakedness, or danger, or sword? 36 Even as it is written that, "On your behalf we are being put to death all the day; we were considered as sheep of the slaughter." 37 But in all these things we overwhelmingly conquer through him who passionately loved us. (8:35-37)*

Paul the Apostle has described the threats and difficulties that Christians experience. In the face of all that, he made the comment that we overwhelmingly conquer through him who loved us. I would argue that verse 37 is the central verse of the book of Romans and the central thought of the book of Romans. Paul has the habit of putting the central thought in the very center of the letters that he wrote. Chapters 1-8 of Romans described how the individual Christian should lead his or her life. Chapters 9-16 of Romans described the place of the Christian community in the world. The book was neatly divided into two parts so that way we can easily tell where the center of Romans is. In the last five verses of chapter 8, Paul stated that we are loved by either God the Father or the Son three times. If you read those last five verses, they describe God's love for us. In the third verse, the central verse of the five, Paul states that we overwhelmingly conquer through him who loved us. That was Paul's central message to you!

The Center of the Center

But in all these things we overwhelmingly conquer through him who passionately loved us. (8:37)

Sometimes we feel blessed, and sometimes we feel defeated, but hardly ever a totally victorious conqueror. More often than not when I speak with Christians, they are discouraged and they certainly don't feel like conquerors. They feel weak. Smacked around by failure and struggling with various sins, they are afraid of God.

Yet when Paul looked at Christians through the lens of God's plan, he saw the Christian as totally conquering. For Paul, we have conquered the world, the flesh, the devil, and the Law. We have conquered the world because our faith has brought us into the Kingdom of God's Dear Son, a different world than our own. We have conquered the flesh because in the Rapture or the resurrection from the dead, our body will be conformed to his glorious body. We have conquered the devil because he who is in us, the Holy Spirit, is greater than he who is in the world. We have conquered the Law because Christ has died according to the Law's demands so that we are liberated from the Law's condemnation. Also, we are given the Trinitarian relationship that allows us to live through the power of the Holy Spirit, and not through "self-will" in keeping the Law. In all of these areas we come out magnificently triumphant through him who loved us.

The Father and Son's Love

For I am completely convinced that neither death, nor life, nor angels, nor angelic authorities, nor things in the present, nor things about to come, nor powers, nor height, nor depth, nor any other kind of created thing, shall be able to separate us from the passionate love of God, which is in Christ Jesus our Lord. (8:38-39)

I**t is quite an amazing thing that two members of the Trinity have a deeply personal love for people like us.**

We can say glibly that we are loved by God, but it is entirely different if we think deeply about this. If we mull this over, our hearts should truly be struck with awe. Here we are finite creatures and two infinitely happy persons, the Father and the Son, have a delighted passion for us, they love us. The majority of times in the New Testament, the emphasis was on the Father's love for his own. In 1 John 4, the text indicates twenty-nine different times that we are loved by God the Father. But in other places in the New Testament, the love of Christ for us is emphasized, such as where Paul said Christ loved him and gave himself for him (Galatians 2:20).

W**e do not need this truth as information. We need to experience this truth emotionally so that it becomes a part of our instincts.**

When that occurs, we can become what God has intended for us, well-loved children who feel secure and who deeply love the Father back and deeply love the Son.

Mastering the 7 Skills of Romans

We are going to proceed to chapters 9-11 which are dramatically different than 5-8. As we do so we will summarize the problems and solutions of Paul that we have seen so far.

PROBLEM	SOLUTION
1. Humanity turned over to its desires (1:24)	1. Believers given the capacity to manage desires and control them (6:11-13)
2. Humanity turned over to its dishonorable moods (1:26)	2. Believers given the capacity to deal with moods through the Holy Spirit (7:5-6)
3. Humanity turned over to a disapproved mind that failed the test (1:28)	
4. Humanity trapped by a chaotic culture exhibiting great immorality (1:18-32)	
5. The Jews adopted a performance based religion resulting in hypocrisy (2-3)	
6. Union with Adam resulting in sin within, death, condemnation, and status as a sinner (5:12-21)	6. Union with Christ resulting in death to sin, life in Christ, justification, and status as a righteous one (5:15-21; 6)
7. The flesh given as the overarching problem resulting from God handing over and the Fall of Adam (7:14, 18; 8:3-10)	7. Walking by means of the Spirit brings liberation from the power of sin within and the flesh (8:1-14)

Chapter 12 will bring further solutions to light, and we will learn of the wonderful privilege we can have within our inner life. These solutions plus our synergistic participation results in skills.

9 | ISRAEL'S REJECTION

CHAPTER SUMMARY: Now Paul addressed the issue of **Israel** and the Church. To say the least, God's setting aside of Israel and the transfer of the blessings of the Messiah to the Church was a shock and scandal to the Jews. How could God betray and **reject** them this way?! Paul in chapters 9-11 addressed those issues in powerful and surprising ways. Even though Israel was unbelieving, Paul argued, God has always selectively worked with a portion of the descendants of Israel, sometimes a very small remnant.

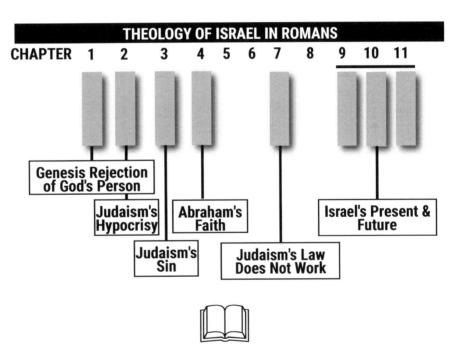

GOD'S FREEDOM AND ISRAEL, THE ELECT NATION

In the remarkable chapters of 9-11, Paul addressed the relationship of Israel to the Church. The underlying issue was the setting aside of Israel and the beginning of the Church. Ironies exist with this because even the term "Church" was taken from "Israel." ἐκκλησία ekklesia "church or assembly" in the LXX was used for קָהָל kahal "assembly," the common Old Testament term for the congregation of Israel. The Church was a true substitute for the previous congregation. For the Roman ἐκκλησία ekklesia, Paul felt the need to go into detail concerning the failure of Israel, the ascendancy of the Gentile church, and the relationship of the two. A deeper reason existed also, he addressed this issue for the honor of God. In this profound change, he argued, Yahweh did not betray his people.

Paul Like Moses

Truth I am speaking in Christ, I am not lying, my conscience bearing me witness in the Holy Spirit, that it is a great sadness and unceasing grief in my heart. For I was on the point of wishing[84] I myself were accursed[85] from Christ on behalf of my brothers, my relatives according to the flesh, (9:1-3)

Paul has similarities to Moses. Moses also wanted to be accursed for the sake of his brethren and he offered to die for the people twice. Paul like Moses felt the same way. After the Passover lamb was sacrificed, Moses became the leader of Israel in its journey to the Promised Land. After Jesus, our Passover Lamb, was sacrificed, Paul became the leader of the Church's journey into the world of the Gentiles. Moses was the great lawgiver to Israel, and the judge for the decisions that were needed to be made for the people in their journey. Paul in a very real sense became the great "law giver" for the church in its journey. Further, we have a life of Moses as given in Exodus through Deuteronomy, and we have Paul's life in the Book of Acts and his letters. When Paul was called, it was in a classic prophetic call similar to Moses. Deity appeared to him in the Person of Christ, and blindness descended on him for several days. Every prophetic call is different, but usually two elements are involved: God's appearance, and some physical reaction from the future prophet like a trance. Paul was our Moses!

After stating his motives and his history, Paul started not with Israel and the Church, but with God. He wanted to protect God from the accusation that he has failed in his purposes.

And it is not as the word of God had collapsed and failed, for not everyone out of Israel, these are Israel. (9:6)

Three issues appeared in chapters 9-11 in addressing Israel's failure to recognize their Messiah.

1. God's freedom in his choices.[86] In chapter 9, Paul made the extended argument that God has freedom to make choices. This defense had to come before he dealt with Israel or the Church because God's freedom of choice was behind the setting aside of Israel and the ascendancy of the Church.

2. The failure of Israel. God's history with Israel was the story of him consistently responding to the repeated failures of the nation. Within this repeated series of failures, Paul noted that God was still fulfilling his purposes and exercising his freedom.

3. The ascendancy of the Church. Paul studiously showed that implicit within the Old Testament was a profound love for the Gentile world that would culminate in the extension of God's grace through the Church to the world. Out of his freedom he pursued the Gentiles.

Chapter 9 was consumed by the issue of the inclusion of the Gentiles within the people of God and the exclusion of many who were descendants of Abraham. In chapter 9, Paul argued that God has a loving and righteous right to include and exclude. As we shall see, a strange harmony existed between God's action and the heart and actions of human beings. His righteous use of his freedom fell within a historical context harmonizing with his decisions.

As he launched into the issue of Israel and the Church, his immediate starting point was to emphasize that the physical descendants of Abraham were not all true Israel. He used Jacob and Esau to make that point.

Just as it is written, "Jacob I loved, but Esau I hated." 14 What shall we say then? There is no injustice with God, is there? Absolutely not! (9:13-14)

A deeper reality was behind the simple statement of God's hate. The quote "Jacob I loved, but Esau I hated" did not come from Genesis but from Malachi. In the quote in Malachi, Esau was more than Esau

---

[84] Robertson, <u>Word Pictures</u>, Vol. IV, p. 380. This is his suggestion for a translation.

[85] ἀνάθεμα anathema "to be cursed" This word in the LXX refers to the cursing of the Canaanites to extinction. It was Paul's strongest expression for calling down God's wrath on false teachers (Galatians 1:8-9).

[86] Note I am not using the word sovereignty because I believe that word suffers from "totality transfer." "Totality transfer" was when a word carried all of its meaning into a context. Sovereignty has become a freighted and bludgeon like term that freezes the brain. Philosophic theology and Reformed Theology has ruined the word.

alone: Esau included his descendants who became the Edomites. Just as with Esau, the Edomites did not need God, but relied on their efforts to recover from the judgment of God upon their nation.[87]

> *"I have a deep passion (love) for you," says Yahweh. But you say, "How have you loved us?" "Is not Esau Jacob's brother?" declares Yahweh. "Yet I have loved Jacob; 3 but I have hated Esau, and I have made his mountains a desolation, and appointed his inheritance for the jackals of the wilderness." 4 Though Edom says, "We have been beaten down, but we will return and build up the ruins"; thus says Yahweh of Armies, "They may build, but I will tear down; and men will call them the wicked territory, and the people toward whom Yahweh is enraged forever." (Malachi 1:2-4)*

What Esau and the Edomites became was the context for the text in Malachi. In some ways, Esau was a more sympathetic figure than Jacob, but Jacob had one redeeming feature. A couple of times he trusted Yahweh. Esau did not. Both Esau and Edomites represent the self-made person who saw no need for God. In God's elective choice (Romans 9:11) of Jacob before either was born, Yahweh pronounced their destiny. Yet in the working out of that destiny, we can see a divine and human harmony in the outcomes, the point being that physical connection was not the defining characteristic for an Israelite. As Paul developed God's freedom of choice, he also addressed the issue whether God's freedom was controlled by God's character.

GOD'S RIGHT TO CHOOSE TO BE COMPASSIONATE

> *What then are we saying? Is there unrighteousness around God? Absolutely not! (9:14)[88]*

Paul then added another question to his first one regarding God's word failing: he asked if there was unrighteousness in God. As he argued for God's freedom to do what he wanted, he made sure to place that freedom in the context of God's righteousness and love.

> *For to Moses he says, "I shall have mercy on whom I might have mercy, and I shall have tender mercy on whom I might have tender mercy." (9:15)*

With this statement, Yahweh stated that grace[89] and mercy were his personal prerogative. No one would deny that a judge and ruler should have that right. God stated it flatly here concerning Jacob and Esau and his descendants. Mercy and grace were the property of the offended party. In some ways, Jacob was more offensive than Esau, but Jacob's saving virtue was not his character, but his faith. Paul then shifted to the time of the Exodus. Paul proceeded to show God's freedom of action in his hardening of Pharaoh's heart.

> *For the Scripture says to Pharaoh, "Unto this very same thing I raised you up , to demonstrate in you my power, in order that my name [character, works, reputation] might be displayed in all the Earth." Therefore, then on whom he desires he shows mercy, and on whom he desires he hardens. (9:17-18)[90]*

It is very important to see the verse in Romans 9:17 as found in the Hebrew and LXX text of Exodus 9:15:

כִּי עַתָּה שָׁלַחְתִּי אֶת־יָדִי וָאַךְ אוֹתְךָ וְאֶת־עַמְּךָ בַּדָּבֶר וַתִּכָּחֵד מִן־הָאָרֶץ׃

> *For now [if] I had stretched forth my hand and proceeded to strike you and your people with the plague, and the result would have been you would be wiped out from the Earth. (Hebrew translation of Exodus 9:15)*

---

[87] David Eckman, <u>Discovering Micah through Malachi</u> (Carmel, New York: Guideposts, 1990), pp. 164-168. This portion examined in detail the implications of this text.

[88] παρὰ **para** "in the presence of around" "Around God, or in the presence of God" is a nice way of avoiding a more direct question, "Is God unrighteous?" That was a nicely Rabbinic way of asking the question. See Harris, <u>Prepositions</u>, pp. 172-173. An excellent book.

[89] In the LXX quote from Exodus 33:19 the text had "I shall have mercy," but in the Hebrew text the verb is actually to be gracious חָנַן.

[90] הֶעֱמַדְתִּיךָ **heechmadtyka** "I made you to stand" (Exodus 9:16) was the Hebrew behind "I raised you up (Romans 9:16)." Contextually the raising up has to be understood as being kept alive and in power. The Greek word also meant "to be raised from the dead." That could mean the LXX translator felt that God could have killed Pharaoh, but instead he kept him alive, like he had been raised from the dead.

Mastering the 7 Skills of Romans

The initial impression of the verse Paul quoted was changed by the content of the Exodus context. Quick judgment was being set aside by Yahweh so as to illustrate his glory to the ancient world. In fact, the entire context of the story changes the initial impression that Exodus quote made. Most who know the story of the Pharaoh of Moses' time are aware of Paul referring to God's hardening. This hardening was much more than an act of pure sovereignty. Paul was not protecting a supreme sovereignty. Instead he was arguing for a righteous and loving freedom. Sovereignty would say God can do whatever he decided for any mysterious reason. The example of Pharaoh is a good one to examine. Freedom says God will do what is right and loving because his actions are always a reflection of his nature.

Let us retell the Pharaoh story by the use of three Hebrew words from Exodus and three Greek words used in the LXX from the same book. I will relate the references to the words in Exodus to their particular Hebrew words and give a translation in the right column and identify who also was the agent.

	"MAKE STRONG"	"TO HARDEN"	"TO MAKE HEAVY"	ENGLISH TRANSLATION OF HEBREW WORDS
1	חָזַק	קָשָׁה	כָּבֵד	Hebrew words
2	σκληρυνῶ Gr. harden	σκληρυνῶ	βαρέω Gr. make heavy	LXX Greek
3	4:21			God predicted he will harden Pharaoh's heart
4		7:3		God will make strong Pharaoh's heart
5			7:14	*God said Pharaoh's heart was heavy, unmoving*
6	7:22			*Then Pharaoh's heart became strong*
7			8:15 Heb. 8:11	*Pharaoh made his heart heavy, unmoving*
8			8:32 Heb. 8:18	*Pharaoh made his heart heavy, unmoving*
9			9.7	*The heart of Pharaoh became heavy*
10	9:12			Yahweh made the heart of Pharaoh strong
11			9:34	*And he [Pharaoh] sinned and made his heart heavy, unmoving*
12	9:35			*Then the heart of Pharaoh became strong*
13			10:1	For I [Yahweh] have made his heart heavy, unmoving
14	10:20			Then Yahweh made the heart of Pharaoh strong
15	10:27			Then Yahweh made the heart of Pharaoh strong
16	11:10			Then Yahweh made the heart of Pharaoh strong
17		13:15		*Then it came to be that Pharaoh hardened his heart*
18	14:4			And I will make Pharaoh's heart strong
19	14:8			Then Yahweh made the heart of Pharaoh strong

When we plot the relationship between Yahweh's hardening the heart of Pharaoh, and Pharaoh either having a stubborn heart (unmoving, heavy) or making his heart heavy, what we see was not a display of sovereignty, but of moral freedom. At the very beginning, we have Yahweh's prediction that he will harden the heart of the god-man of Egypt. Yet in the telling of the story, it was Pharaoh who took the initiative in making his own heart heavy, unmoving, or stubborn. Note the italicized material (Exodus 7:14, 22; 8:15, 32; 9:7), and how it preceded the hardening activity of Yahweh which began in 9:12. Then, in 9:34-35, Pharaoh "sinned and made his heart heavy, unmoving." Following that in 10:20, 27; 11:10, Yahweh proceeded to harden the man's heart. In commentary on the death of the first born of Egypt, the writer of Exodus stated that the plague was directly connected to Pharaoh hardening his own heart (13:15). As the people fled Egypt once again, Yahweh hardened the heart of Pharaoh which led to the demise of his army and probably himself (14:4, 8).

Paul certainly knew the details of the Exodus story and he chose to emphasize God's freedom in hardening the heart of Pharaoh. In a way, what Yahweh eventually did in response to Pharaoh making his heart hard was not unreasonable. When Yahweh hardened his heart, he was simply letting Egypt's leader have what he really wanted. I would argue, what we have here was not a display of blind mysterious sovereignty, but a display of God's use of righteous (relative to Egypt), loving (relative to Israel) freedom.

GOD'S RIGHTS AS CREATOR

To summarize his point, Paul gave a brutally straightforward illustration. In 9:20-24, he shared the illustration of the potter and clay: how the potter freely made a choice with how he will use the clay. Some of it will be used for honorable or valuable use and another portion for dishonorable or not so valuable use. The stark strength of the illustration showed the threatening intensity of what Paul faced. Great opposition existed to Paul taking the Gospel to the Gentiles. Some wanted to kill him for doing such. In his argument in chapter 9, Paul emphasized God's rights. Paul, however, was not defending himself. He was defending God. In the apology for God in this illustration, Paul reduced his defense to the absolute minimum. Does not the God of the Universe have the same rights as a humble potter?

Granted, clay and human beings are not the same. As Paul continued his argument, he actually described in detail the quality of clay that God worked with. In doing so, Paul attempted to justify the loving and righteous freedom of his "Heavenly Potter." Yet this illustration was not original with Paul. The potter illustration was God's idea, and it was used by Yahweh both in Isaiah and Jeremiah. In Isaiah, Yahweh compared himself to a potter.

> *Woe to the man calling his maker (potter) into court! A pot among the pots of the ground. Can the clay say to his potter, "What are you doing?" And your work say, "There are no hands (handles) to him!" (Isaiah 45:9)*[91]

The potter and clay illustration was used to justify the call of Cyrus the Persian as the Messiah delivering Israel from captivity in Isaiah 45:1-13. Note carefully that the act of this "Heavenly Potter" was to form an event in time for the rescue of his people by a Gentile king. The illustration was used to justify Yahweh's freedom to do something radically gracious and loving for Israel. The potter illustration was not used in the context of something sovereignly decreed in eternity past. Instead it was used to justify God's use of a Gentile to rescue Israel at a very low point in its history. It was a defense of God's freedom to act righteously and lovingly. The text in Jeremiah 18 also emphasized God's righteous freedom. Jeremiah was to go to the potter's house and observe him working. What was on the potter's wheel displeased the potter so he redid the clay again.

> *And the vessel he was making was marred in the hand of the potter which he was making with the clay. Then he turned and he proceeded to make it another vessel even as it was right in the eyes of the potter to do. (Jeremiah 18:4)*

Then Yahweh applied what Jeremiah saw to the people of Israel. Did he not have the same right to do what the potter did? In his justification of the right, he referred to the character and actions of the people. The clay possessed no moral movements within itself. With clay, it was sheer sovereignty on the potter's part to redo the vessel. That was where the comparison was not completely applicable with people. Yahweh proceeded to say that if a nation relented of evil, he would repent of the judgment he was going to bring upon it.[92] And if a nation or kingdom that was virtuous pursued evil, Yahweh would repent of the good he intended and judge it (Jeremiah 18:7-10). Therefore, the potter illustration was not there to emphasize Yahweh's arbitrary sovereignty, but his radical freedom to act in a morally loving and righteous way. With Paul, Isaiah, and Jeremiah, the use of the illustration of the potter was historically conditioned. Change occurred within history and the "Heavenly Potter" changed what he was doing with the "pot."

---

[91] See also Isaiah 64:8 (Hebrew 64:7) "And now Oh Yahweh you are our Father, we are the clay and you are our Potter (Maker), and all of us are the work of your hand."

[92] וְנִחַמְתִּי **winaghemty** "and I will feel differently and change, repent." Note how Yahweh has a vital relationship to the actions of his creatures.

With the illustration, Paul was also responding to Jewish prejudice that they were the chosen people and God was obligated to them through his promises to the Fathers, Abraham, Isaac, and Jacob. He wanted the Jews and Gentiles to recognize that it was not physical descent from Abraham that mattered, but having the faith of Abraham (Romans 4:11-17). Further, God was free to express his love and righteousness any way he wanted. The potter illustration was similar to what John the Baptist did. The Pharisees came to him to be immersed, and he told them not to say Abraham was their father because God could turn the stones into the children of Abraham if he wanted (Matthew 3:7-9)!

With the illustration of the potter, he asked a question to those listening to the Book of Romans.

> *And if (and it is true) God is desiring to display the wrath* [future eschatological wrath] *and to personally make his power known put up with complete patience vessels of wrath* [Gospel rejecting Jews and Gentiles] *having become fully qualified for destruction,*[93] *in order that also he would make personally known the wealth of his glory upon vessels of mercy which he prepared before unto glory; even us, and he called us not only out of the Jews, but also out of the Gentiles. (9:22-24)*

As Paul continued the illustration of the potter, he emphasized that God was more than willing to judge, but he even more so wanted to display the wealth of glory on those like Paul and the believing Jews and Gentiles who have trusted the Gospel. Indeed the "Heavenly Potter" was making two kinds of pots: those to be blessed and those to be cursed.

Immediately turning to the Old Testament, Paul referenced Israelites who made themselves "fully qualified for destruction" (9:22). Again, a relationship existed between the type of pot and the moral motions of the human clay. Two prophets, Hosea and Isaiah, were given as examples of this preparation for judgment. Hosea spoke of those who no longer were the people of God and now were. Those who were rejected were then accepted (Hosea 2:23). In contrast to Hosea, Isaiah spoke of how though Israel might become many, only a remnant will be saved. Only a small part of Israel will be delivered. This was similar to Paul's earlier point that not all of Israel will be blessed. In Isaiah's example, it was very few (9:27-29). Was all of this arbitrary?

God's Critical Principle

No, because God realistically discerned what the moral qualities of the "clay" were. He discerned not the moral strivings of the clay, their moral performance, but the clay's ability to discern its need of the Gospel. Paul asked a summarizing question, "What shall we say then?" His answer was that the Gentiles who did not look for mercy have found it, and the Jews did not find it because they looked to their own moral performance. The discerning reality that judged both groups was the Christ. Paul answered why this happened.

> *On account of what?* [Because the Jews pursued this] *Not out of faith but works. They stumbled against the stone of stumbling. Even as it was written, behold I am placing in Zion a prepared stone of stumbling and a rock of scandal, and the one believing upon him will never be ashamed. (9:32-33)*

Assuming this stone was Christ, Paul finished this chapter the way he started it by talking about Christ. At the start, he referred clearly to Christ the Messiah. At the end, he stated the Messiah who was Jesus was not understood by his own people. As a result, the "Heavenly Potter" chose part of the clay he was working with for an honorable use, and another part for dishonorable. This was not an arbitrary sovereign choice. Instead it was a loving and righteous action of God's freedom. The "clay" actually had different qualities. Human beings are not inanimate, malleable clay. They have the capacity for moral motions and faith choices. In chapter 9, Paul strongly defended the honor of God in his righteous and loving freedom as it was displayed in the rejection of corporate Israel and the acceptance of the Gentiles.

---

[93] **κατηρτισμένα katertismena** "fully prepared or qualified." This perfect passive participle implied that the unbelief and rejection of God plus God's own judgment was what prepared them for judgment. It was not a mysterious choice in eternity past but the natural result of interaction between man and God.

10 | ISRAEL'S UNBELIEF

CHAPTER SUMMARY: Deliverance was available to **Israel** in the past and it is present now. Israel though has a consistent pattern of an unbelieving response to the revelation of God. Paul, the Moses of the Church, took Moses' very last plea to Israel in Deuteronomy and turned it into a Gospel invitation. Further, he showed that God was pursuing the Gentiles in the face of the **unbelief** of the Jews.

I have been reading a fascinating book entitled <u>The Memoirs of Gluckel of Hameln</u>.[94] Begun in 1690 it is the memoirs of a German Jewish woman that she wrote for her children of which she had fourteen. Paul in chapter 10:2 said that he witnessed that the Jews had a zeal for God but not according to personal knowledge. One can see what he meant by reading her book. Everything in her life was seen through the prism of Orthodox Judaism. All things were connected to God's approval or disapproval. In the midst of the story she described how her father-in-law and many of the Jews of Europe came to believe in a contemporary Messiah. The false Messiah Sabbtai Zevi created hysteria among the Jews and many wanted to migrate to Palestine where he was. The Moslems objected to his claims, tortured him and as a result, he converted to Islam. This shocked all of the Jews of Europe. Rigorously practicing the Law as they understood it, they believed in a false Messiah who betrayed them instead of the true Messiah who died for them. In chapter 10 of Romans, Paul described the unbelief of Israel and its zeal for the Law.

The beginning of chapter 9 and that of 10 were focused on Paul's attitude towards Israel, and God's relationship to the nation. The first four verses of the tenth chapter created a natural break between chapter 9 which emphasized God's righteous and loving freedom, and chapter 10 which emphasized the failure of Israel to respond to God's offers of deliverance.

> *Brethren, the good intention of my heart and the specific request on their behalf to God is for salvation. For I witness for them that they have a zeal for God, but not according to a personal knowledge for while being continually ignorant of the righteousness of God and seeking to establish their own, they have not become submissive to God's righteousness. For Christ is the termination of the Law for righteousness for everyone believing. (10:1-4)*

---

94 Gluckel of Hameln, <u>The Memoirs of Gluckel of Hameln</u>, tr. Marvin Lowenthal (New York: Schocken Books, 1977), p. 295.

Paul then made a dramatic turn to the contents of the Old Testament and the Torah of Moses. He said that the Israelite within the system of the Law had to live within those laws.

> *For Moses writes concerning the righteousness out of the Law that the man having done these things* [statues and judgements] *shall continue to live in them. (10:5)*[95]

The Message to Israel

But Christ offered a completely different alternative. To underscore that alternative, Paul selected one of the most significant portions of the Torah (the first five books of Moses), the final appeal to Israel for obedience. In Deuteronomy 30, Moses said this obedience to Yahweh and the Law must take place within the human heart. Paul made the most remarkable use of the final appeal of Moses at this point in Romans. He took the conclusion of Moses' speeches where the Lawgiver of Israel answered the question of how an Israelite can enter into the obedience of the Law. To recognize how powerful and clever this was, we have to look at the outline of Deuteronomy.

Three addresses constitute the bulk of Deuteronomy.

- The history of deliverance (1-4:43)

- The expectations of God (4:44-26:19)

- Blessings for obedience or cursings for rebellion (29:1-30:20)

Within the context of these addresses Moses predicted the failure of Israel and its captivity. To be in the audience must have been an overwhelming experience. On the one hand, he was giving the nation the Law essentially for the second time, thus the name **Deuteros,** or "second," **Nomos,** or "Law," which became Deuteronomy. On the other hand, he prophesied the failure of the nation and its acceptance of idolatry. What hope did he give at the end of his third address? The third address was the last one before the Book of Deuteronomy spoke of the death of Moses. At the very end of that address in Deuteronomy 30:6-20, he told the people that Yahweh would return them from captivity, and he would circumcise their hearts so that they would love Yahweh with all their heart and soul. Then Moses went on to tell the audience before him how to respond.

> *For this particular commandment which I myself am commanding you this day it is not too wonderful (or miraculous) for you, and not too distant. It is not in the skies for you to say, "Who shall go to the skies for us so that he can take it for us in order that we might keep it?" And it is not beyond the sea so that you say, "Who shall pass over for us the sea so that he can take it for us in order that we might keep it?" For the matter (or word) is very close to you, in your mouth and in your heart to keep it.*
> *(Deuteronomy 30:11-14)*

Moses then said life and good and death and wretchedness were before them, and he commanded them that day to love Yahweh their God.[96] This was the high point of Moses' exhortation to Israel. Every religious Israelite in ancient times and the present day religious Jew would be aware of this pivotal passage.

> The message they have heard must be integrated into their hearts and lives.

---

[95] "shall live in them," The "in" is the preposition **ἐν en** can mean "in" or "by." The challenge of translating ἐν is because it was the most common of prepositions and over time it became so elastic in meaning it ceased being used in Greek. Harris, Prepositions, pp. 116-118. In Hebrew the Greek ἐν was translating the Hebrew preposition ב **"Be"** which clearly meant "in them," not "by means of them." Therefore, I would understand Paul was saying that with Christ a person was taken completely out of the sphere of the Mosaic Law while Moses was saying the Israelite had to live within the statutes and judgments.

[96] This sounds very much like a recapitulation of the choice before the Tree of the Knowledge of God and Evil. Much of the Hebrew vocabulary was common to both.

Paul took this final and critical exhortation by Moses and made it the literary parallel to the final and critical message of the Messiah Jesus. Moses and the Law said one thing, but the righteousness of faith said something quite different and quite specific. Paul used the words of Moses' exhortation to raise the issue of faith in Jesus to the highest pinnacle possible.

> *The righteousness out of faith thus speaks, "You should not say in your heart, who shall ascend in to Heaven, that is to bring Christ (the Messiah) down, or who shall descend down into the abyss that is to lead Christ (the Messiah) out of the dead?" But what does it say, "The utterance is next to you in your mouth and in your heart, that is the utterance of faith which we are proclaiming that if you should confess Jesus as Lord (Yahweh) and you should believe in your heart that God raised him out of the dead, you shall be saved. For by the heart a person believes unto righteousness, and by the mouth a person makes a confession unto salvation. (10:6-10)*

The Saving Confession

At Qumran, archaeologists found what looked like thick leather belts. These were actually phylacteries. They were designed to be worn around the forehead and also on the hand. Sown into the leather were Old Testament verses. Wearing those, the Jews would make a daily confession that Yahweh was their God and he was one. They would say out loud what is called the Shema (Hebrew for "you hear") Deuteronomy 6:4, "Hear Oh Israel, Yahweh[97] is our God. Yahweh is One." Further, that verse with several others would be sewn into their leather phylacteries. Every Jew was aware of that confession and religious Jews would proclaim that profession with their mouth out loud every day. The name Yahweh, the personal name of God, occurred over 6000 times in the Hebrew Bible. Invariably it was translated as "Lord" in the English Bible and that was usually written as "LORD." In the Greek Old Testament (LXX) it was translated as **κύριος Kurios** "Lord," the same term Paul used in the confession. The Jewish Christian would probably see much more than just the title Lord in what Paul wrote. Because of the context of Romans 9-11, and the use of Lord as the substitute for Yahweh, it would be impossible not to believe that the confession entailed admitting Jesus was Yahweh or deity.

WHAT PAUL DID WAS EXTRAORDINARY

1. He strategically took the very final admonition of Moses and turned it into a clarion Gospel proclamation for the confession of Christ

2. He became the second Moses who invited Israel into the household of faith

3. He declared that Christ already had mounted to the skies, and come from the abyss, and all the Jews had to do was believe

4. He took the Shema of Israel and turned it into the Shema of the Church

5. He forcefully equated the Yahweh of the Old Testament with the Jesus of the New

> **M**any, many people try to establish "bottom up" righteousness.
> **Being so preoccupied with what they are doing and whether they are righteous or not, they forget to see what God has provided in Christ.**

They are preoccupied with religious rules and make additional rules of their own while they don't think of subjecting themselves to God's rules. What is God's rule? He has ruled that trust in Christ is the end of the Law. The Law has nothing to say to the believer. God has granted his righteousness to those who trust in Christ. God has placed us in Union with Christ so that we have the righteousness of God in him. We have need of nothing.

---

[97] Instead of Yahweh they would say Adonai, "Lord" out of superstitious reverence.

Mastering the 7 Skills of Romans

Therefore, we need to have "top down" righteousness. This is a righteousness that comes from God and not from the Earth. The challenge is that people instinctively believe that their conduct determines God's relationship to them. The opposite is true. What God the Father has done through his Son Jesus is what matters. Paul has said any number of ways in Romans that we are not under the Law, that we have died to the law. He also said that we are justified with God by faith in his Son. Ultimately what God has done for us matters, not what we do for God.

Israel Rejected the Message

In Romans 10:11-13, Paul made the point that both Jew and Gentile will be saved if they call upon the name of the Lord. Salvation was open to all. He now considered the question: has Israel been granted a fair opportunity to accept this message? Israel has failed to accept the invitation and to make the confession that Jesus is Yahweh. Whose fault is it? Israel or God's? Paul proceeded to answer that question. He described what was predicted in the Old Testament about Yahweh pursuing the Gentiles because of the disinterest of Israel. He connected those predictions to the creation of the Gentile Church and described God's activity and Israel's faults. First, Israel was sent Evangelists.

Israel Was Sent Evangelists

The message was taken to them. He referenced Isaiah 52:7 that spoke of the proclamation of the good news of Israel being released from captivity from Assyria (Isaiah 52:1-12). The feet of the one who brought the good news were lovely. In Isaiah 52:7, it was one man who was announcing the good news, but in Paul's rewriting of the familiar verse, he made it many men who were evangelizing with the good news. The quote was from the context of Israel being redeemed out of a great captivity. The neighborhood the verse was from was quite significant. Isaiah 52:13-15 began the great Song of the Suffering Servant and there appears to be a linkage between the great deliverance from captivity and the greater deliverance of the Suffering Servant.

> Yahweh has stripped off the arm of his holiness before the eyes of the nations (the Gentiles) with the result the ends of the Earth will see the salvation of God. (Isaiah 52:10)

This deliverance from captivity would be made known to the entire Earth, but in an amazing contrast, the truly great arm of Yahweh's holiness would not be observed. Isaiah in Isaiah 53:1 asked who had seen the arm of Yahweh (with the assumption that no one had). Further, in complete contrast to the worldwide revelation of the rescue of Israel from captivity, the Kings and rulers of the Earth were just shocked by the revelation of the Suffering Servant (Isaiah 52:15). The contrast between the deliverance of Israel in Isaiah 52 created the contrast to Isaiah 52:12-53. In the earlier part of Isaiah 52, the nation was delivered gloriously while in 53 the Servant was ingloriously humiliated. As we said, the incredible display of power at the crucifixion was hidden. In Romans 10:16, not all the Jews, Paul stated, listened carefully so as to obey.

Israel's Failure In Spite of the Gospel (10:14-21)[98]

Paul then said that even though the message was taken to them, Israel did not respond. He quoted Isaiah 53:1 which rhetorically asked who believed the reported message. The implication was no one believed or very few did. Paul pointed out that hearing was required for the message to have a chance of being believed.

The Message Went to All the Jews Everywhere

Paul then pointed out that the message that needed to be heard was spread far and wide. As an illustration of the intense penetration of the message, he quoted from Psalm 19:4 where the message of God's creation has gone to the ends of the Earth. Paul used a very nice metaphor. As the sun rays envelop everything on Earth, so also this Gospel has gone to all the Jews. The issue at hand was not whether the whole world had heard the Gospel, but whether the Jews in the known world did. Paul was rather confident that they had. Other Apostles were taking that message to them. Particularly, Peter was to take the Gospel to the circumcised

---

[98] E.W. Bullinger, The Companion Bible (Grand Rapids, Michigan: Kregel Publications, 1922), p. 1680. The outline is from Bullinger, a genius if there ever was one.

(Galatians 2:7-8). What should be remembered about the Day of Pentecost in Acts 2 is that Jews from all over the known world were in Jerusalem and heard the message of the resurrected Messiah. Those who were there would return to the "ends of the Earth" with that message.

Moses Had Warned Israel of God Going to the Gentiles

In Deuteronomy 32, Moses taught the people a song about their future apostasy and their future judgement. Paul quoted only part of the line that said God would provoke the people of Israel with those who were not a people and with an outrageously foolish nation.

> *They themselves have made me jealous with a no-god. They have provoked me with empty things (idols), and I myself will make them jealous with a no-people, with an outrageously foolish nation I will cause to provoke them. (Deuteronomy 32:21)*

Paul left out the part about idolatry, but he showed that in the future of Israel, the nation would be scandalized by a provocative nation. The term for foolish is נָבָל **nabal** "foolish, senseless." Nabal was the husband of Abigail (1 Samuel 25:25). He was an outrageously provoking fool. In Hebrew, that was exactly what Nabal meant. This nation would also be a no-people. The Church is not a people because it is made of many different people, and it is a foolish provocation to the ways of the people of the Earth.

Israel Chose Unbelief

The greatest of Lawgivers, Moses, spoke of God turning to the Gentiles, and the greatest of the prophets, Isaiah spoke of the same.

> *And Isaiah is being very bold and he says, "I have been found by the ones not seeking me, manifest I came to be to the ones not making requests of me." (10:20)*

> *And to Israel he says, "All the day I stretched out my hands to a continually unpersuaded and arguing people (10:21)." [Quoted from Isaiah 65:1-2]*

This verse from Isaiah 65:2 began God's diatribe against his people Israel. Isaiah 65:1-16 contained a long complaint about Israel, and the refusal of the people to listen and obey. Instead of obeying, they argued with and insulted the Holy One of Israel. It was a striking condemnation of Israel, and after 65:16 were promises of redemption and rescue. Paul described the process of belief, and how Israel was pursued by God's message to no avail. Then, God was turning to the Gentiles so as to provoke Israel.

11 | ISRAEL'S DELIVERANCE

CHAPTER SUMMARY: Israel has completely failed to respond to God's intentions, but that did not mean they were utterly rejected. Paul gave three reasons for this. Even though a hardening and blindness has happened to Israel, first, a remnant of believing Jews exist. Secondly, Israel was and is the natural place of blessings, and the future holds a time of complete **deliverance** for Israel when the fullness of the Gentiles comes into the Body of Christ.

The previous chapter painted a dim picture of the obedience of Israel. They were not persuaded by Moses, nor persuaded by Jesus the Messiah, nor by Paul. Did that mean that God has no place for them? Paul gave an unequivocal answer. God is unequivocally committed to his people.

God Has Not Rejected His People

I am saying then, has God rejected his people? Impossible! For also I myself am an Israelite, out of the seed of Abraham, of the tribe of Benjamin. God has not rejected his people whom he knew personally beforehand. Or do you not know what the Scripture says in Elijah, as he intercedes to God against Israel? "Your prophets they have killed, your altars they have torn down, and I alone am left and they are seeking my soul." But what did the oracle say to him? "Seven thousand men I have left to myself. These are the kind who have not bowed the knee to Baal." Therefore then, now in the present time there is a remnant according to the election of grace. (11:1-5)

As usual, the Apostle began in his typical way: he asked a question. Since in chapters 9 and 10, Paul stated the failures of Israel to respond to Yahweh their God, the natural question was, has God rejected his people? In answering the question, Paul went back and forth from his present day realities to the history and prophecies of the Old Testament. His first point was that being Jewish did not preclude a person from trusting in Christ and belonging to God's new thing, the Church. A remnant of the nation has been incorporated into the Body of Christ. Even in times of great apostasy in the Northern Kingdom Israel, God still had a remnant. A remnant existed in the Northern Kingdom Israel, and a remnant of Israelites exist within the Church.

Scripture taught that God was not finished with the nation of Israel. This was very important to the Apostle Paul. In order to show that God was not through with the nation of Israel, Paul pointed out that he along with other Jews had become Christians. This shows that God was more than willing to accept the individual Jew if they believed in Jesus his Son. Paul also pointed out that in Elijah's time, a small percentage of Jews believed in Yahweh and refused to worship Baal. Paul gave that as an illustration of the fact that there were faithful believers even in the darkest times of Israel's history. Even darker than the time of Elijah was the time of Christ when the Son of God was rejected by his own people. Even in that darkness, Paul said God was not done with Israel. He will be faithful to his promises to them as he will be faithful to his promises to us.

Israel Has Been Placed Into A Spirit of Stupor (11:7-10)

But the reality was that a hardening had occurred in the hearts of the people of Israel to the Gospel of Christ. As usual, Paul buttressed what he said with Old Testament quotes and as was his usual habit, he quoted major figures from the Old Testament, Isaiah and David, as he had done before in Romans.

> *Even as it was written, God gave to them a spirit of bewilderment, eyes not being able to see, and ears not able to hear until today. (11:8)*

In the above, Paul used a paraphrased quote from Isaiah 6, the so-called commissioning of the prophet Isaiah.[99] Isaiah was sent to the people, and he was told to render their hearts fat, which was understood as making them insensitive (Isaiah 6:10). The image seemed to suggest feeding them with so much prophetic truth and repeating it so often that the people were bloated from it and became incapable of responding. Their ears and eyes would become dull and dim respectively. What was fascinating in Romans 11 was it appeared that the "fattening" of their hearts was "sovereign," but it seemed in Isaiah 6 that the "fattening" was due to repeated rejection of Isaiah's message. After referencing Isaiah, Paul turned to King David to further buttress what he saw as God's judgment on Israel in his day.

> *May their banquet table become a trap, and as for their well-being may it become a snare. Let their eyes be darkened from seeing and their loins continually shaking. (Psalm 69:23-24)* [Hebrew Bible]

The Inclusion of the Gentiles (11:11-15)

Paul did not leave his people in their lost state. He now proceeded to speak of their future. As usual he asked a question to indicate that he was transitioning.

> *I am saying then, did they stumble with the result they have fallen? Absolutely never! But by their trespass salvation [deliverance] came to the Gentiles to make them thoroughly jealous. And if and it is true their trespass is the wealth of the world and their failure is the wealth of the Gentiles, how much more their fullness. (11:11-12)*

Earlier Paul said it was strategically beneficial to view the failure of the Jews and Gentiles (3:9) as a means to open the door of the Gospel to both. In Romans 11 also, he said the advantage of the hardening of the nation of Israel would lead to using the Gentile Church as a means to provoke Israel to jealousy. Then, he made the remarkable transition to speak of the future deliverance of Israel. He used the language of "remnant" and "fullness" to signal the change. **τὸ πλήρωμα ta pleroma** "the fullness" was translated by the NAS as "fulfillment," the New Jerusalem Bible as "restored," and the RSV as "full inclusion." "Fullness" was much better because it was obviously in contrast to **λεῖμμα leimma** "remnant."[100] The fullness stood in contrast to the small remnant of Jews that were saved within the Body of Christ. Paul then specifically said to the Gentile Christians in Rome that he wanted to elevate his Apostleship to the Gentiles so as to rouse jealousy among the Jews. Then, he asked a question of the Gentile believers.

---

[99] Isaiah 6 occurred in the year of King Uzziah's death. Isaiah by this time had ministered for years.

[100] See also Romans 9:27.

For if their casting away is the reconciliation of the world, what is the reception except life out of the dead? (11:15)

What a remarkable twist! If the failure of the Jews opened the door of the Gospel to the entire world, then their return must even have a greater effect. The effect will be "life out of the dead." Is this mere hyperbole or actual designation of a future fact? Based on what we know of Paul's eschatology, his reference was almost certainly to a resurrection, probably the resurrection and rapture of 1 Corinthians 15:23-54. The joining of a future fullness of Israel accepting Christ, and the great event of the resurrection made for an irresistibly powerful message, a spiritual resurrection of the nation and physical resurrection of the dead. After his implication that there was a future for Israel, Paul then described a possibility for the Gentiles that was already true for the Jews.

The Olive Tree (11:16-21)

Concerning the Jews, he explained how the Church superseded the nation; now he related the future restoration of the nation to the largely Gentile Body of Christ by giving his third illustration of the Olive Tree in the Book of Romans. The Olive Tree was considered a beautiful tree. In Psalm 52:10, the Psalmist compared himself to a green Olive Tree in the House of God. Hosea spoke of God's passionate delight in Israel, and how he intended to make Israel's beauty like that of the Olive Tree.

I will heal their turning away, I will passionately love them willingly, for my anger has turned from them, I will become like the dew to Israel; he will blossom like the lily, and his roots will be like the trees of Lebanon. His shoots will sprout, and his beauty will become like the olive tree, and his fragrance like Lebanon. (Hosea 14:4-6)

Yahweh called Judah a beautiful Olive Tree, but judged it in Jeremiah 11.

Yahweh called your name, A Green Olive Tree of beautifully formed fruit, for a great rushing wind has started a fire upon it, and snapped her branches. Indeed, Yahweh of Armies who planted you has spoken evil against you, on account of the evil of the House of Israel and the House of Judah because of what they did to provoke me for they have burned incense to Baal. (Jeremiah 11:16-17)

Israel then was represented in the Old Testament as an Olive Tree of beauty that fell under the judgment of God, but would also be restored like a lovely Olive Tree.

Paul took this imagery from Hosea, Jeremiah, and other references in the Old Testament, and brought it forward to make a future prophecy concerning Israel and the Church. In Romans 11:17-24, Paul described how branches from Israel were broken off so that the Gentiles (being a wild Olive Tree) might be grafted into the tree of Israel. The Israelite Tree was holy and it appeared to be the generations of the people of Israel starting with the Patriarchs. The Gentile Christians must remember they were grafted in as a foreign wild Olive branch. The Gentiles should not then feel pride towards Israel, but humility. For if God could set aside the natural branches, then he could certainly set aside the unnatural branches of the Gentiles.

It is quite true they were broken off due to unbelief, and you[101] are standing by faith. Do not have a proud perspective, but fear. For if it is true God did not spare the natural branches, neither shall he spare you. (11:20-21)

The Mystery – All Israel Will Be Saved (11:25-36)

Then, Paul told the Roman Christians to carefully look at what he was saying. He wanted them to understand the implications of how God worked in history. Paul assumed God worked in predictable patterns based upon the response of those whom he had called.

---

[101] The "you" in the verses (11:18-24) is a second masculine singular not as one would expect a second masculine plural. This is reminiscent of Moses address to Israel in Deuteronomy where all of Israel was addressed as a second masculine singular even though hundreds of thousands were gathered before Moses hearing him speak. I suspect Paul was addressing the Gentile Christians as a collective similarly to how Moses addressed Israel as a collective personality.

Take a look at [Behold], then, the kindness and severity of God, on the one hand on the ones having fallen severity, and on the other hand, upon you the kindness of God, if you should remain in the kindness, otherwise you yourself also will be cut off. (11:22)

Then, he told the Gentile Christians that if Israel ceased their unbelief, God could graft them back in. In fact, it would be easier to do so since they were the natural branches. After speaking of that possibility, he then said it was a certainty. He told them a "mystery" **μυστήριον mysterion** "a doctrinal secret that is revealed." Paul stated elsewhere in Romans that a mystery was a doctrinal secret that was hidden for ages and generations and now was revealed to the Church (Romans 16:25; Ephesians 3:9, and Colossians 1:26).

For I am not desiring you to be ignorant, brethren, of this particular mystery [doctrinal secret] so that you would not be wise ones from yourselves, that a hardening out of a part came to Israel until the fullness of the Gentiles should come in and thus all Israel shall be saved, even as it was written, the Rescuer shall come out of Zion turning away ungodliness from Jacob. (11:25-26)

Romans 11:12 spoke of the fullness of Israel coming to belief as causing life from the dead, a resurrection. In 11:25-26, it was the coming fullness of the Gentiles that caused the "spiritual resurrection" of Israel. Ungodliness (their rejection of Christ) was turned away from Jacob. Paul's quote came from Isaiah 59:20 and the context spoke of Yahweh coming to conquer the Earth and deal with transgression and iniquity (Isaiah 59:16-20). Chapter 60 spoke of Zion being restored in faithfulness and the Gentiles coming to its splendor.

In an incredible twist, Paul stated that God's strategy was to allow the Gentiles and Jews to continue in unbelief. The degeneration by the Gentiles into idolatry was permitted and the degeneration of the Jews into hypocrisy was also permitted. As we read through Romans, Paul presented these judgments by God, and each judgment became the basis of a wondrous transformation or twist of taking the darkness and turning it into light.

The God of the Condemnations and the Great Deliverances

In five critical places, God allowed sin and failure to increase. With each of these disasters, God brought forth or will bring forth a greater blessing to believing humanity.

THE FIVE GREAT TRAGIC JUDGEMENTS IN ROMANS		
JUDGEMENT	**REVERSAL**	**COMMENTARY**
1. The handing over of the idolaters to their own insides, their lusts, emotions, and thinking (1:24-28)	For the law (Torah) of the Spirit of life in Christ Jesus has set you free from the Law (Torah) of the sin and of the death. (8:2)	After the description of God handing humanity over to its own insides in chapter 1, the subsequent chapters of 6, 7, and 8 showed the path of deliverance by the astonishing opportunity of living life in the presence of the Trinity. Humanity was taken from the disastrous inheritance from Adam of sin, to the incredible inheritance of godliness through Christ.
2. The handing over of humanity in Adam to sin and death (5:13-21)	And the undeserved gift is not like through the one having sinned; for on the one hand, the judgment from one act resulting in condemnation, but on the other hand, the grace gift from many trespasses resulting in justification. (5:16)	With Adam came sin, death, condemnation, and established life as a sinner. As a result of Christ, we have eternal life, the Holy Spirit, justification, and establishment as righteous ones. In the face of Adam's one trespass, Christ died for the endless sins of humanity and brought freedom and deliverance.

THE FIVE GREAT TRAGIC JUDGEMENTS IN ROMANS		
3. The handing over of creation to deterioration (8:20)	For the creation was subjected to futility, not willingly but because of him who subjected it, upon hope 21 because the creation itself also will be set free from its slavery to corruption into the freedom of the glory of the offspring of God. (8:20-21)	Through the Fall, we have been rendered mortal and deteriorating. At the same time, all of creation has been rendered pointless because the masters of creation have become pointless. At the time of the Rapture and resurrection, creation too will experience the glorious freedom of the offspring of God. Limitations will be reversed and glory will be enthroned.
4. The handing over of Israel to hardening so as to place Gentiles in the Olive Tree of Israel's blessings (11:8-10)	Now if and it is true their trespass is the wealth of the world and their failure is wealth for the Gentiles, how much more will their fullness be! (11:12)	With the hardening of Israel, God opened up the door of blessing to the Gentiles. This hardening was an Old Testament reality and with the rejection of the Messiah, the majority of the nation entered a deep spiritual slumber. Yet the future remains bright for Israel. The fullness of Israel, not just a remnant, will come to faith, and with that life from the dead, a resurrection too!
5. The handing over of the Gentiles and Jews to ἀπείθεια apeitheia "being unpersuaded or unbelieving" (11:30-32) συγκλείω sunkleio "lock up or shut up"	For God has shut up all together in unbelief and a refusal to listen that he might show mercy to all. (11:32)	With the setting aside of Israel with its privileges and prerogatives, the door was opened to the Gentiles. With the spiritual rebellion of all, God decided to have mercy on all through the message of the Gospel. As both Jews and Gentiles were shut up into the prison of sin, God offered both justification through the Gospel.

On the one hand, what is crystal clear is that humanity, which is made in the Image of God, is an inherent disaster without a relationship to God. The wondrous freedom a human being has who was made in the Image of God finds that freedom a curse because the ability to choose was now under the baleful influence of sin within. On the other hand, God rescues humanity from its misuse of freedom with a far greater blessing than what they originally had.

Paul's Paean of Praise

What were profound negatives became the foundation of wondrous positives. In exaltation, Paul turned to praise God for his wisdom. In appreciating Paul's praise of God's wisdom, we must realize what seemed to be motivating the Apostle. His praise at the end of chapter 11, was based on the "problem-solution" pattern of Romans. God's ability to judge human sin on the one hand, and then through grace, take those circumstances and mutate them into wondrous blessings on the other hand, brought forth a song of praise from Paul. We can see this was motivating Paul's thought by the vocabulary he used in his praise.

> *Oh, the depth of the riches and wisdom and knowledge of God, how unfathomable the judgements of him and unsearchable his paths (ways). (11:33)*

τὰ κρίματα ta krimata "the condemnations or judgments" referred to what a judge decided as the punishment or judgment. Examples of its usage are Romans 2:2, 3; 3:8; 5:16; 13:2. Yet in the context of Romans, these judgments led to greater, even astonishing benefits. The juxtaposition or placing the bad next to the resulting good was breathtaking.

Who has known the mind of the Lord or his fellow counselor come to be? [102] *Or who has given to him, and he shall pay him back? (11:34-35)*

The answer of course was no one. The God of the Bible was beyond human understanding, and was not needing human counsel. Nor was he obligated to anyone because no one was truly capable of giving anything to him.

because everything is directly from him, and through him, and unto him. To him the glory unto the ages, Amen! (11:36)

This brings the curtain down on the relationship of Israel to the Church. It also brings the conclusion of the great inversions wherein God judged human sin, yet like the ugly cocoon and the lovely butterfly, and through the dead Christ in the tomb and the glorious resurrection, God brought forth something vastly greater and gracious in response to human sin.

Transition

In the first three chapters of Romans, we have the collapse of human culture: chapter 1, humanity has lost its identity, chapter 2, humanity's moralism was useless, and chapter 3, human relationships became dangerous. The Book began with the collapse of human culture, and at the end of the Book, Paul gave God's answer to the collapse. Now with chapters 12-16, we have a new human culture introduced, the culture of Heaven!

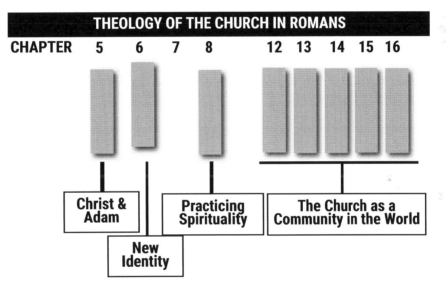

The 7 skills to be mastered in the Book are the bridge from the collapse of culture in chapters 1-3 to the establishment of the culture of Heaven in the Church, the Body of Christ on Earth (chapters 12-16). The last two skills are found in this last section; they are the skills of a transformed mind and the skill of an other-centered heart. Romans is unique in the writings of Paul because he fully develops what he sometimes referred to in his other writings. These seven skills form the other half of the problem-solution approach we are using to analyze the Book. Let us go on to the colony of Heaven on Earth: the last five chapters.

WE CAN SEE THREE STEPS IN THE PREVIOUS PROGRESSIONS:

1. A rebellious choice on the part of humanity
2. An allowance of degeneration and catastrophe for humanity or in the case of creation a disaster of pointlessness
3. A divine rescue which is gracious and at the same time creative, a higher and better level of existence is introduced

---

[102] Isaiah 40:13 in the Greek Old Testament (LXX). The Hebrew translated as, "Who has measured the Spirit of Yahweh, and a man of his counsel who has caused him to understand?" The LXX translator used the Greek word mind for the Hebrew word for Spirit. That was similar to how Paul combined spirit and mind in Ephesians 4:23, ". . . be made new in the Spirit of your mind." The implication from the LXX and Paul was that spirit and mind were the same.

12 | THE NEW CULTURE-GRATEFUL SERVICE

CHAPTER SUMMARY: To participate in the Church, the **Culture** of Heaven, Christians will need a transformation of heart and mind. In addition, what motivates the soul should be deep affection for others, and what makes for effective ministry is using the gifts of the Holy Spirit.

THE CORPORATE MISSION OF BELIEVERS (12:1)

In a few words and in one verse, Paul declared a revolution. The Apostle made a one-verse pivot from considering the catastrophe of Israel and its eventual glorious future, to quickly speaking of the church. Three chapters consumed with Israel preceded this one short verse. In a sudden transition, Paul told the Christians who they were, how they were to change their hearts and thinking, and what they should do after the inglorious failure of the Jews. In chapters 3-8, he emphasized the deliverance of the individual Christian (even though he spoke using the plural "you"), but now Paul spoke of the corporate goal of all Christians.

We must stop and think about the immediate implications of the quick transition. Israel was a nation of people with a land and a country, a capitol, and a common ancestry. Practicing a religion centered on the Temple, their priesthood slaughtered sacrifices and presented them to God. The most obvious element of Israelite religion was the slaughter of sacrifices so that the priests could make the people ceremonially clean. Being clean, they could enter the Tabernacle or Temple to be heard by God. All of those very physical elements have been pushed aside by Christ to be replaced by a new people, the church, whose worship and citizenship is group-centered, not cultic or Temple-centered, and faith-centered, not ancestry-centered. The practices of Israel had been left behind with their Temple. The new Temple is the Church because the members of the church are the habitation of Christ through the Holy Spirit. If ever there was a revolution, this was it.

> "Our Christian experience with God should be the direct opposite of the non-Christian world which disapproved of God and his ways. As we accept the renewal, it opens the door for what Paul described in the rest of the chapter."

Picking up where he left off in chapter 8 which finished with the love of the Father and Son, Paul told the believers in this first verse at the beginning of chapter 12 how their uniquely created spirituality would be similar to and distinctly different from the very physical spirituality of the Old Testament.

After chapters 9-11, which showed Israel was set aside in favor of the church, Christians are told they can be a living sacrifice. Calling the believers to be a living sacrifice, Paul brought the absolute center of the Old Testament system to bear. Chapters 9-11 are unique in Paul's writings, and we must notice that he used a unique phrase to transition away from Israel. It is the only place where he said the body of the believer can be a living sacrifice θυσία, **thusia**. In fact, it was not common for Paul himself to use that phrase of Christ. He spoke of Christ as a ἰλαστήριον **hilasterion** "place of atonement" in Romans 3:25. Just once he mentioned Christ as a sacrifice **thusia** in Ephesians 5:2. Otherwise, he called his own sacrifice **thusia** (Philippians 2:17) and the sacrifice of the Philippian church in sending him a gift of money **thusia** (Philippians 4:18). It is fascinating that Paul wrote often about the work of Christ on the cross and its benefits to us (usually based on our union with him), but the terminology of sacrifice was used to emphasize the spiritual sacrifices of believers as a response to God's grace.[103] Presenting the body was called an acceptable sacrifice. The previous three chapters made a point of saying present Israel was unacceptable to God, but Paul said the believers are acceptable.

We should meditate on the nature of Old Testament sacrifice so as to appreciate this transition. An Old Testament sacrifice did not take away sin: a sacrifice was primarily for removing the uncleanness of the people while at the same time satisfying God.[104] Otherwise the people nor the priesthood could approach Yahweh or do anything for him. A sacrifice also created a sense of satisfaction within God, and it became a sweet-smelling aroma ". . . a soothing aroma" (Exod. 29:18 NAS) in his nostrils. From Genesis to Numbers, this effect on Yahweh was mentioned 38 times. That soothing aroma was only experienced by Yahweh when the requirements were met for the type of animal, the quality of the animal, and the correct procedures by the priests and Levites in the sacrifice of the animal. The sacrifices had a two-fold purpose: one was to satisfy God and the other to remove uncleanness. Five different sacrifices were expected of the people of Israel. <u>God defined the five sacrifices as acts that would specifically please him, a soothing aroma.</u>

> Not only would the believers be a living sacrifice they would also have
> the role of the priesthood. Just as Christ was a sacrifice and priest
> so also the Christians have the same privileges.

The other critical Greek word besides sacrifice **thusia** meant serving as priests. λατρεία **Latreia** "service" is the LXX term for priestly service. This was again a revolutionary change because it was universally understood as Paul pointed out in 9:4 the divine service in the temple belonged to Israel and particularly the priests.

> who are Israelites, to whom belongs the adoption as sons and the glory and the covenants and the giving of the Law and the <u>temple service</u> and the promises, (Romans 9:4 NAS)

הָעֲבֹדָה **ha-achvodah** "the divine service" and "to serve the divine service" לַעֲבֹד אֶת־עֲבֹדַת **le-achvod eth achvoddhath** (Num. 3:8) was the central work of the priests and Levites. <u>Only the priests and the Levites were allowed to come into the presence of God, and to do spiritual work for God.</u> With those two principles in mind, God defined and limited what was an acceptable sacrifice, and only the priests and Levites could offer them.

Not only has Israel been set aside, the church has taken over its ministry and sacrificial system in a thoroughly spiritual way without the physical dimensions and practices of the Israelite religion. Now, those who believed in Christ were the true spiritual, acceptable, priesthood.

> Only Christians were those who were the acceptable living sacrifice,
> and now only Christians, both female and male, were those who had the right to
> live in the presence of God and do things for God.
> Christians were the sacrifice (albeit a living one) and the priests just like Jesus!

This is so strange and at the same time a great challenge to the individual Christian. On the one hand, we are granted two great privileges: we are a living sacrifice and each of us can function as a priest. On the

---

[103] It is in Hebrews with its emphasis on the Great High Priest Jesus where **thusia** is used of Christ on the cross (Heb. 8:3; 9:23, 26; 10:12). Spiritual sacrifices of believers were mentioned in Hebrews 13:15, 16 and Peter does the same in 1 Peter 2:5.

[104] See Excursus I, pages 160-161.

other hand, the body being blessed with these ministries is inhabited by sin as a force, with desires needing taming, and perspectives left over from our non-Christian life. This new spiritual way was mediated through the mortal body with sin within. As a result, we have a paradox: the body has sin within, but as we continue to live, our body will be alive with the life of Christ and the empowerment of the Holy Spirit.[105] Romans 6:6, said the body of sin has been nullified so the slavery to sin was ended, and 6:12 told us we will not have to listen to the lusts of the body because of the new life within. The mortal body belongs to the realm of death, yet the believer has true life within because the Spirit of Jesus enlivens us (12:10-11) whom God the Father has placed within us. Bodily sinful practices can be ended and true life can be experienced (12:13). The human body now has the privilege of being a living sacrifice, and by its activity would bring pleasure to God the Father.

THE SIXTH SKILL

To fully participate in this new kind of service to God, a revolution has to take place in the mind and heart of the Christians. Most of the time the new Christian recognizes the need but does not know how to proceed. The sixth skill of Romans addressed that. Metamorphosis of the inner life must occur. Paul anticipated this in Romans 7. After describing the struggles of the inner life, and how the Law did not offer any solution, he gave the solution at the end of the chapter.

> *Thanks be to God through Jesus Christ our Lord! So then, on the one hand I myself with my mind am serving the law of God, but on the other, with my flesh the law of sin. (Romans 7:25 NAS)*

The human mind will be the solution the as it relates to God. How is this to be done?

The Metamorphosis of the New Testament Believer (12:2)

Based upon Paul's very impressive way of building one thing upon another in his Book, I am assuming that the command of 12:2 is the next skill. 12:1 is a transitional statement wherein the church becomes the "sacrificial system" of the Old Testament and takes over the priestly ministry of the Old Testament. 12:2 is cumulative (the practice of the first five commands were assumed) and an additional commanded skill because **μεταμορφοῦσθε metamorphousthe** "be transformed" (Romans 12:2) is a present imperative passive:

1. The present means that it should be taking place now and continuing into the future

2. The imperative means it is a command to be obeyed

3. The passive means we are under the influence of another agent who is changing us

This other agent is obviously the Holy Spirit and the change will be within the mind **νοῦς nous**. The nature of the change is a complete renewal, meaning the change will be qualitatively different from the previous state of the mind. What is the nature of our cooperation? As we practice the five skills of the previous chapters, we are told to analyze the changes occurring within us as to their beneficiality, their acceptability, and their completeness. The analysis is to see if we find them positive. The verb for approve is **δοκιμάζω dokimadzo**. The verb is important in the classical and common Greek of the time. Referring to usually a serious appraisal, it should then result in the approval of something significant. The term was used of an assayer of precious metals, and an examiner of goods.[106] Paul was calling for a reflective examination of God's way of sanctification. He wanted the Christian to be convinced that God's will was a "perfect fit." In this way humanity's disapproval of God in 1:28 is reversed through the salvation of believers:

---

[105] John M. G. Barclay, Paul and the Gift (Grand Rapids, Michigan: Eerdmans, 2015), pp. 500-519. His observations are very keen but the density of his prose makes it hard to understand.

[106] Liddell and Scott, Lexicon, p. 442. "**δοκιμαστής dokimastes, οῦ, ὁ,** (**δοκιμάζω**) an assayer, scrutineer, Plat., Dem."

And just as they <u>did not</u> approve (**δοκιμάζω dokimadzo**) *of having a personal knowledge of God any longer, God gave them over to a disapproved* (**ἀδόκιμον adokimon "a rejected mind"**) *mind, to do those things which are not proper, (1:28)*

More than just a blanket presentation of the body is asked for. A transformation of the mind was needed to begin the task of creating a truly vibrant church. For Paul, what we do as Christians was dependent on who we are in our hearts. Obviously if we approve strongly of God's new and revolutionary ways, we will become involved in a self-perpetuating cycle. As we experience more deeply the Father's and Son's love and participate in the life change brought about by the Holy Spirit, we can then become more effective in our Christian life. Our Christian experience with God should be the direct opposite of the non-Christian world which disapproved of God and his ways. As we accept the renewal, it opens the door for what Paul described in the rest of the chapter. 12:1 dealt with the past and the substitution of the church for Israel. 12:2 addressed the present pagan culture. The church is not to be outwardly conformed to the present age. 12:2 **συσχηματίζω su-skematidzo**, "to conform one thing to another." The verb without the prefix is very common. It means conforming to a shape, to hair styles, conforming to almost anything. As a noun it refers to the shape of things, the externally observed realities of the ancient world. Instead, he called for a profound change. This was basic to Paul's thought. With his call to the inner conversion of the heart, Paul not only rejected the practices but also the thinking and wisdom of his world. Paul said not to be outwardly conformed to the age. His thinking though went far beyond hairstyles. He expected that the wisdom of God transcended anything the age could offer.

> *Yet we do speak wisdom among those who are mature; a wisdom, however, not of this age, nor of the rulers of this age, who are passing away; 7 but we speak God's wisdom in a mystery, the hidden wisdom, which God predestined before the ages to our glory; 8 the wisdom which none of the rulers of this age has understood; for if they had understood it, they would not have crucified the Lord of glory; (1 Corinthians 2:6-8 NAS)*

He also expected that the Christian view of reality would be seen as silly and foolish, and he encouraged Christians to embrace such divine foolishness.

> *Let no man deceive himself. If any man among you thinks that he is wise in this age, let him become foolish that he may become wise. (1 Corinthians 3:18 NAS)*

Sin is self-perpetuating because the desires of the flesh are being satisfied. Through the command of 12:2, Paul commanded believers to step into a similar (in its attractiveness), but profoundly different (in its source- the Holy Spirit) process of satisfaction as we discover the benefit, pleasure, and completeness of our life with God. The benefit will be in how we experience and practice life; we will be effective. The satisfaction will come from experiencing life as something lovely and rich emotionally. The completeness will be the completion of our humanity: we were made to know God and now we do.

T his sixth skill of metamorphosis is so strategically important.
Out of a satisfied heart, believers will be able to change their perspectives,
their activity, and their relationships. The metamorphosis will be the energy source for
the seventh skill which is living the other-centered life.

The Priestly Ministry of the New Testament Believer (12:3-8)

Strikingly after using language carried over from Israel, sacrifice and priestly service, he then went on to challenge the central ethos of the ancient world. That central ethos was an honor-shame culture of self-centered and hierarchical competition. As we proceed in Romans 12, we will develop more deeply what Paul said. Suffice to say he was not only calling for humility, he was introducing a revolutionary principle of interdependent affectionate service. Challenging directly the ethos of the ancient world, Paul proclaimed the **Culture of Heaven.** Since he wanted the mind to be transformed, he pointed out the direction the process should take. Note my expanded translation:

For in explanation of the implications of 12:1-2 above, through the grace given me, I am saying to everyone among you not to be <u>high minded</u> beyond which it is necessary to be <u>thinking</u>, but instead to be <u>thinking</u> as to have a <u>healthy perspective</u>, as God has measured to each one a measure of faith. (Romans 12:3)

The verb **φρονέω phroneo** occurs in verse 3 in four different underlined forms underscoring that Paul went from discussing a metamorphosis of the mind to the activity of the mind in creating perspectives. **phroneo** means to have a way of thinking or to have a perspective. The Apostle expected the Christians to transition from a shame-honor based way of thinking to a loving, other-centered way. Note carefully how the first word in the column appears in the other four words of the column. The bottom four words are from the Greek text of 12:3.

- **φρονέω phroneo** <u>"to have a perspective"</u>

- **ὑπερφρονεῖν huperephronein** "to have a proud perspective"

- **φρονεῖν phronein** "to think or have a perspective"

- **φρονεῖν phronein** "to think or have a perspective"

- **σωφρονεῖν sophphronein** "to have a healthy perspective"

One cannot escape the insight of Paul that the renewed mind would produce renewed perspectives. These renewed perspectives would be driven by the satisfaction of the heart caused by the divine metamorphosis. The metamorphosis will make the Christian response instinctive and other-centered, not calculated to promote pride or self-promotion.

We should talk about the relationship between the Greek word for "mind" **νοῦς nous** and the verb for "having a perspective" **φρονέω phroneo**. Clarity about those terms is important because Paul's whole approach to the Culture of Heaven expressed through the church is based on the metamorphosis of the mind. I will do a literal rendering of Romans 2:4 and point out where derivatives of **nous** "mind" and **phroneo** "to think or have a perspective" appear that illustrate the relationship of the two words. In 2:4, Paul accused the Jews of having a false picture of God in their minds that led them to have a negative perspective which despised the kindness of God. He told them they needed, through faith, a repentance or profound change of mind. Though they were not present to read or hear Romans, in the verse he addressed them. This Pauline methodology of addressing such a group was to instruct the Roman Christians.[107]

*Or are you looking down on [**kata-phroneo** literally having a <u>perspective</u> that looks down] the wealth of his kindness and forbearance and long suffering, having a <u>mind</u> [root of word is **nous**] ignorant of the fact that the kindness of God is leading you to repentance [**meta** change of mind, **noian** from **nous**]? (Romans 2:4)*

Note that Paul observed that the Jewish mindlessness concerning God's kindness led them to have a perspective of despising God's kindness. What the mind contains, the way the mind sees reality, determines the perspectives the mind develops.

Perspective or thought flows from the assumption, beliefs, and pictures within the mind.

To repent, in Greek, means to have a profound change of mind. With that, change will come, a change in perspective or how we think.

Let's express this in principles:

1. The mind is the repository of our beliefs and pictures or how we see the reality of ourselves, others,

---

[107] E.W. Bullinger, <u>Figures of Speech Used in the Bible</u> (Grand Rapids, Michigan: Baker Book House, 1968), pp. 898-899.

the world, and God.[108]

2. Out of the mind flows our perspectives and habits of thought.

3. The mind is changed or repents through faith.

4. With the change within the mind comes the change in perspective.

5. That change through faith is called repentance or in Greek **μετάνοια Metanoia** or a complete mind change.

As the mind meditates on God's will or desires for us, Paul assumed it will conclude that such a will is beneficial, pleasing, and a completion of our humanity. The Apostle then shared the perspectives that should then flow from the renewed mind, and how it will be expressed through our bodies in the life of the church. Shifting quickly, he gave concrete examples of how our bodies can become a living sacrifice.

> *For just as we have many members in one body and all the members do not have the same function,5 so we, who are many, are one body in Christ, and individually members one of another. (Romans 12:4-5 NAS)*

Just as the members of the human body are interdependent, human life as expressed in the church should be an other-centered and interdependent. Sharing a unity with the Head, Christ, we are connected to one another for each other's benefit and for the glory of God. We benefit each other by the individual gifting the Spirit has given. He then enumerated seven gifts that different Christians will have. In other places Paul mentioned additional gifts, but here he gave a sample using the number seven, the Hebrew number of completeness. Of these seven gifts, three are speaking gifts, and four are various forms of service. The word for gifts is derived from the verb "to be gracious" so the gifts are "grace gifts." Just as grace has granted salvation, so grace gives gifts to the individual believers so they can serve one another.

> "With this metamorphosis Paul assumed that the emotional environment of the heart will be under the influence of the Trinity, therefore, love will be the atmosphere of the heart."

The first gift mentioned was prophecy. Probably because it was first of importance. Like the gift of Apostleship (which Paul mentioned for himself), prophecy provided revelation. Along with Apostleship, prophecy was one of the foundational gifts of the church (Ephesians 2:20) with Christ being the chief cornerstone. Prophecy has to be in harmony with the analogy, or in conformity with the content of the faith. An analogy **ἀναλογία, analogia** shows the correspondence between two things in a "right relationship, comparison, proportion."[109] Obviously we get our word "analogy" from this Greek word. A prophet had to function as a true prophet.

With the next six, Paul emphasized a very important principle: the gifted person should concentrate on using the gift the Spirit has given him, and by implication not presume to have others beside his or her own. As a retired seminary professor, my observation is that many students in seminary and many pastors in the churches have a different gift than what is required for their ministry. Such are serving from preference and not from giftedness, and their results show it. The one serving, literally the one serving as a deacon, should focus on serving. The teacher should stay with her or his teaching; the exhorter with the exhortation, and the giver with the giving. The one who is leading should act with zeal or diligence, and the person exhibiting mercy should be cheerful.

Paul has shared the pattern that will give the Christians the opportunity to be a living sacrifice and be a participant in a priestly service similar to, yet profoundly different than the Old Testament priest. Calling the believers to a metamorphosis, both in mind and perspective, he set before them the ministry of spiritual gifts. With this metamorphosis, he assumed that the emotional environment of the heart will be under the

---

[108] Essentially, we exist within these following existential realities: God, self, others, and the world. Another way of putting it is that the mind contains beliefs or pictures of existential values that we have to absolutely relate to: God, self, others, and the world of people. Perspectives or thinking is the way we understand those existential values.

[109] Joseph Henry Thayer, A Greek-English Lexicon of the New Testament (New York: American Book Company, 1886), pp. 39, 408. Earlier Paul mentioned functioning according to the measure of one's faith (12:3). In that instance he was addressing the subjective experience of trusting God. In 12:6 he referred to the content of the faith. We are always to walk by faith, and he who proclaims has to be in harmony with the content of the faith of Christianity.

influence of the Trinity, therefore, love will be the atmosphere of the heart. At this point he did a reality check to make sure that the metamorphosis was real. He described what the symptoms of such love are.

The Motivation of the New Testament Believer (12:9-13)

From the metamorphosis of the mind flowing out to the perspectives, now Paul touched upon what should be the deep and predictable emotions of the heart. Such emotions should be driven by love. Emotions are important. Emotions are the energy source of the mind and perspective: essentially, the energy source of the heart. His description of the nature of that loving energy is crucially important.

One would think that Paul should have had the section about gifts and service after this section about love. Is not love the source of effective service, and also more important than service itself? Yet Paul did a similar thing in First Corinthians where chapter 12 was on spiritual gifts and chapter 14 continued on the same subject. The Apostle put chapter 13 on love between the two. Interestingly in both 1 Corinthians 13 and Romans 12:9-13 he did not command anyone to be loving. Instead, he commented on what love can do in the heart and relationships of a person. In 1 Corinthians 14:1 he told the Corinthian Christian to pursue love, an interesting turn of phrase. Not saying "be loving," but he said all of you pursue the experience of love, and be zealous about spiritual gifts.

This section of chapter 12 confronts a fundamental question going to the heart of the purpose of this book Mastering the 7 Skills of Romans. It also goes to the fundamental issue of verses 3-8. Will the mutual service of the church be based on a "concept-body response" wherein the heart is not engaged, or an "overflow of a loving heart approach"? The issue is: can the heart be commanded to love or does God's implanted love within have to be foundational before that command can be obeyed? The evangelical sickness sadly is just a concept of loving others in the mind and the body directed to act accordingly. Does this qualify as Paul's definition of love?

The context of Romans has the answer. Romans 5 and 8 mention God's love for his own. Romans 5:8 spoke of God recommending his love to us. In Romans 8:35-39, the Son's love for us was mentioned twice, and the Father's love once. Being placed at the very center of the Book of Romans, it explicated the passion driving redemption and our adoption. Not until 12:9 was the believers' love for one another mentioned. Prior to that, the five skills did not mention love for one another once. Obviously while the five skills commanded responsive obedience, no place so far expected believers to love God or man. One can say we certainly should love God and man, yet so far Romans did not. Could it be because Paul has a different strategy than just demanding it? Could it be that the cumulative acquisition of the six skills, including of course the one concerning the metamorphosis of the mind, naturally produces affection for God and people? Let us see how 12:9 and the following answers the two previous questions.

Paul described from chapters 1-11 a remarkable set of truths illustrating God's great love for his own. Without the metamorphosis of the mind mentioned in 12:2 and the acquisition of the other-centered perspective (12:3-8), what immediately follows (12:9-12) would be impossible. If God's love is not absorbed, understood, and experienced, nothing would change in the human heart. With such a metamorphosis as described in 12:2, Paul assumed human love would be very present and very evident in 12:9-10. Here is my translation:

> *Love is without play acting or hypocrisy* [love must be genuine]. [Those who have it are] *Ones continually despising malicious evil, and continually joining themselves to what is beneficial, in relationship to affection of the brethren for each other having tender family affection, in relationship to honor giving preference to the others,*

It is very different from the New American Standard Version.

> *Let love be without hypocrisy. Abhor what is evil; cling to what is good. 10 Be devoted to one another in brotherly love; give preference to one another in honor (Romans 12:9 NAS)*

The New American Standard Version has five commands. My translation, not one. I am translating directly what Paul wrote. He did not write one command, let alone five. I believe he is making an observation about how love functions in the mind and heart that has gone through metamorphosis. We can see that he is not talking about "acting" loving but being truly loving. He does not want love to be a performance art, an act of hypocrisy.[110] He was not describing something we do, but something flowing out of us because the transformed heart has the fruit of the Spirit within. Unfortunately, some can become so good at religious acting that they do not notice their own fakery. When they see an observation about what love is like, they turn it into a command instead of leaving it as a description.

So why does the NASV have five commands, and I have none? The reason is called a "verbless clause." In the Greek Paul wrote, he did not write any verb at all. Directly translated, he wrote "The Love unhypocritical." Being hypocritical means the outer observed person appears loving, but inwardly is a white washed tomb. No delight in the other person's well-being exists, nor joy in the other's presence is present. Paul presumed love, Agape love, is always an inward disposition before it became an activity. Steven Runce, who is an expert in Discourse Grammar, commented on the verbless clause in 12:9.

> *Many want to take the verbless clause of v. 9 as an imperative, as well as some participles (e.g., LEB, NASB). This option was available to Paul, and doing so would have made all the ideas equally important rather than subordinated under the general heading of love being unhypocritical.*[111]

The typical and recommended way of dealing with a verbless clause is simply to insert an "is" as I did in my translation.[112] In other words, Paul described the symptoms of love as opposed to commanding love. Note how emotional those symptoms were: despising (12:9), affection for the brethren (12:10), tender family affection (12:10), and rejoicing (12:12).

This love coming from the inside out depends upon the metamorphosis of the mind and heart. One might consider this emphasis on the verbless clause as a mere academic distinction. It is not. Issues of great significance ride on the difference between the verbless clause describing the realities coming forth from love within, and the imperative emphasizing what we should do without. Romans 12:1-2 calls for a profound inner change. After that call it speaks of an other-centered ministry using spiritual gifts. Then, Paul made his observation on unhypocritical love. That observation is strategic because it presumes something inside the Christian will flow out.

Let's look at this through the prism of five other Pauline passages. In Galatians 5:22 Paul stated that love was a fruit whose source is the Holy Spirit. Just as divine love from the Father was brought to the heart of the believer in Romans 5:5, so the human response of loving God, Christ, and particularly others is from him too. Instead of the works of the flesh (Galatians 5:19-21), an inward riot of selfishness and pain, the Spirit produces an inward disposition of tranquility and affectionate love for others. In our next passage, Paul in Ephesians implied how the Christian received the influence of the Holy Spirit.

> *And do not allow yourself to be drunk with wine, by which is dissipation, but in contrast allow yourself to be presently filled with qualities from the Spirit. (5:18)*[113]

---

[110] Liddell and Scott, Lexicon, p. 1886.

[111] Steven E. Runce, Discourse Grammar of the New Testament, (Peabody, Massachusetts: Hendrickson, 2010), p. 265. Participles following a command are normally assumed to be part of the command. Participles following a copula (an "is" statement) or a verbless clause are considered descriptive. Daniel Wallace in his significant grammar assumes the participles in 12:9 function as commands. Yet he says normally they have to be preceded by an imperative, a command. The dilemma is that a verbless clause is not a command, and the context of Romans 12 and the context of Paul's writings presumes love is a by-product of an effectual relationship with God. Any issue of grammar as Wallace states and I agree ultimately has to be decided by context. I believe in this context Paul was making an observation about the nature of love and how love flows from the transformed heart and mind. Daniel B. Wallace, Greek Grammar: Beyond the Basics (Grand Rapids, Michigan: Zondervan, 1996), pp. 650-651.

[112] Another way of approaching this is that we have an Anacoluthon meaning "lacking sequence." The participles following the verbless clause are not grammatically connected to the verbless clause deliberately so as to force thought upon the reader. A good example of understanding it that way was in James D.G. Dunn, Word Biblical Commentary: Romans 9-16 (Dallas, Texas: Word Book Publishers, 1988), p. 738. He set it in what he called note form: "9 Genuine love: hating what is evil, devoted to what is good." That communicates without using a command or an imperative. At the same time, it is not a grammatically perfect sentence; it is an Anacoluthon.

[113] Page 98-99 [of this section] defines "to be transformed" as a present imperative passive, so is the command in Ephesians 5:18. This means we are passive as an agent, the Holy Spirit, changes our character. Indeed, a synergism exists: we have to practice the 7 skills. Yet without the aid of the Spirit all of our cooperation is useless.

Mastering the 7 Skills of Romans

Notice that the agent wine and the agent Spirit were both capable of influencing the Christian. Both agents were present and fully capable of bringing influence to bear. The Christian's responsibility was to submit to Spirit-filling, or in other words, the influence of the Spirit. In a truly beautiful touch, Paul then said we can make melody in our hearts to the Lord. "Make melody" **ψάλλω psallo** means to pluck the strings usually of a harp. In our case, the harp is our heart. Spirit-filling leads to a human response of great beauty welling up from our depths. Influencing our character within, it leads to positive results without (Ephesians 5:19-33).

The third illustration are passages from Romans 2. In them, Paul contrasted the Jews with certain Gentiles who did not have the Law, yet were spontaneously keeping the Law from within their hearts.

> *For when Gentiles who do not have the Law do instinctively the things of the Law, these, not having the Law, are a law to themselves, (Romans 2:14 NAS)*

The phrase translated "do instinctively" is literally in Greek "by nature the things of the Law would be doing" (**φύσει phusei** means "by nature" or "naturally"). In 2:29 he says that this was from the Spirit. In Romans 2:14-16, Paul spoke of those Gentiles, then he picked up the same subject further in the chapter. If we recognize believers were not called Christians at the time of the writing of Romans, it should occur to us that he is contrasting Jews with gentile Christians. Without the commands of the Law (since the Gentiles never had them), the gentile believers through the Spirit were keeping the expectations of the Law.

> *If therefore the uncircumcised man keeps the requirements of the Law, will not his uncircumcision be regarded as circumcision?. . .*
>
> *28 For he is not a Jew who is one outwardly; neither is circumcision that which is outward in the flesh. 29 But he is a Jew who is one inwardly; and circumcision is that which is of the heart, <u>by the Spirit</u>, not by the letter; and his praise is not from men, but from God. (Romans 2:26, 28-29 NAS)*

The principle is that Paul did not have a command approach to changing the human heart. He had a process approach. The seven skills represent the process wherein the believer goes through a transformation and loves naturally and thus fulfills the legal expectations.

The fourth passage is 1 Corinthians 8:1-3:

> *Now concerning things sacrificed to idols, we know that we all have knowledge. Knowledge makes arrogant, but love builds up. If anyone thinks he has learned, not yet he has really known, as it was necessary to have known. Yet if anyone would be presently loving God, this one has had a relationship with him and has been known by him. (1 Corinthians 8:1-3)*

The implication follows that loving God is a product of God having had an established relationship with the person. This, of course, starts with the skill of counting ourselves continually alive to God in Christ (6:11). God established a basis of relationship with the believers in Christ (Romans 5-6). As believers assumed themselves continually alive to God and related to him, out of that flowed character change and the fruit of the Spirit. Love never starts with us.

The final passage is 1 Corinthians 13 where Paul contrasted drastic human sacrifice with the heart's disposition of love.

> *And if I give all my possessions to feed the poor, and if I deliver my body to be burned, but do not have love, it profits me nothing. (1 Corinthians 13:3 NAS)*

If love is not present within, delivering one's body to be burned is unprofitable in the spiritual realm. Verse 3 is fundamentally important to Paul's thought.

Inward disposition must precede outward activity.
Otherwise, Christianity is a sham and hypocritical, merely a performance art.

In a remarkable portion in Cranfield's commentary on Romans, the author quoted Calvin, and then followed it with an astute comment.

> *Calvin p. 271: 'It is difficult to express how ingenious almost all men are in counterfeiting a love which they do not really possess. They deceive not only others, but also themselves, while they persuade themselves that they have a true love for those whom they not only treat with neglect, but also in fact reject.' The recognition that the state of the man who believes that he is loving, when he is not, is even worse than that of the man who pretends to be loving, knowing that he is not, is important.*[114]

A partnership, we must remember, exists between the Christian and the Holy Spirit. Allowing herself to go through a profoundly transformational inner experience, the Christian can then, from the inside out, do loving acts. Love within can come out. A Christian reading my translation of 12:9 (regardless of what is on the written page) may automatically presume they have to act loving: in other words, play-act. Their legalism blinds their eyes to the fact that the New Testament assumes the Holy Spirit kindles love within and we have to manage its outward expression. Instead, they unconsciously act hypocritically.

One may think giving five examples and spending so much time on the verbless clause, a fine grammatical point, is an excessive amount of effort. Such thinking is missing the crisis of the church. It is the difference between reality and shadow. It is the difference between living our lives in the presence of the Trinity, and living our lives trapped within our own thinking. It is the difference between being preoccupied with Heaven, and being preoccupied with our own thoughts. Let us leave the five examples behind and continue on with our text, and look again at 12:9:

> *Love is without play acting or hypocrisy* [love must be genuine]. [Those who have it are] *Ones continually despising malicious evil, and continually joining themselves to what is beneficial,*

Such love has strong emotions within its thrall or power. The normal and commonly used word for hate is **μισέω miseo**. Much stronger than that is **ἀποστυγέω apostugeo** found in verse 9, meaning to hate violently. I translated it as "despises." **στυγέω stugeo** means to abhor. With the preposition **ἀπο apo** "away from," it means to hate and turn away. As a noun it means "abhorrence." The object of the hatred was malicious evil or **πονηρός poneros**. Satan is called the evil one using this word. Naturally a heart of affectionate love wanting the best for others would have a sense of repulsion in the presence of maliciousness, while beneficiality would have a magnetic attraction. Notice the matrix of emotions: affection for people, abhorrence of viciousness, and an attraction to benefitting others. One of the major tools of language analysis is antonyms or words meaning the opposite of each other. In this case, we have "love" and "hatred." The latter is a very strong emotion. Indeed, it follows that love indeed should be as strong an emotion or stronger. Both responses are found in the same person who has undergone metamorphosis.

Why would Paul so quickly have joined love to such a negative response? Obviously, he believed that Agape love was a powerful emotion that affected all other emotions within. Another reason was that Agape love could be expended on that which was unworthy. Agape love is a human emotion. It can be used positively or negatively. Let's think about this. Notice first that Agape love is the deepest possible affection within the human heart. Such love can be used on God or on that which is opposite to God. Agape love from the heart can easily embrace this present darkness with passionate delight.

> *And this is the judgment, that the light is come into the world, and men <u>loved</u>* [Agape] *the darkness rather than the light; for their deeds were evil* [**poneros** maliciously evil]. *For everyone who does evil <u>hates</u> the light, and does not come to the light, lest his deeds should be exposed. (John 3:19-20 NAS)*

---

[114] Cranfield, <u>Romans</u>, Vol. 2, p. 631.

Mastering the 7 Skills of Romans

Agape love is a powerful human emotion that can be used on a good object or person or an evil object or person. Since love is always an act of preference, humanly speaking, such love naturally partners with hate or dislike. In John 3:19-20 it is partnered with hate **μισέω miseo**. Paul partnered healthy Agape in Romans 12:9 with a stronger word than hate, disgust. Healthy Agape love comes with a dislike of malicious evil. At the same time, it has a deep fondness for God and other believers, and instinctively joins itself to what is beneficial. Without healthy and strong emotions, a believer's spirituality is not what it is supposed to be. Christian activity without accompanying correct and strong emotions is hypocrisy; it is play acting. Strong emotion, love, and strong prejudice, hate and abhorrence, lead to strong attachment and tenderness.

> . . . *in relationship to affection of the brethren for each other they have tender family affection, in relationship to honor they give preference to the others, (Romans 12:10)*

The phrase "affection for the brethren" should be hyphenated "affection-for-the-brethren." It is all one very familiar word: "Philadelphia" or brotherly love. **τῇ φιλαδελφίᾳ ta Philadelphia** or "as to brotherly love" is the beginning phrase. Paul then elucidated the kind of brotherly love coming forth from Agape love. It is **φιλόστοργοι philostorgoi** translated "tender family affection." In its Greek literal meaning in 12:10 it is "those-loving-like-affectionate-family-members." In classical Greek it is defined as "loving tenderly" and is frequently used of family affection.[115] In Koine Greek, the common Greek of the time, it was frequently used in wills when a bequest was made and the person receiving it was described as being "tenderly loved" in the will.[116] Wanting to be very clear in what he was communicating, Paul reinforced the "Philadelphia" phrase with an unambiguously clear word for deep affection. This is in harmony with what is found in my other writings and is expressed in this aphorism:

> What we do in our emotions will almost always predetermine
> what we do with our will and relationships.[117]

One of the realities flowing out of love is to honor other believers. Jayson Georges and Mark Baker make a powerful point about honor. "Honor is a good thing when people seek it from God and use it for his glory. Christians should not abandon the proper pursuit of honor. Rather they should passionately pursue the right kind of honor."[118] Western Christians sometimes overlook a critical point: if we honor Christ by believing the Gospel, God the Father will honor us for doing so. Those who believed the Gospel, as Paul said in Romans 2:7, were pursuing glory and honor from God (just as the Son sought honor from his Father John 8:49), and in 2:10, God honors those who were persuaded by the Gospel with glory, honor, and peace (just as the Father honored the Son John 17:1, 4-5). Love honors those who are the recipients of such affection. To live within the life of the Trinity is to live in an atmosphere of mutual affection and honor. Naturally such affection and honor should be extended to all members of the Christian family.

Concepts in the mind and bodily activity without accompanying affectionate other-centered emotions is simply hypocrisy. With affection driving the process of practicing these other virtues, it makes for a powerful and attractive display. Paul went onto say what love can do.

> *In relationship to zeal, not lazy ones, in relationship to the Spirit boiling, in relationship to the Lord serving (12:11)*

The Apostle shared how love relates to different areas of the Christian life: to zeal, to the Spirit or possibly human spirit, and to the Lord. Love revealed itself in the following ways: in relationship to hope rejoicing, concerning persecution or stress remaining faithful, concerning prayer being obstinately involved, and concerning the needs of the saints sharing. Essentially, this was the same principle Christ shared:

---

[115] Liddell and Scott, <u>Lexicon</u>, p. 1940. Every usage appears to have an intensity about it. The word was also used within very romantic passages in classical Greek.

[116] Moulton and Milligan, <u>Vocabulary</u>, pp. 669-670.

[117] David Eckman, <u>Becoming Who God Intended</u> (Pleasanton, California: BWGI Publishing, 2005), p. 29.

[118] Jayson Georges and Mark D. Baker, <u>Ministering in Honor-Shame Cultures</u> (Downers Grove, Illinois: InterVarsity Press, 2016), p. 211.

*"The good man out of the good treasure of his heart brings forth what is good; and the evil man [**poneros** maliciously evil man]out of the evil [**poneros** maliciously evil] treasure brings forth what is evil; for his mouth speaks from that which fills his heart. (Luke 6:45 NAS)*

At this point he ended the section of his "concerning or in relationship to statements" to simply state "continually practicing hospitality" (12:12-13). Paul used a series of participles and two nouns to describe how the good person out of the good treasure of his heart brings forth beneficial things as Christ described.

Unhypocritical love [manifests itself this way]:

- Hating evil (Participle) v. 9
- Joining to good (Participle) v. 9
- Ones-loving-like-family (Noun) v. 10
- Honoring others (Participle) v. 10
- Not lazy ones (Noun) v. 11
- Boiling spiritually (Participle) v. 11

- Serving the Lord (Participle) v. 11
- Rejoicing hopefully (Participle) v. 12
- Enduring stress (Participle) v. 12
- Stubbornly praying (Participle) v. 12
- Sharing (Participle) v. 13
- Pursuing hospitality (Participle) v. 13

The two nouns and ten participles describe activity. Naturally a sincere Christian will ask her or his heart whether such activity is happening. If it is not, the response should not start with, "I must get busy!" The response should be, "I must examine my heart and see if I am really practicing the first sixth skills of Romans."

ASK YOURSELF, AM I . . .
1. Focusing on the Father and staying in his presence (6:11-13)
2. Assuming our Union with Christ (6:11)
3. Not "listening to our appetites" (6:12)
4. Following the prompting (walking by) of the Spirit (7:6, 8:4)
5. Having a Heavenly perspective (8:5-6)
6. Allowing my mind to be renewed (12:2)

SKILLS OF ROMANS

That will give the serious Christian the interest and the energy to get busy. Each element of these six skills puts the believer in a place where the Spirit of God can produce the fruit of the Spirit and a Heavenly perspective. If those activities are not preceded by the systematic and sequential practice of the six skills, then to merely exhort ourselves to such an activity is fundamentally ineffective. If what Paul described was merely dependent upon the believers acting in the expected way, then the commands would be cruel indeed. To command someone who is without energy and crippled to race is not what Paul intended. He earnestly believed the Holy Spirit would give the necessary emotional energy and perspective to act.

The Response of the New Testament Believer to Opposition (12:14-21)

Romans 12:9-13 is one verbless clause followed by one long sentence. The entirety described how love effects relationships and activities. Affirming the symptoms of love and particularly how it should result in mutual care and self-giving, Paul turned his attention to how love should respond to those who hate Christians. Verse 14 begins a new sentence and a relatively new subject dealing with persecution. It actually contains a command, as the previous verses from 12:9-13 did not.

You be blessing the persecutors, you be blessing and not cursing. (12:14)

This is as close to the language of Jesus as one can get. Obviously, Paul was aware of what Jesus taught. He slightly changed the language when he said the believers should not be cursing the persecutors while Jesus said bless those who curse his followers.

bless those who curse you, pray for those who mistreat you. (Luke 6:28 NAS)

Mastering the 7 Skills of Romans

We must underscore that Paul was repeating in his own words the ethics of Jesus Christ. Some of the vocabulary and phrases are the same as the two passages where Christ spoke of dealing with those who would misuse believers. One passage was from the Sermon on the Mount:

> *"But I say to you, do not resist him who is evil; but whoever slaps you on your right cheek, turn to him the other also.*

> *44 "But I say to you, love your enemies, and pray for those who persecute you 45 in order that you may be sons of your Father who is in heaven; for He causes His sun to rise on the evil and the good, and sends rain on the righteous and the unrighteous. (Matthew 5:39, 44-45 NAS)*

The other was from Luke 6 and the section is often called the Sermon on the Plain because it is similar to the one on the Mount.

> *"But I say to you who hear, love your enemies, do good to those who hate you, 28 bless those who curse you, pray for those who mistreat you. 29 "Whoever hits you on the cheek, offer him the other also; and whoever takes away your coat, do not withhold your shirt from him either. (Luke 6:27-29 NAS)*

Romans 12:14-21 appears to be a restatement of Luke 6:20-49.[119] That section of Luke was a briefer statement of the Sermon on the Mount. Not only does it reflect what is in Luke, but it also includes Paul's own reflections on it. To not relish revenge, to not return evil for evil, and to be generous to one's enemy demands a power source which leaves the heart content, peaceful, and affectionate under the most dire of stress and persecution. This power source was described in verses 9-13 and its influence must also permeate the response to being wronged.

Verses 16 and 17 return to previous subjects touched upon earlier, sympathy and perspective. In the latter verse he piled up the use of perspective as he had in verse 12:3. Forms of perspective (**φρονέω phroneo** "having a perspective") occur three times.

> *Be having the same perspective with each other, not having high things controlling your perspective, but be associating with the humble. Don't become ones of a high perspective among yourselves. (12:16)*

Paul gave a conceptual presentation of how a person sees things by using the word "perspective." The believers should not consider themselves better than others. In Luke 6 we find the same idea speaking of humility about perspective in the midst of the section on persecution. Contrasting Paul's statement with Christ's, we find the language of Jesus more picturesque and unforgettable.

> *"Or how can you say to your brother, 'Brother, let me take out the speck that is in your eye,' when you yourself do not see the log that is in your own eye? You hypocrite, first take the log[120] out of your own eye, and then you will see clearly to take out the speck that is in your brother's eye. (Luke 6:42 NAS)*

Returning to Paul, he emphasized kindness to enemies. So that the enemies would become embarrassed.

> *17 Never pay back evil for evil to anyone. Respect what is right in the sight of all men. 18 If possible, so far as it depends on you, be at peace with all men. 19 Never take your own revenge, beloved, but leave room for the wrath of God, for it is written, "Vengeance is Mine, I will repay," says the Lord. 20 "But if your enemy is hungry, feed him, and if he is thirsty, give him a drink; for in so doing you will heap burning coals upon his head."[121]*

Kenneth Bailey in his commentary <u>Paul Through Mediterranean Eyes</u> has a lovely illustration of what

---

[119]   Luke was a companion of Paul's in the travels in the Book of Acts. Paul may have had access to Luke's material on the life of Christ, but not necessarily what was in Matthew.

[120]   Liddell and Scott, <u>Lexicon</u>, p. 443. **δοκός, ἡ**, later **ὁ, (δέχομαι)** a bearing-beam, in the roof or floor of a house, generally, a balk or beam, the bar of a gate or door. Essentially in modern terms Christ was describing a telephone pole!

[121]   The thought that this refers to embarrassing one's enemies is the most common understanding of the "coals of fire" reference.

Paul was talking about. When Paul was in Corinth, he was opposed by the leader of the Synagogue named Sosthenes (Acts 18:12-17). He brought charges before the Roman judge. The judge wanted no part of it and Sosthenes ended up with a vicious beating by the onlookers. Yet later we have a man named Sosthenes well known to the Corinthians being called a co-author of Corinthians by Paul. Bailey made the suggestion that after the beating Paul may have visited the Synagogue leader, treated him kindly, and led him to Christ. It is a nice thought and if true, it illustrates kindness to the opponent and persecutor.[122]

Again, Jesus has the same thought but adorned it with artistry.

> 29 *"Whoever hits you on the cheek, offer him the other also; and whoever takes away your coat, do not withhold your shirt from him either. (Luke 6:29 NAS)*

Romans 12:17-21 ends with this principle:

> 21 *Do not be overcome by evil, but overcome evil with good.(Romans 12:21 NAS)*

In the same spirit Christ previously underscored that ethic:

> 27 *"But I say to you who hear, love your enemies, do good to those who hate you, (Luke 6:27 NAS)*

Summary of Chapter 12

Chapters 1-8 took us from the moral disaster of the Greco-Roman world, and the legalism of the failing Jewish religion to the wonder of what Christ has done for humanity and the church. Chapters 9-11 explained how God's righteous and loving freedom chose to take the failure of Israel, and through their failure establish the church of his beloved Son. Chapter 12 opened to the vistas of the Trinity's desire to extend the Culture of Heaven to the Earth. The first two verses of the chapter showed how the church was a substitute sacrifice (though a living one), and a substitute priesthood (though encompassing all believers, both female and male). This profound shift called for humility on the part of Christians and a willingness to use the gifts God the Holy Spirit has given to the church. In the approximate middle of the chapter, Paul shared the energy source of this new movement and life, love. Describing how love works itself out in the lives of healthy believers, he emphasized the avoidance of hypocrisy and the embrace of a Spirit-filled life. In the conclusion of the chapter, Paul dealt with the persecution and abuse of Christians. Paul was in accord with what Christ taught in Matthew and Luke. Even with enemies, a loving response should be pursued and practiced. With this chapter we have the sixth and seventh skills presented: the transformation of the mind and heart, and the other-directed life. The skills represent our participation in the life of the Trinity, and our participation in the life of the church.

What is particularly striking is that Christian ethics are worked out within the community. "Ethics is ultimately the formation of Christian community-ekklesia. Paul grounds his moral vision in the formation of God's new covenant people."[123] Chapter 12 began the Culture of Heaven. Beginning with an encouragement for a profound change of heart and perspective, the Apostle began by emphasizing the mutual and reciprocating ministry the sisters and brothers should have with one another through the use of spiritual gifts. As he transitioned from the use of grace gifts, Paul then emphasized how Agape love should lead to a communal life filled with affection for one another. Israel has been set aside and the church builds its unity not on a common language, common land, common ancestry, but on a diverse community united by deep family affection as experienced within the Trinity.

As we have worked through the problems Paul isolated in earlier chapters, we now come to the last solution to the "handing overs" dealing with humanity being left with a disapproved mind, a mind that failed the test of recognizing the true God and Creator.[124] We now have added another solution, the renewal of the mind, to the problems addressed by the Book of Romans.

---

122   Kenneth E. Bailey, Paul Through Mediterranean Eyes (Downers Grove: Illinois, Inter-Varsity Press, 2011), P. 58.

123   Georges and Baker, Ministering in Honor-Shame Cultures, p.213.

124   See page 98 of this chapter for the full discussion on the mind approving of God's will.

PROBLEM	SOLUTION
1. Humanity turned over to its desires (1:24)	Believers given the capacity to manage desires and control them (6:11-14)
2. Humanity turned over to its dishonorable moods (1:26)	Believers given the capacity to deal with moods through the Holy Spirit (7:5-6)
3. Humanity turned over to a disapproved mind that failed the test (1:28)	Believers have an approved mind that approves God's ways (12:1-2)
4. Humanity trapped by a chaotic culture exhibiting gross immorality (1:18-32)	
5. The Jews adopted a performance based religion resulting in hypocrisy	
6. Union with Adam resulting in sin within, death, condemnation, and status as a sinner (5:12-21)	Union with Christ resulting in death to sin, life in Christ, justification, and status as a righteous one (5:15-21; 6)
7. The flesh given as the overarching problem resulting from God handing over humanity and the Fall of Adam (7:14, 18; 8:3-10)	Walking by means of the Spirit brings liberation from the power of sin within and the flesh (8:1-14)

As we have progressed through Romans we have been given a list of the spiritual skills we need to acquire. Those skills are based on God's solutions to the problem. Yet having a solution does not mean we have learned to take advantage of the solution. That is where the skills come in. After the commentary section on Romans 16, we will present how those skills are acquired and practiced.

13 | THE NEW CULTURE-RESPECT FOR GOVERNMENT

CHAPTER SUMMARY: The New Culture of Heaven on Earth, the Church, is required to be obedient to earthly authorities. The members of the Body of Christ are called to love others and thus fulfill the Law, and to be spiritually awake and not live in darkness.

THE CULTURE OF HEAVEN AND EARTHLY AUTHORITIES

This New Heavenly Culture has to exist in this old world. In chapters 12-16, Paul gave the constitutional document of the Gentile church. Generally, he described how the members should treat each other, but in various sections he described the church's relationship to the world. This section on earthly authorities begins as follows:

Every individual be under submission to the existing authorities. For there is no authority except by God, and the existing ones have been appointed by God. (13:1)

When I am studying a biblical text, I normally have not only the English Bible open but also other language Bibles. For New Testament study I frequently would have a Hebrew translation of the New Testament open because I enjoy seeing how knowledgeable translators of the Old Testament would translate Greek into Hebrew. Often, I find interesting and sometimes helpful the vocabulary and syntax they chose. In addition, I like to have the Syriac Peshitta open. That is a later version in the Aramaic language, and a very early translation of the New Testament. With both versions I found translations for verse 1 that caught my eye. My translation from the Hebrew New Testament is below.

For there is no authority except that being placed by the mouth of God.[125]

The "appointed by God" in Greek became "by the mouth of God" in Hebrew. That seemed to be a powerful way of translating the Greek, and true to the spirit of the Old Testament. It is the commands coming from the mouth of God that establishes reality for this earth. Then, the Peshitta struck me poignantly.

Every soul should serve to the authority [the sultanate] *of the great ones. (Romans 13:1 Peshitta)*

---

[125] כִּי־אֵין מֶמְשָׁלָה זוּלָתִי הַנְּתוּנָה עַל־פִּי הָאֱלֹהִים Romans 13:1 Hebrew New Testament 1886/1999/2013. Salkinson-Ginsburg.

Mastering the 7 Skills of Romans

At the time of the first century A.D., the Syriac word Sultan meant authority. Only later with the Moslems did it refer to specifically Islamic rulers. Even so, that brought to mind the fifteen hundred years when many of the Orthodox Churches had to survive and thrive under the Moslem authority. That was a history filled with sadness and sometimes deep persecution. Yet the Orthodox submitted themselves to the teaching of Paul and strove to be good citizens. Those two translations reflect the contents of 13:1-7: the expectation of God that we will render to Caesar what is Caesar's, and the sad reality of suffering often accompanying the command.

The truth of this is sublimely illustrated by the Book of Daniel and the experience of Nebuchadnezzar. In interpreting the vision of the four world empires in the king's vision of the statute of gold, silver, bronze, and iron and clay, Daniel spoke this truth to the king.

> "And it is He who changes the times and the epochs; He removes kings and establishes kings; He gives wisdom to wise men, And knowledge to men of understanding. (Daniel 2:21 NAS)

In order to teach the king this truth a decree was made.

> "This sentence is by the decree of the angelic watchers, And the decision is a command of the holy ones, in order that the living may know that the Most High is ruler over the realm of mankind, And bestows it on whom He wishes, and sets over it the lowliest of men." (Daniel 4:17 NAS)

The king, as a result, was driven away from humanity and essentially became insane. The purpose was to teach him that the most high is the ruler over mankind (Daniel 4:25). After that horrible experience, his sanity was restored and the king confessed this:

> "And all the inhabitants of the earth are accounted as nothing, But He does according to His will in the host of heaven and among the inhabitants of earth; And no one can ward off His hand or say to Him, 'What hast Thou done?' (Daniel 4:35 NAS)

This is the consistent teaching of the Old and New Testament that the rulers of this earth hold their positions through the decision and wisdom of God. Whether they were good or evil, they were placed by God. Paul was so convinced of this that he supported it with quite dramatic language.

> So that the one continually resisting the authority, has opposed the mandate of God, and the ones who have continually resisted shall receive a judgment on themselves. (13:2)

It is interesting to observe that verse two emphasized a continual resistance to established authority. The language was strong because it challenged a stubborn resistance to government. It is much the same as Christ's observation to Peter, "For the ones having taken up the sword shall die by the sword (Matthew 26:52)." Moreover, he placed the authorities on a par with other servants of God, the priesthood. Twice he called authorities the deacons of God (13:4). Once he called them the **λειτουργός leitourgos** or servant of God. Paul used this same term in 15:16 wherein he described himself as a servant **leitourgos** ministering as a priest the Gospel of God. In the Septuagint Greek Text, the same term is used of angels as servants of God (Psalm 103:21) and also priests (Isaiah 61:6). In addition, it was used of the servants of King Solomon (1 Kings 10:5). The text stated that these authorities existed to deal with the evils of this world.

The goal of the Christian, then, would be to win praise from them for well-doing. **ἔπαινός epainos** "praise" is quite interesting in its usage as a noun here or as a verb. The word emphasized very positive praise usually done in a public context.[126] Often this praise was done as a panegyric or complimentary address. In the context of the Greco-Roman world, such addresses were sought by the rich and proud in order to draw attention to themselves. Certainly, Paul would not have thought of Christians bolstering their egos, but much more likely he was emphasizing that Christian virtue was not just a private affair but something to be lived out before the world. As Jesus said, believers should be like a city set on a hill (Matthew 5:14), not set there to be noticed, but instead to be impossible not to be noticed. A number of scholars connect this text to benefaction,

---

[126]   Liddell and Scott, <u>Lexicon</u>, pp. 603-604. See also James Dunn, <u>Romans 9-16</u>, p. 703.

or doing things of public benefit, a customary practice in Roman life. Jackson Wu, a Christian teacher in Asia who uses a false name for security purposes, made telling comments.

> *Paul urges Christians to do works that serve the public good. He does want his readers to be moral citizens with private spirituality. His exhortation has explicit expectations – local officials will praise believers' good works. This implies such works are public and so are noticed. Through public benefaction, believers will "do what is honorable in the sight of all."*[127]

In fact, the Apostle said quite clearly that if the Christian desires to be unafraid of the authority, she or he should do what is beneficial, and the authority will notice and give **ἔπαινός epainos** "praise."

In 13:6-7, Paul touched upon the mundane, the paying of taxes. This emphasis was repeated by him several times to the extent one would think he did not want to leave Christians an out. A reason may have been that in Rome, in the approximate years when Romans was written, much resentment was building up concerning taxes. Tax collectors and what are called "tax farmers," those who paid fees to be tax collectors, were highly unpopular and considered quite dishonest by everyone.[128] Paul wanted to be very certain that Christians were not accused of fomenting problems with Roman officials so he used:

- **φόρος phoros** tribute paid by subject nations to Rome. This obviously would apply to Christians outside of the City of Rome.

- **ὀφειλή opheile** obligation of any sort. Sometimes this would include involuntary participation in state work projects.

- **τέλος telos** to toll. This could include almost any type of tax.

- **φόβος phobos** fear, respect. This word is two-edged: it assumes respect but also fear of disobeying.

- **τιμή timae** honor, and sometimes payment.[129] The Greco-Roman world placed a high value on showing respect.

What Paul had to say was in the stream of Old Testament thought which was reinforced by other New Testament writers.

> *My son, fear Yahweh and the king; Do not associate with those who are continually changing* [with respect to Yahweh and the king]; *22 For suddenly their calamity will rise, and who knows the disaster coming from both of them? (Proverbs 24:21-22)*

This teaching naturally resulted in the church becoming a conservative institution. Normally, Christians should not be those who push for radical change and government change. We have better things to do.

The Culture of Heaven and Everyone Else

Paul was a stylist in how he wrote his letters. What I mean is that he would use particular elements of rhetoric or speech communication to get his message across. For example, at the end of the first half of Romans chapters 1-8, he used a chiastic form of five verses to rhapsodize about the Father's and Son's love for believers. [130] A chiasm or chiastic form literally means "an X form" where the key idea is at the center of the "X" or, in that case, the center of the five verses. And at the beginning and end of the verses are a similar thought. A chiasm is usually used to bring a thought to a sense of rest. That is exactly what he did at the end of the eight chapters. Now in chapter 13, he brings that section to rest with a three-verse chiasm and a four-verse exhortation (13:11-14). This chiasm is worth looking at carefully because the short paragraph says something about the Law, and also the importance of the seven skills.

---

[127] Jackson Wu, Reading Romans with Eastern Eyes (IVP Academic: Downers Grove, Illinois, 2019), p.171.

[128] James Dunn, Romans 9-16, p. 766.

[129] John D. Harvey, Exegetical Guide to the Greek New Testament: Romans (B & H Academic: Nashville, Tennessee), pp. 318-319.

[130] See pages pp.76-77.

Mastering the 7 Skills of Romans

In a compact three-verse chiasm, Paul left the topic of earthly authority behind, and turned to address the Christian's relationship to everyone else in humanity. Having established that the church functions on reciprocal love relationships, he then emphasized that those who are not members of the Body of Christ should have love extended to them. Here is a diagram form of the verses:

To no one nothing you be owing except to <u>love</u> the others. For the one continually loving the other of a different sort has brought the <u>Law</u> to completion. (13:8)
For the [following quote says]
don't commit adultery,
don't murder,
don't steal,
don't desire [what is not yours],
and if any other kind of commandment, in this word it is being summed up, you love your neighbor as yourself. (13:9) <u>Love</u> does not do evil to the neighbor. Therefore, <u>love</u> is the completion of the <u>Law</u>. (13:10)

Notice how verse eight and ten have quite common vocabulary; they are the ends of the "X." "Love" is twice in verse eight and ten. "Law" is once in eight and ten, and "completion" is in both verses. In the middle verse are four commands from the Ten Commandments (Exodus 20; Deuteronomy 5) plus the word for individual commandment. That is the center of the "X."

Paul firmly believed that the reciprocal love relationship between the Father and the Son should flow over to believers, and we should enter in and participate in the circle of love which is the Trinity. Flowing from these reciprocal relationships would be love for our brothers and sisters in Christ. Flowing beyond them, it should be shared with those outside of Christ. Of necessity, this means that Agape love has to be relational, and deeply emotional, otherwise it would not have the capacity to move the human heart to embrace the lives of others. This short chiasm contains the essence of the Book of Romans. God the Father and the Son has been motivated by love and not Law; we should be motivated by love and not Law. In doing so, the Law comes to its completion in time and completion in its purpose to make human interactions noble and good. Paul's radical idea is that living life within the Trinitarian relationships makes the Law as a system useless (except for its ability to tell us what is sin). Love circumvents the legal system and yet produces the morality the Law so desperately sought. Romans has 77 uses of the word Law. The last two references to Law in the Book are in 13:8 and 13:10. Something has set the legal system of the Old Testament aside: it is the simplicity and power of deep affection for another.

A chiastic form, if observed, carefully brings a topic or an idea to a rest point. And so it brought chapter 13 to a rest point. After that, a final exhortation closes off chapters 12 and 13. Before he entered into a fresh topic in chapter 14, he brought the previous two chapters to a conclusion.

Chapters 12-13
↓
Rest Point 13:8-10 Chiasm
Closing Off 12-13
↓
Exhortation, Wake Up 13:11-14

After all of this very positive encouragement and sublime language of 12 and 13, he ended on a very realistic note: he said, if as a Christian you are spiritually asleep, now was the time to wake up. " . . . because now already is the hour you must wake out of sleep (13:11)." Sleep brings two realities: a lack of awareness, and a lack of action. In the present Evangelical Church and Catholic Church, a lack of awareness is rotting out the soul of both institutions. A working knowledge of the Trinity is uncommon. An emotional sense of God the Father's love is missing even in the most biblically conservative churches.

Sadly, a life-changing knowledge of our wondrous Union with Christ is largely unknown.

As one thoughtful Chinese American brother who attends a huge Chinese Church on the West Coast said to me, "I never heard anything about my Union with Christ for all the years I attended there." Just today, a Caucasian Christian who grew up in conservative churches and as a pastor's son said to me, the churches he knew were preoccupied with knowledge with little understanding of the power of a relationship with God. A knowledge and experience of the Spirit's leading was largely lost. Ask a Christian or a Catholic to explain how the ministries of the different Members of the Trinity interrelate for our benefit, and the best you may get is a quizzical look and maybe a glimmer of interest. The other lack coming with "spiritual sleep" is a loss of activity and emotion. Sometimes what exists (and this is better than what normally occurs) is a conceptual knowledge of some truths about the Trinity. At least knowledge of our relationships to the Three is present in the mind. Laying fallow, the truth does not grow and blossom because integration has not occurred in the heart. Therefore, the heart is emotionless, and the Christian's living-out of the truth is moribund or corpse-like. If we don't learn these truths now, I could imagine Paul the Apostle waiting in Heaven to offer us two courses: one on the life of the Trinity, and another on what it means to be in Union with Christ. My fear is some Christians may not attend or take a nap in class and not even listen to him in Heaven.

Paul exhorted the Christian to recognize the season, the **καιρός kairos**. The word does not refer normally to a period of time, but instead it emphasizes the character of the times. The **kairos** for a believer is the period of expectancy for the return of Christ, and the time of opportunity to live a godly life. The night has been cut short and the day had drawn near so that his coming is the next immediate thing in the plan of God. The same language occurred in James.

> *8 You too be patient; strengthen your hearts, for the coming of the Lord is the next immediate thing. 9 Stop groaning, brethren, against one another, so that you yourselves may not be judged; behold, the Judge has taken a stand right at the door. (James 5:8-9)*

The verb at the end of verse 8 "is the next immediate thing," and the verb "has taken a stand" at the end of verse 9 are both Greek perfect tenses. That means nothing exists between the coming of the Lord and the believers, and nothing is between the door of verse 9 and the Judge standing at that door. For both James and Paul this season is the season of expectancy: the coming of the Lord Jesus is the next immediate thing.[131]

Based on that expectancy, Paul used the language of clothing to exhort the Christians in Rome. We should put away like clothing, the works of darkness, and put on like clothing, the weapons of light. Paul has used the metaphor of taking off and putting on clothing to represent what we should present to others in the relationships of life (also used this way in Ephesians 4:22, 24; Colossians 3:8, 12). Clothing people see, and our moral or immoral activity people see. Paul called what we should put on, the armor of light. The result should be that the Christian will have a life lived nobly and well. At the same time carousing, sexual immorality, and jealousy were avoided. At the conclusion of this section Paul summed it all up.

> *All of you put on like clothing the Lord Jesus Christ, and don't make fleshly forethought on behalf of its lusts. (13:14)*

Where Paul began this section on the Culture of Heaven with the mind (12:2), he now ended the section with the mind. The word for forethought is **πρόνοια pronoia**. The **noia** part of **pronoia** derives from the word **νοῦς nous**. **Nous** occurred in 12:2 where Christians were told to allow their mind to be transformed. At the end of 13, Paul told believers not to have spiritually asleep hearts and minds, nor to allow the mind to be preset to satisfy the lusts of the flesh. What they were to do was to so practice the 7 skills so that as they stepped into the relationships of life, the very life of Christ would be emanating through them. Their Heavenly weapons would be the character of Christ and the perspective of the Trinity.

---

[131] Of course, this implies strongly a pre-tribulation Rapture. If you know of no such things or have a different view of when Jesus will come, be assured such is not the focus of this book. The focus of this book is learning and living the 7 skills.

Practicing the 7 Skills

Chapter 13 was largely concerned about human authorities and at the end, treating those outside the church with love. These two exhortations obviously were presupposing the practice of skills 1-6. Such skills will give us what Christ described in John 14:27.

> 27 "Peace I leave with you; My peace I give to you; not as the world gives, do I give to you. Let not your heart be troubled, nor let it be fearful. (John 14:27 NAS)

Paul and Christ presumed the world and its authorities will generate plenty of stress and sometimes persecution. Believers, then, need to have a peace and joy insulated from the chaos of this world. Precisely, that is what the 7 skills do. As citizens of another world, Heaven, we have more than a right to have hearts satisfied with living life in the presence of the Trinity. Having the fruit of the Spirit and the perspective of the Father, experiencing the Father's deep affection for us, and contemplating the incredible gift of the God-Man dying for us should be sufficient to make the gloomiest circumstances bearable. This joy Jesus spoke of was dependent upon the believer's relationship to each member of the Trinity. As the Christian assumed she was continually alive to the Father (skill 1) in Christ (skill 2) and assumed to be dead to sin within by thoroughly ignoring it (skill 3), the Spirit would grant the fruit of the Spirit (skill 4). From that would develop a spiritual perspective from the Spirit (skill 5). As time passed and this process was repeated over and over again, the mind and heart would be transformed (skill 6). Within the person was a self-sufficient and self-contained source of joy. This peace and joy makes for a happy Christian and a powerful witness for the truth. What is the reality behind that truth? We are loved by the Father and Son, and blessed emotionally and mentally by the Spirit.

If we do not practice skills 1-6 in the face of the world's chaos, we will be enslaved to the continually passing crises. In a sense, we live in a world where we can pick and choose what human misery we can fret about. Or we can revel in our Heavenly relationships. We are now in a position to see how these skills create the Culture of Heaven within a local church or within the Body of Christ.

In chapters 12 to 13, Paul exhorted the believers in Rome to master the last two skills and we will see how they are critical for the challenges of chapters 14-15 of Romans.

	MASTERING THE 7 SKILLS OF ROMANS
1.	Mastering the skill of focusing on the Father and staying in his presence (6:11-13)
2.	Mastering the skill of assuming our Union with Christ (6:11)
3.	Mastering the skill of not "listening to our appetites" (6:12)
4.	Mastering the skill of following the prompting (walking by) of the Spirit (7:6; 8:4)
5.	Mastering the skill of having a Heavenly perspective (8:5-6)
6.	Allowing my mind to be renewed (12:2)
7.	Mastering the skill of allowing our mind to be thoroughly renewed by the Spirit (12:2)
8.	Mastering the skill of being other centered and ministering to others (12:4-6)

In Romans 14-15 are explicit examples of how these skills can be used to create a unified and vibrant church, the Culture of Heaven. Chapter 16 gave the results of these skills in the deep and loving relationships of Paul and his sisters and brothers in the house churches of Rome.

14 | THE NEW CULTURE- RESPECT FOR ONE ANOTHER

CHAPTER SUMMARY: The clash of **cultural** backgrounds of the Gentile Christians and the Jewish Christians is addressed. The spiritually strong should not despise the spiritually weak, and the weak should not judge or penalize the strong.

THE CULTURE OF HEAVEN AND CLASHING CHRISTIANS

God used Moses to perform 10 miracles that delivered Israel from Egypt. In a similar way, God used miracles to deliver the church from the religion and life of Israel. If God the Holy Spirit had not intervened as described in the Book of Acts, the Body of Christ would have become a minor and despised sect within Judaism. As we shall see, the Great Commission of Christ was in great danger of being strangled by the Jewish culture, Law, and traditions. To appreciate chapter 14, we have to look at the history of the Great Commission and the history of the early church. The fact that the Gospel of Matthew is considered the most Jewish of the Gospels makes its ending most striking. It ends not with the nation of Israel, but the Gentile nations.

> *19 "Go therefore and make disciples of all the nations, baptizing them in the name of the Father and the Son and the Holy Spirit, 20 teaching them to observe all that I commanded you; and lo, I am with you always, even to the end of the age." (Matthew 28:19-20 NAS)*

Only Jewish disciples were present, and they were the ones who were told to go to all the nations, the Gentiles, to disciple them while baptizing them, and commanding them to obey all that he commanded them. In the history of Acts and the history of the church, those who were present were frozen in place and did not do it, and did not even attempt it. Without the intervention of Christ and the Holy Spirit, the Gospel would have stalled and rusted in Jerusalem. Why they did not make such an attempt was played out in the Book of Acts. A reading of Acts will show that the Holy Spirit and the Risen Christ had to have a strategy to make the command in Matthew 28 a reality for the Jewish disciples. Our Apostle, Saul of Tarsus, was to play a leading role in their strategy.

In Jerusalem, the conversion of the Jews started with Acts 2. Peter was a central figure and preacher in that process. Christ had told him he would have the keys of the Kingdom of Heaven (Matthew 16:19), and Peter opened the door to that Kingdom on the Day of Pentecost. The miracles and the message were restricted to

3733885292920

the circle of the Jews in Judea and the Hellenistic Jews, Greek-speaking Jews, who were there.[132] In subsequent chapters we see the circle expanding. Thousands were gathered into the church. Remember though, it was an all-Jewish church.

Philip took the next step of expansion with the Samaritans. The first significant extension of the Gospel was to the Samaritans (Acts 8:4). The Samaritans were a mixed race of Jews and Gentiles who accepted the five books of Moses, but not the rest of the Old Testament. Being considered heretics, a great animosity existed between the Samaritans and the Jews. Nevertheless, a Spirit-filled Philip overcame such prejudices and Samaria welcomed the Gospel.

The first true, recorded Gentile conversion was the Ethiopian eunuch who had come to Jerusalem to worship showing that he was a God-fearer who tried to conform to the Jewish Law (Acts 8:27).[133] Being a eunuch, for him the issue of circumcision was irrelevant. Philip again was instrumental.

Finally, we come to the last step, but in a true sense, a first step in a long and arduous process of establishing an effective mission to the Gentiles. The transition to the Gentiles was done by bringing two ideal men together (Acts 10-11). One was Cornelius, a centurion. He was a devout man meaning he did not worship idols and a God-fearer, a Gentile who tried to conform his life to the Law without being circumcised. Further, he financially supported the local Jewish population and was a man of excellent reputation. The other man was Peter, who was going to use the keys again from Christ to additionally open the door of the Kingdom of Heaven to the Gentiles. An angel first appeared to Cornelius telling him to send for Peter whereupon he sent three men to summon him. Peter was a bit more problematic. God had to address his false pictures of the Gentiles, God, Jesus Christ and himself. Peter had a vision, actually called an ecstasy in Greek, in which a sheet was lowered three times filled with unclean animals, animals Jews were not permitted to eat. At the first appearance of the sheet, Peter was told to kill and eat. Refusing, he said that he had never eaten anything unclean. With this he showed the power of family and cultural background. God himself was telling him to eat unclean animals and he refused! Shortly thereafter, three Gentiles sent by Cornelius summoned him. Three times the sheet had come down, and afterward three Gentiles were at the door. Because of the vision he went along. Note carefully, it took this vision to move Peter in the direction of opening the door to Gentiles. Recognizing that he was there to preach the Gospel, he spoke as follows:

> And he said to them, "You yourselves know how unlawful it is for a man who is a Jew to associate with a foreigner or to visit him; and yet God has shown me that I should not call any man unholy or unclean. (Acts 10:28 NAS)

What was the problem? Peter illustrated the difficulty. He who proclaimed the risen Christ repeatedly in Jerusalem and in Galilee was commanded by the God-Man to take the good news to the Gentiles. Instead of responding, he was frozen in place, frozen by a lifetime of tradition and prejudice. The vision showed the picture in Peter's heart of the Gentiles: unclean animals who needed to be avoided. Proclaiming the Gospel to the crowd of Gentiles in the home of Cornelius, Peter watched as the Holy Spirit fell upon the group and they spoke in foreign languages they had never learned.

> 44 While Peter was still speaking these words, the Holy Spirit fell upon all those who were listening to the message. 45 And all the circumcised believers who had come with Peter were amazed, because the gift of the Holy Spirit had been poured out upon the Gentiles also. 46 For they were hearing them speaking with tongues [different languages] and exalting God. Then Peter answered, 47 "Surely no one can refuse the water for these to be baptized who have received the Holy Spirit just as we did, can he?" (Acts 10:44-47 NAS)

Note again it took a miraculous display of divine power to authenticate what Peter was doing in preaching the Gospel to the "unclean." Later on, Peter was assailed for preaching the Gospel, and he stoutly defended

---

[132] Ἑλληνιστής **Hellanistas,** Greek speaking Jew was differentiated by Luke with the Ἐβραῖος **Hebraios,** Hebrew or Aramaic speaking Jews (Acts 6:1), and the Ἕλην **Hellan** who was a Gentile Greek speaker.

[133] This is an assumption because the possibility existed that he was a Jewish man serving an Ethiopian queen. But many Jews were in Jerusalem from foreign lands so such a conversion of a Jewish eunuch would not have been that unusual. This conversion was obviously unusual.

himself. Essentially his defense was the miraculous vision and the pouring out of the Holy Spirit.

The next event involved not the immediate circle of Apostles or the Apostle Paul. It involved certain men from Cyprus and Cyrene who evangelized in Antioch.

> *20 But there were some of them, men of Cyprus and Cyrene, who came to Antioch and began speaking to the Greeks also, preaching the Lord Jesus. (Acts 11:20 NAS)*

Those in Antioch were called Ἕλλην **Hellan** which was a Gentile Greek speaker and that should be differentiated in the context of Acts from an Ἑλληνιστής **Hellanistas** who normally would be a Jew speaking Greek and who largely conformed to a Greek style of life. It appears that these from Cyprus and Cyrene had a separate experience, motivation, and mission which was not described in Acts. Within a short time, Paul became involved with the church in Antioch as a teacher and leader.

But prejudices and background die hard. Peter regressed back to the frozen state. Cornelius' conversion is typically placed at around 36 A.D., and the next event is considered to be ten years later. The conversion of Cornelius could have been a happy ending, but Peter's prejudices showed up again. Our basic instincts often surface when we are under tension. Peter was caught in a situation similar to his denial of Christ. Except this time, it did not involve the execution of the Savior, it just was the issue of whose company should he keep at dinner. Paul wrote about it.

> *But when Cephas came to Antioch, I [Paul] opposed him to his face, because he stood condemned. 12 For prior to the coming of certain men from James, he used to eat with the Gentiles; but when they came, he began to withdraw and hold himself aloof, fearing the party of the circumcision. 13 And the rest of the Jews joined him in hypocrisy, with the result that even Barnabas was carried away by their hypocrisy. (Galatians 2:11-13 NAS)*

No threatening soldiers stood around with clubs and swords. Social pressure and the fear in his own heart captured him and made him a hypocrite. The arrival of those from James generated tension. Peter and his group knew these men certainly confessed Jesus as the Messiah. They knew the visitors kept the Law of the Old Testament and the traditions. They also knew that they were deeply prejudiced against the Gentiles whether the Gentiles confessed Jesus as the Christ or not. Like mischievous children being caught at home by parents who have just returned from a party, Peter and his group acted like nothing had happened. Nothing had changed. Seemingly Paul was not surprised by Peter's hypocrisy, but the surprise was Barnabas, a good and spirit-filled man (Acts 11:24), went along with it too. Barnabas' response, not Peter's, showed how engrained the prejudice was.

To finally address these issues, Paul and Barnabas went up to Jerusalem to settle the question as to whether the Gentile converts were to be under the Law, particularly the cleanliness laws and dietary restrictions. Peter first spoke to the assembly about his own experience with Cornelius (Acts 15:7-11). Then Barnabas and Paul shared their experience emphasizing the miracles that authenticated their mission to the Gentiles.

> *And all the multitude kept silent, and they were listening to Barnabas and Paul as they were relating what signs and wonders God had done through them among the Gentiles. (Acts 15:12 NAS)*

The messages of the three speakers seemed to have swayed the discussion, and James concluded the gathering by saying the Gentile Christians were not under the precepts of Judaism. Yet he included in his resulting declaration a respect for the dietary laws.

> *"Therefore it is my judgment that we do not trouble those who are turning to God from among the Gentiles, 20 but that we write to them that they abstain from things contaminated by idols and from fornication and from what is strangled and from blood. (Acts 15:19-20 NAS)*

Two things should be underscored. First, miracles brought Israel out of Egypt, and miracles were what brought the church out of Israel. It took the miraculous to break the hold of prejudice and tradition. Second, that tradition still had its impact because James recommended an aspect of the Israelite law forbidding eating strangled animals which left the blood in the bodies, and the eating of blood itself (Leviticus 17:13-14). In the message James sent forth by Judas and Silas (interestingly not Paul) to the Gentile Christians, the brother of Christ James said that these rules were **ἐπάναγκες epanagkes** or necessary (Acts 15:28).

This background is important in understanding the tension reflected in Romans 14-15. The tension was directly related to the contents of the proclamation of James. We begin by translating the last verse of chapter 13 and the first verse of chapter 14. We should connect 13:14 closely to 14:1 because the conjunction **δὲ de** normally was used for advancing a previous argument or action.

> *But put on the Lord Jesus Christ, and make no provision for the flesh in regard to its lusts. In addition, the one being weak in faith you receive unto yourself, not for divisive discussions. (Romans 13:14-14:1)*

This last verse of chapter 13 underscored something of critical importance. Paul told us in Romans 5-6 we are joined to Christ's person and his life is within. Using metaphorical language Paul now said to clothe ourselves with Christ. The Christ who is within should be manifest on the outside of our lives. **ἐνδύνω endunó** "to be clothed" was Paul's standard term for what we should wear into relationships. Clothing is what others see on the outside of us, and, indeed, our ultimate and best clothing is the life of Christ within coming out. Thayer in his lexicon said it beautifully, ". . . to become so possessed of the mind of Christ as in thought, feeling, and action to resemble him and, as it were, reproduce the life he lived."[134] We must carefully note the word "lust" also in that verse. In the context of chapters 14-15, Paul was not referring to covetousness, fornication or sexual desire. In the thirteenth chapter he did. In 14-15 another type of work of the flesh was addressed: " . . . enmities, strife, jealousy, outbursts of anger, disputes, dissensions, factions," (Gal. 5:20 NAS). Divisions occurring within the church will be the subject of 14-15. These divisions revolved around food.

With verse 14:1 we have the key word of the two chapters, "receive."

You <u>receive</u> the weaker brother 14:1

↓

As God has <u>received</u> him 14:3

↓

As Christ has <u>received</u> all of you 15:7

14:3 spoke of the way God received believers into the experience of salvation.

> *The one eating let him not despise the one not eating, and the one not eating let him not judge or penalize the one eating. For [the principle is] God has received him. (Romans 14:3)*

15:7 spoke of the way Christ has received us. Like the reception of the two key members of the Trinity, the kind of reception we are to offer the person we differ with should reflect Heaven itself:

> *Wherefore receive one another even as Christ has received all of you for a glorious display (**δόξα doxsa** "glory") of the character of God. (15:7)*

The acceptance that Paul stated Christians were to be dressed with was the Trinitarian reception and acceptance. As Christ and the Father has received the children of God for the glorious display of the character of God, believers were to display the same towards one another. This acceptance of the Father and Son was not mere tolerance but a positive honoring of the believer for their faith in Christ. Westerners often lack an appreciation of honor or honoring one another, but it is an essential part of Trinitarian truth. God honors those he loves. The verse is very powerful. How believers were to treat each other is to imitate him. Earlier Paul defined family affection using the terms love, acceptance, honor, and glory.

> *. . . in relationship to affection of the brethren for each other they have tender family affection, in relationship to honor they give preference to the others, (Romans 12:10)*

---

[134] Thayer, <u>Lexicon</u>, p. 214

To "receive" has a deep meaning behind it. We are to receive other Christians the way the Father and Son have received us. We have been received with great affection, honor, and glory. Glory to be experienced now, as the beauty of salvation enters our lives, and the future glory of being made like Christ.

Why have we been treated so? Because we have done the miraculous act of believing the Gospel. On account of this, Christ and the Father honor and give glory to the children, those who believed the Gospel. In the darkness of this world, the believers have done the incredible. When they looked upon the man on the cross, they saw God dying for them. What the leaders of Israel, the Roman authorities, and the rulers of the world could not see, they saw. All the important people saw was trouble and danger.

As we said, honor and glory are unfamiliar concepts for the Western mindset. Glory essentially means having and presenting an esthetically positive picture of someone. Honor is to treat someone with high regard. Peace is the tranquility existing in a relationship. This is what God gives to those who were persuaded by the Gospel and accepted it.

> *but glory and honor and peace to every man who does good, to the Jew first and also to the Greek.*
> *(Romans 2:10 NAS)*

Doing good in the context of Romans 2 was to accept the gift of righteousness by accepting the Gospel. In John 12:42-43, The New American Standard Version has the word "approval" instead of the word "glory" which is the common translation of **δόξα doxsa** "glory or high opinion." The Greek word is much more positive than mere approval: it is more like spectacular appreciation.

> *Nevertheless many even of the rulers believed in Him, but because of the Pharisees they were not confessing Him, in order that they should not be put out of the synagogue; 43 for they passionately loved* [Agape] *the glory* [**δόξα doxsa** "glory or high opinion"] *from men rather than the glory* [**δόξα doxsa** "glory or high opinion"] *from God. (John 12:42-43)*

What exists within the reciprocal relationships of the Trinity, love, glory, acceptance, and honor are what is granted to the person believing the Gospel.

Chapters 14-15 reflect an important aspect of the Culture of Heaven on Earth. The Church should accept one another the way the members of the Trinity accepted us. Often times we do not see that within the churches. Bickering, arguments, angry disagreements are present. As a brand new Christian who was seventeen, I was speaking to an elderly Christian man who shared with me he was a Christian. He and his wife seemed like fine people. He said he no longer attended church, because of how poorly he and his wife were treated. Instead of hearing from them about the glories of God, what I heard about was the corruption and hurtfulness of God's people. It left me disappointed and confused about my new life in Christ. Paul argued in these chapters that the things which unite us are so great that they transcend our differences and should result in peace.

The differences to be addressed in these chapters involve leftover issues from Judaism and the Law which the early church had to struggle through. Seventy-one times Paul referenced the Law or law and pointedly wrote numerous times that Christians were not under it. Saying so in reality did not make it so for Jewish Christians. In the face of the false pictures of reality carried over from the past, Paul argued for tolerance. We need that as much today as we did back then. These chapters will give us the principles we need to navigate the present church and experience the Culture of Heaven.

But put on the Lord Jesus Christ, and make no provision for the flesh in regard to its lusts. In addition, the one being weak in faith you receive unto yourself, not for divisive discussions. (Romans 13:14-14:1)

The word "weak" was a strong term in the ancient world. The term "weak" was used three ways in the New Testament: 1) for being sick such as Lazarus who died from his sickness, 2) for ones being physically weak who need to be helped (Acts 20:35), and 3) for those who are weak in faith. Obviously the weak in faith is the metaphorical use of the verb and noun. From examining the first usage we can see it refers to a debilitating and possibly dangerous illness, and from the second usage, it refers to those who were physically weak who need help. We also have a rather unique use in Romans 5:6 where humanity was so spiritually weak it could not help itself; it needed a redeemer. The New American Standard Version translated the word as "helpless." The metaphorical use appears to mean being "restricted in their ability to exercise faith."

Receiving one another was not to result in a continuous bitter argument: **διάκρισις diakrisis** "examination and judgment". It's not a friendly word. It is used for disputes and discerning who is at fault and who is right.[135] What was the source of argument? It was about what was proper to eat for a Christian. James Dunn did an excellent job in his commentary of bringing light on the issues involved.[136] The issues of 14-15 were particularly Jewish in nature and fits into the Book of Romans as much as the discussion in chapter 7 about the Law and its use by sin, and chapters 9-11 dealing with the failure of Israel and the Gentiles. What is of particular importance to notice is that the Law and aspects of Judaism were unsettled issues in the church. Parties and arguments were present. Paul had to deal with those issues or else the church life would be one very large squabble. The issues of clean and unclean foods and festivals were mentioned in the chapter. What marked Judaism in the diaspora was dietary rules and the observance of special days. The fact that these were points of contention in the church at Rome, and in the Christian movement at large shows how important Romans was in its declaration and protection of this movement of God towards the gentile world.[137] Half the Book dealt with the Old Testament and Judaism and 77 references to the Law really form the backdrop to what Paul said in chapters 14-15.

> *But for Jewish Christians, or Gentiles who had long been associated with Judaism before they heard the gospel ("judaizing" God-worshippers or proselytes), much more was at stake. Nothing less than a crisis of identity . . . The depth of the sociopsychological problem which the practice of the gentile and freer thinking Jewish Christian caused the more traditional Jewish and judaizing Christians should not be underestimated or played down.[138]*

To address these things, Paul argued this way: since God accepted the person and can make the person stand spiritually, we should accept the person too. His goal was to make the differing parties do what they do out of faith and gratitude, and not despise or judge each other. Bracketed between the command to receive the weaker brother (verse 1), and the observation that God has received him (verse 3) was the command to not despise the weaker brother, and not condemn or penalize the stronger brother. Paul noted that the more sophisticated Christian who understood grace would be tempted to despise or look down on the person who differed. He also noted that the weaker brother's attitude could easily become punitive. The strong brother would sense that what we ate made no difference and setting apart one day or other made no difference. Being punitive about it would make no sense, but the very human temptation would be to look down on that "superstitious legalist" would be very real. **ἐξουθενέω exsoutheneo** is a very strong word: it means to look

---

[135] Liddell and Scott, Greek Lexicon, p. 399. The word carried with it in a number of different contexts coming to a decision or doing something decisive: a judicial decision or "medical diagnosis," examination or revision of accounts. "a decision by battle," "Separation of tumor from blood vessels."

[136] James Dunn, Romans 9-16, pp. 800-801.

[137] We must remind ourselves that the Book of Hebrews and James and the Book of Acts also grapple with "Jewish issues." Sometimes that struggle is overlooked and a very important aspect of understanding the New Testament is ignored.

[138] James Dunn, Romans 9-16, p. 811. In the Head to Heart Discipleship Program run by our organization, we see many go through a similar crisis of identity when they actually learn Trinitarian truth and understand the Gospel of grace. It unsettles their world. Many are deeply appreciative of experiencing those truths. At the same time the journey to appreciation and joy was at times very uncomfortable.

at someone with contempt. The weaker brother with his moral scruples about food and days would consider it something to be condemned by God and therefore, should be condemned by him. That attitude easily could become punitive. **κρίνω krino** "to judge" means to pass a judgment. Normally it is more than having a negative opinion.

My own experience with church squabbles both involving me personally and observing the "Christlike" squabbles of other Christians, is that God goes out the window and is just looking in on the recriminations thrown at each other. God the Father just becomes a word to be dragged through the argument without any redeeming purpose. Paul wanted to avoid having such happen. Forcefully, he attempted to give a number of different ways of looking at the debate.

Paul in chapters 14-15 gave his reasons why God's kindly reception should be practiced by both parties, so an explosive and divisive result would be avoided. The basic principle was in 14:3 and 15:7 as we have already written about. God has received us without disdain or judgment. The disputants should practice the same. He then developed these following arguments.

1. God is able to make the weaker brother spiritually stand even with an incorrect belief (14:4-6)

2. God is the ultimate judge; we are not (14:7-13)

3. Nothing is unclean and also do not stumble anyone (14:14-23)

4. Christ's example should be our model (15:1-7)

5. Unclean Gentiles are part of God's program (15:8-14)

6. Paul's example also should be our model (15:15-33)

God is Able to Make the Weaker Brother Spiritually Stand (14:4-6)

All of us carry false pictures or beliefs about reality around in our hearts. All of us have incorrect thinking. John in 1 John 1 said that if we think we do not have sin within us manifesting itself in our thinking, desires, emotions, and relationships, we are deceiving ourselves and the truth in not in us. Sin certainly is inside us. Yet the wonderful thing John also tells us through 28 different ways in 1 John 4 is that God the Father loves us and can make us stand spiritually. In 1 Corinthians 8, Paul said that we do not understand spiritual things as we ought to, but if we love others in an emotionally healthy way, we have been and are loved by God.[139] Perfection is not a prerequisite to be perfectly loved by God. He can make us stand. This must also be understood by the Christian (Jew most likely) who is on the verge of penalizing the strong believer.

> *Who are you the one presently judging the household servant of another? To his own Lord he is standing or falling. Indeed, he shall stand, for the Lord has the capacity to make him stand (14:4).*[140]

Forcibly, Paul said that the person being penalized was a household servant of God. That being the case, it was up to God to decide how to treat him and not the other believer. Again and again in this section he will call upon Trinitarian Theology to address this division or potential division in the Roman church. Here he called upon God as the one who penalizes or does not penalize his servants. More than that the Apostle emphasized God's ability to work with the stronger brother who was not keeping the dietary restrictions.

Paul then addressed another particularly Jewish issue, that of keeping certain days sacred. In verses 5 and 6, he placed spiritual preconditions on the relationship to days. In the former verse, he said the believer should be fully convinced or confident in his own mind. That harks back to 12:2 where the believer should be approving of God's will within the mind. **πληροφορέω plerophoreo** means to be fully satisfied or fully convinced.[141] It was used earlier in Romans 4:21 of Abraham who was fully convinced that God would keep his promise of a son. Because the believer was fully convinced and was approving of this as God's will for

---

[139] See page 103.

[140] This echoes back to Romans 2:1, 3 as noted by James Dunn, Romans 9-16, page 803.

[141] Thayer, Lexicon, p. 517. As a noun Thayer translated it as "full assurance, most certain confidence."

her or him, Paul stated such a belief should result in thanksgiving to a good God. That is interesting. The person who was not confident would want to convince the opponent of his belief so he could be confident and at peace with his own belief. The peaceful and confident person, however, would not have to convince anyone. Paul then rounded out his section by saying no one lives a solitary life, whether alive or dead, each is intimately and completely connected to the Lord (14:7-8). This then opened up another avenue of addressing the contention in the church.

God is the Ultimate Judge; We are Not (14:7-13)

Paul was addressing a potentially disastrous problem in the Roman church. If the Gentile Christians and the Jewish Christians (plus those Christians who had first followed Judaism before they converted to Christ) should become sharply critical of each other, a split might occur and the unity of the Body of Christ in Rome might collapse. To ameliorate that, the Apostle strategically gave a series of different perspectives on the controversy over food and the observing of special days. After saying that God the Father can make the weaker brother stand spiritually, he went onto say something obvious. Sometimes the obvious is the best thing to say.

> *For no one of us lives to himself and no one dies to himself. If we should live, to the Lord we are living, if we should die, to the Lord we are dying. If then we should live and if we should die, to the Lord we belong. (14:7-8)*

Our lives as Christians are "divinely entangled." Both entangled with the Lord and entangled with eternity. Often times we all need to realize that life holds much more than just the contents of a squabble. A trillion years from now we will continue to exist in the Father's love. As was his practice, Paul drew the dimensions of the issues out to eternal measurements. He addressed the weaker brethren and asked why they were judging their brother, and to the stronger brethren, why they were despising their brother. With those questions in mind, he said all of us will stand before the Judgment Seat of God.

This is fascinating. What seemed to be of prime importance in the Epistles of Paul and the other Epistles was how Christians treated each other. How we sustain our relationships to the members of the Heavenly family, our brothers and sisters in Christ, matters very much to God.

> Paul took jurisdiction out of the hands of the Roman church
> members and transferred it to Heaven, the proper court.
> How we treat each other as Christians is of crucial importance to God.

We can see this in the Lord's prayer where Christ said that how we forgave others was the basis of how our Father would forgive our trespasses (Matthew 6:14-15). In 1 Corinthians 11:32-34, Paul admonished believers to treat each other well at the church's love feasts and communion so that they would not fall under the Lord's discipline or child-training. He told the congregation that discipline comes from the Lord and that was why they should wait for each other and eat at home so as to not embarrass other Christians. John said in 1 John 2:9 that the one who said he lives in the light should not hate his brother, and in 3:16 we should lay down our lives for our brothers. It matters to God how we treat each other.

The believer was to appear before the judgment seat or **βῆμα Bema** "platform, judgment seat."[142] The same term was used in 2 Corinthians 5:10 for the judgment seat of Christ. In the context of going to be in the presence of the Lord, Paul told believers they will receive back what they have done whether it was beneficial or worthless. The same thought was echoed in 1 Corinthians 3:14-15 where believers were told that they will receive a wage or reward for what they have built upon the foundation of Jesus Christ in his church. Whatever the result, loss or reward, the believer was still saved (3:15). He added the additional thought that Christians are the inner sanctuary of God, the place where God dwells since the Spirit is within them (1 Cor. 3:18). That being the case what was done in the context of the church matters. In what Paul wrote to them, the believers in Rome should be brought up short to think seriously about their acts and attitude. Making it even more sobering, individuals will have to give an explanation or a speech to God about their behavior. The

---

142   Thayer, Lexicon, p. 101. This could be a place of just giving a speech, or a place of judgment.

term for speech was **λόγος logos** explanation or story. Christ, the Logos, was God's explanation of himself to us, and we have to return an explanation of ourselves to God.[143] Paul was determined to address the issue of judgmentalism. As we consider his approach, we must remember that judging in the ancient world was much more than an attitude, it normally involved a punitive action. At all costs the Apostle wanted to prevent any disruptive reaction from the weaker brother. He then admonished them to practice a different sort of judgment with a different sort of action.

> *No longer then, we should judge each other, but this you should immediately judge* [as a judgment] *rather, to not be placing a cause of offense before the brother or a cause of stumbling. (14:13)*

The admonishment was placed in the context of appearing before God and having the actions in the church judged by him. To escape a negative result the brethren were told not to judge. After talking about God's future judgment, Paul transitioned and gave his theological judgment on the issue before the church.

Nothing is Unclean and Also Do Not Stumble Anyone (14:14-23)

The Apostle recognized how engrained the belief about certain unclean foods was. One of the great challenges of true discipleship as opposed to mere information dissemination was to lead Christians to true heart change. Such change was a labor-intensive project. In giving his own opinion as truth from Christ, he still granted the power behind incorrect belief.

> *I know and I am persuaded by the Lord Jesus that nothing is unclean in itself, except to the one reckoning something to be unclean, to that one it is unclean.[144] (14:14)*

The verb reckoning **λογίζομαι logidzomai** means to have an assumption within the mind. Paul used the word frequently in his writings, twenty-seven times. As an example of the significance of the word, Romans 6:11 commanded Christians to reckon or assume they were continually alive to God the Father in Christ Jesus. Reckoning was the result of a faith commitment so that what was believed became an assumption and so a reality in one's life. Reckoning created the pictures of reality inhabiting the heart and mind. The weaker brother lived in a world where he

> "One of the great challenges of true discipleship as opposed to mere information dissemination was to lead Christians to true heart change."

pictured things as being clean or unclean, a place of dangerous contamination. Even though Paul no longer believed in the Old Testament and Rabbinic rules on uncleanness, he certainly respected the power they had over the person's life.

Jesus' teaching in the Gospel of Mark, his own private teaching to Paul, and that wonderful vision of Peter's where God told him to eat unclean animals (Acts 10:10-16) were very clear on the abrogation or cessation of the laws of uncleanness when it came to food. The Messiah spoke clearly and bluntly on the topic.

> *18 And He said to them, "Are you so lacking in understanding also? Do you not understand that whatever goes into the man from outside cannot defile him; 19 because it does not go into his heart, but into his stomach, and is eliminated?" (Thus He declared all foods clean.) 20 And He was saying, "That which*

---

[143] Liddell and Scott, <u>Greek-English Lexicon</u>, pp. 1057-1059. **λόγος logos** was an important word that was used in many different contexts of speech. Within such usage was always the sense of giving an explanation. The omniscient God allows us to explain ourselves!

[144] To be pure or impure was critically important in the Old Testament. Without it one was not acceptable to God. This expressed on its own terms the principle of being acceptable or unacceptable to God as presented in the New Testament. F. Maass, "**tema** to be unclean" <u>Theological Dictionary of the Old Testament</u> vol. 2 (Peabody, Massachusetts: Hendrickson, 1997, pp. 495-497. Uncleanness as a word and its usage is extensive in the Old Testament. The verb occurs 160 times and the noun 89 times. To become clean or pure occurs 94 times and the noun 95 times. "**tehor** to be pure" F. Maass, <u>Theological Dictionary of the Old Testament </u>vol. 2 (Peabody, Massachusetts: Hendrickson, 1997, pp. 482-486. After the time of the Old Testament the rabbis made the rules of cleanness and uncleanness massive and burdensome. So it was no wonder that the Jewish converts to Christianity carried with them the picture of an unclean world with multitudes of unclean people within it. "The revocation of rabbinic formalism in the determination of clean and unclean is among the revolutionary innovations of early Christianity." F. Maass "**tehor** to be pure" p. 486.

proceeds out of the man, that is what defiles the man.21 "For from within, out of the heart of men, proceed the evil thoughts, fornications, thefts, murders, adulteries, (Mark 7:18-21 NAS)[145]

Ritual uncleanness involving food was a condition within the mind, and not something existing any longer in the real world. Paul based this upon the teaching authority of the true Messiah of Israel, Jesus. What Jesus taught seemingly was perfectly clear to himself, and he appeared to upbraid his disciples for their lack of spiritual insight by questioning their understanding and their mind's capacity for thought (Mark 7:18). Peter was obviously present for that teaching but it had no effect on him since the old prejudice was blatant in his refusal to obey God and eat unclean animals in Acts 10. Almost certainly the same held true for the Jewish Christians in Rome. Making no difference to them, these weaker brethren continued in their belief.

Paul stated clearly his position on the cleanness of all food, but he did not berate the weak. Instead, he turned to those, the strong, who assumed all foods were clean and instructed them on how to think and act. Telling them to walk in love, Paul pointed out to the strong that if they flaunted their freedom, the weaker brothers would be afflicted with significant emotional pain, and their spiritual life might be destroyed (14:15). This was so very similar to 1 Corinthians 8:11 where Paul said the strong through eating food sacrificed to idols might destroy the weaker brother for whom Christ died. Besides Rome and Corinth, the issue seemed to be present in many of the churches. What he emphasized instead of the issues of food and drink were the emotional values stemming from the Trinitarian relationship: love, joy, peace. God's Kingly authority was based upon those qualities (14:17). This issue had the potential to tear the early church apart. Paul said that bluntly.

On account of food don't you tear apart the work of God. Everything is clean, but an evil thing to the man eating when the result is a stumbling stone. (14:20)

"Tear apart" was a serious term. Paul's teacher in Judaism, Gamaliel (Acts 22:3), used it to say to his fellow leaders that if this new movement concerning Jesus was not from God, it would be destroyed or be torn apart (Acts 5:38). Paul squarely placed the responsibility for the continuity of the work of God on the shoulders of the strong. Not only were they given that responsibility, he reminded them again their liberty may well have a devastating effect on the weak. The strong were told that it would be noble not to eat or drink something unclean that may lead the weak to stumble. In the face of their liberty, Paul recommended to the strong joy, peace, love, and nobility. They were to keep the faith they had before God and not declare it before others who would be damaged by it.

In a remarkable conclusion to this chapter, Paul underscored the advantage of the strong. He pronounced a beatitude over them. Blessed was the person who is not condemning himself in what he has decided to approve (14:22). The strong has a great advantage: they can eat anything in a carefree matter. The weaker brother always has the possibility of self-condemnation whenever he eats. The real issue, however, is not food but faith. In contrast to the blessed, the person who was continually examining, continually doubting, who was unsettled if he should eat, will be condemned. The weaker person who was <u>fully convinced</u> or confident in his own mind and was filled with gratitude (14:5-6) would not be condemned. For condemnation does not arise from the eating. Not having faith in a good God while eating or not eating created the judgment. Any act of a Christian should have faith dripping off of it. For anything which is not directly out of faith is sinful (14:23).

F or Paul, motivation was everything. The motivation flowing from the practice of
the 7 skills of Romans as brought forth through a partnership with the
Holy Spirit will have the elements of faith, love, and gratitude.

---

[145]   Jonathan Klawans, "Concepts of Purity in the Bible," in <u>The Jewish Study Bible: Featuring the Jewish Publication Society</u> (Oxford: Oxford University Press, 1985), p. 2046. In this thoughtful article, Klawans pointed out that the Old Testament had ritual uncleanness involving of course certain foods and other things, and moral uncleanness which involved such things as adultery, murder, and idolatry. In Mark, Christ declared all foods clean. Certainly a revolutionary thought. But he also added conditions of the heart to that which was morally unclean (Mark 7:21). To take away that uncleanness of heart in Christianity involved confession (1 John 1:9).

2 Corinthians 5:7 states that the Christian organizes his life around faith. Without love, giving one's life Paul declared a meaningless act (1 Corinthians 13:1-3). With the Apostle, what was said or done should always be accompanied by an excited gratitude (Colossians 3:17). Faith, love and gratitude should be the preoccupying realities of the Roman congregation. To lower themselves to debates about what to eat and drink and what days to observe would set up Christianity for a catastrophic collapse. The essence of the faith, what makes it of monumental importance is participating in the life of the Trinity. With the mutual trust of the Trinity as the essence of the Christian's faith relationship to the Father, with the love binding the Father and the Son being the love that binds the children of God to one another, and with the thankful thrill of gratitude coming from the well-loved hearts of the offspring of a Heavenly Abba, we have Christianity.

Practicing the 7 Skills

With the other-centered approach taught by Paul in chapters 14-15, we have a very important example of the Culture of Heaven lived on Earth. An absolutely opposite example is the Thirty Years War. That war fought in Europe between the Protestants and Catholics in 1618-1648 was an extreme example of the Culture of Heaven not being lived out! The sorry experience of that conflict led to a rejection of Christian churches by many.

The two chapters we are focusing on are filled with principles on managing church conflict. Despising one another and judging one another by various forms of punitive behavior are at the heart of church conflict. The principle in solving any such conflict is elucidated in 14:1,4 and 15:7: receive one another the way our Heavenly Father and his Son Jesus Christ have received us. To do this, we have to master the 7 Skills of Romans.

SKILLS OF ROMANS

	MASTERING THE 7 SKILLS OF ROMANS
1.	Mastering the skill of focusing on the Father and staying in his presence (6:11-13)
2.	Mastering the skill of assuming our Union with Christ (6:11)
3.	Mastering the skill of not "listening to our appetites" (6:12
4.	Mastering the skill of following the prompting (walking by) of the Spirit (7:6; 8:4)
5.	Mastering the skill of having a Heavenly perspective (8:5-6)
6.	Allowing my mind to be renewed (12:2)
7.	Mastering the skill of allowing our mind to be thoroughly renewed by the Spirit (12:2)
8.	Mastering the skill of being other centered and ministering to others (12:4-6)

Without the previous practice of numbers 1-6, having the Culture of Heaven would be impossible. These skills are interlocking. One is always dependent upon the previous one, with the first skill, counting ourselves alive to the Father, being the most important. Out of the central and focusing relationship, we tap into the resources of the Trinity.

Whether it is an argument about what paint to use on the outside of the church or what color carpet to put in the sanctuary, or whether it is an ugly argument among church members or a financial loss caused by one Christian to another, the principles Paul shared have their applicability. The motive always should be other-centered love and the action should always be helpful and gracious.

Mastering the 7 Skills of Romans

As we can see in the chart, the problems Paul described in the Book of Romans now have his answers presented. The chaotic culture (problem 4) has its solution in chapters 14-15. Those two chapters illustrate the problem-solving capacity of the lifestyle described in chapter 12. The goal of those three chapters was to create a community that is in complete contrast to what is in the world. Finally, the world has found a place of refuge and peace, the Church of Jesus Christ.

PROBLEM	SOLUTION
1. Humanity turned over to its desires (1:24)	Believers given the capacity to manage desires and control them (6:11-14)
2. Humanity turned over to its dishonorable moods (1:26)	Believers given the capacity to deal with moods through the Holy Spirit (7:5-6)
3. Humanity turned over to a disapproved mind that failed the test (1:28)	The Solution is 7:23, 25. Believers have an approved mind that approves God's ways (12:1-2)
4. Humanity trapped by a chaotic culture exhibiting gross immorality (1:18-32)	The Solution is 8:3-13. Believers practicing the culture of Heaven (14:1, 4: 15:7)
5. The Jews adopted a performance based religion resulting in hypocrisy (2-3)	Believers living by the Law of the Spirit of life in Christ Jesus (8:2)
6. Union with Adam resulting in sin within, death, condemnation, and status as a sinner (5:12-21)	Union with Christ resulting in death to sin, life in Christ, justification, and status as a righteous one (5:15-21; 6)
7. The flesh given as the overarching problem resulting from God handing over humanity and the Fall of Adam (7:14, 18; 8:3-10)	Walking by means of the Spirit brings liberation from the power of sin within and the flesh (8:1-14)

15 | THE NEW CULTURE-OTHER CENTERED MINISTRY

CHAPTER SUMMARY: As God the Father and Christ has received the believers so Christians should receive **one another**. Both Jews and Gentiles make up the **Culture** of Heaven, and they should reflect its values.

Christ's Example Should Be Our Model (15:1-7)

Paul had continuously placed the burden of initiative upon those whom he called the strong and he placed himself among them. At the same time, he compassionately recognized the enslaving limitations of the Jewish Christians. He used a remarkable term to describe it.

> *To continue the thought we ourselves, the strong ones, ought to bear the weaknesses of the powerless ones and not just be satisfying ourselves. (15:1)*

Paul chose the word **ἀδύνατος adunatos** "powerless" in describing the condition of the weaker brothers. This term appeared in Acts 14:8 to describe a man crippled from birth. Nothing within these weaker brothers would be able to change them in their current condition. Interestingly Paul maintained that even in that state, they could exercise faith so as to be at peace and be loving towards the Gentile believers. In chapters 14-15, Paul gave six reasons why the strong and weak believers should accept one another and work through their deep differences. We will now look at the last three.

1. God is able to make the weaker brother spiritually stand even with an incorrect belief (14:4-6)

2. God is the ultimate judge; we are not (14:7-13)

3. Nothing is unclean and also do not stumble anyone (14:14-23)

4. Christ's example should be our model (15:1-7)

5. Unclean Gentiles are part of God's program (15:8-14)

6. Paul's example also should be our model (15:15-33)

Three times in the first two verses, he used the verb "to please." The first two times he wrote that we should not just please ourselves, but we should also please our neighbor for their edification. Then, he gave the example of Christ who did not please himself but suffered on behalf of the purposes of God the Father.

For even Christ did not please Himself; but as it is written, "The reproaches of those who reproached you fell upon Me." (15:3 NAS)

This was a quote from Psalm 69. The text described the experiences of King David. Yet at the same time, it was understood to also speak of David's greater son, the Christ. The first half of the full verse was quoted in the Gospels as referring to Christ's zeal for his Father's house, the temple (John 2:17).

For zeal for Thy house has consumed me, And the reproaches of those who reproach Thee have fallen on me. (Psalm 69:9 NAS)

In the same Psalm the Psalmist spoke of being given gall and vinegar to drink (69:22) and Paul quoted Psalm 69:23 in Romans 9:10-11 with reference to Israel rejecting Christ. Jesus was presented by the Apostle as someone who chose to suffer on behalf of God the Father. By implication, Paul pointed to Christ's suffering for all of humanity and for the Father's children. In every possible way Christ did not please himself. Romans 15:4 stated that these things from the Old Testament were written to give believers instruction, perseverance, and encouragement.

On the basis of the example of Christ, he called the weaker brethren and the stronger brethren to receive each other as equal partners in the Gospel.

Now may the God who gives perseverance and encouragement give you to have the same perspective with one another according to Christ Jesus; 6 with the result that with one accord you should with one voice glorify the God and Father of our Lord Jesus Christ. 7 Wherefore, receive one another, just as Christ also received us to the glory of God. (Romans 15:5-7)

As Paul progressed through his six perspectives and accompanying pictures calling upon the strong and the weak, his first three sections from chapter 14 gave concrete observations and commands as to how they should treat each other. In chapter 15, sections 4 and 5 gave positive principles of conduct. The fourth section with its principle is interesting because of its call to have a spiritual perspective. We have emphasized over and over that perspective flows out of the beliefs and pictures in the mind.[146] When Paul encouraged believers to have the same mind or same perspective, he was not at all saying they should see everything the same way. The perspective that he was encouraging was that believers should serve one another the way Christ served them. As an example, in Philippians 2:5, "Have this attitude in yourselves which was also in Christ Jesus," (NAS) the Apostle was calling Christians to emulate Christ in the way he counted others to be more important than himself and the way he served them. The picture behind that truth is Christ washing his disciples' feet and then dying for them. As the Roman Christians practiced such a picture and principle, they would present a glorious picture of God the Father to one another and the world (15:6). Then, the section was completed with the repetitive emphasis on a godly reception of one another the way Christ received us as partners, friends, even family.

Unclean Gentiles are Part of God's Program (15:8-14)

Just as Abraham was the father of the circumcision, the Israelites, and the father of the believing Gentiles (Romans 4), so Christ also had a relationship to both groups (15:8-9). He by his presence confirmed God's promises to Israel; indeed, he was the promised Messiah and his presence confirmed all the rest of the promises. Communicating a serious commitment **βεβαιόω bebaiao** "confirm" is not a casual term. This was vastly important because with the rejection of the Messiah, all the future kingdom promises to Israel were put on hold and in abeyance. Paul argued that the Messiah's mere presence guaranteed Israel had a glorious future even if they rejected him. On the one hand, Jesus' very presence in Judea was the ultimate confirmation. Even though the promises would be postponed, they will be fulfilled because the most important person has come, the Messiah himself to confirm them. With the Gentiles, on the other hand, his presence meant the extension of mercy to them.

---

[146] See chapter 12, page 98. Today as I read a book review in the *Wall Street Journal* about a master negotiator, a helpful quote from the book was there: "We see things not as they are but as we are." *Wall Street Journal*, May 6, 2022, p. A15, book review, *My Dad the Deal Maker*.

Paul then gave a series of Old Testament quotes to show that the Gentiles were included in the Old Testament promises of God. Psalm 18:49, a Psalm of David, showed that Gentiles would participate in the praise of Yahweh. Moses in Deuteronomy 32:43 concluded a song that he gave to the people of Israel saying the Gentiles should rejoice with his people. In the two-verse-long Psalm 117, the first verse called upon the Gentiles to praise and extol Yahweh. Finally, he quoted the Septuagint translation of Isaiah 11:10. The Hebrew text is translated as follows:

Then it will come about in that day the root of Jesse, who will stand as a banner of the peoples, unto him the nations will pursue, and his resting place will be glorious. (Isaiah 11:10)

A banner in the world of the Old Testament typically was a sign of hope and encouragement.[147] The Septuagint translators took the metaphor of the banner and simply said he who will arise will be the basis of their hope.

And again Isaiah says, "There shall come the root of Jesse, And He who arises to rule over the Gentiles, In Him shall the Gentiles hope." (Isaiah 11:10)

Paul selected King David, the greatest King of Israel, Moses, the lawgiver, a Psalmist, and Isaiah, probably the greatest Old Testament Prophet, to illustrate that the Gentiles were included in the promises of God. This would give the weaker brethren, most likely Jewish Christians, a greater respect for the Gentiles who almost certainly were the stronger brethren. This would give the Jewish Christians a renewed picture that the Gentiles were included in the promises of God.

Paul then transitioned from that issue to call the church to a walk of faith, joy, peace, and hope. Wanting to turn their attention from the contentious issue, the Apostle hoped that they would be consumed by joy and peace.

*Now may the God of <u>the</u> hope fill all of you with every variety of joy and peace in the process of believing, for all of you to be abounding in **the** hope by the power of the Holy Spirit. (15:13)*

The hope in verse 13 may be referring to the hope who is Christ in the Isaiah 11:10 quote. Obviously, he was calling them to use the 7 skills so that they would be consumed by the greatness of what they were called to, and not be consumed by contention. Concluding this section, Paul told them that he was more than persuaded that the parties were motivated by goodness, being perfectly filled up with all knowledge so that they can confront each other so as to work through any difficulty. The term for confronting or admonishing, **νουθετέω noutheteo**, means to talk as to change another's mind.[148] This is very similar to Colossians 3 where Paul said the "umpire in their hearts" should be peace.

And upon all these things put on love, which is the perfect bond of maturity. 15 And let the peace of Christ act as an umpire or judge[149] in your hearts, to which indeed you were called in one body; and all of you become inherently thankful ones. (Colossians 3:14-15)

Both in Colossians and here in Romans, Paul was firmly underscoring the fourth and fifth skills of Romans, the ability to have the fruit of the Spirit in the heart and a perspective from the Holy Spirit. The great indicator that such was happening was the presence of true peace. Out of that, Paul told the Roman Christians they could work through their differences in love and harmony. It is fundamentally important to realize that Christian differences can be brought to a resolution only in an atmosphere of affection and tranquility.

---

[147] See Exodus 17:5 where a banner is a sign of protection and hope. "And Moses built an altar, and named it The LORD is My Banner; (17:15 NAS). This is considered one of the names of God יְהוָה נִסִּי **Yahweh Nesi** "Yahweh my banner."

[148] Thayer, <u>Greek Lexicon</u>, p. 429.

[149] Liddell and Scot, <u>Lexicon</u>, p. 327. This term was used for the umpires or judges who gave prizes in the Greek games. In other contexts, the word would mean to arbitrate or judge.

Paul's Example Also Should Be Our Model (15:15-33)

Starting with verse 15 Paul would appear to be going in another direction and leaving behind the contention between the weak and the strong. A careful reading might show something else. Paul reminded them that he was a minister of Jesus Christ who was ministering as a priest and his priestly offerings were the gentile believers. Everything he had and did was from Jesus Christ and his boast is in him. This mission for Christ was accompanied by signs (pointing to Christ) and wonders (occurrences stunning the observers). He did this work from Jerusalem to Illyricum (modern day Albania). Illyricum was directly across the sea from Italy.

His missionary goal was not to preach where Christ was already known, but where he was not (15:19-20). Using an interesting term **φιλοτιμέομαι philotimeomai** "to love and seek honor," Paul said he wanted that honor. In classical Greek it meant to be ambitious. Greco-Roman culture was an honor-based culture. Sometimes, even in an honor-based society, the verb might carry with it a bad sense of overreaching ambition so that was a curious term to use.[150] Since he knew he was despised by the Greco-Roman world (he spent enough time in jail and being beaten to be convinced of that), the person he was seeking honor from was God. He had a sincere emotional desire to please and delight God. Such was meaningful to him and the same should be meaningful in our own lives. The strategy of many churches is to repeat the Gospel endlessly to those who have rejected it. Paul's approach to evangelism was very different and very wise. He left behind those who rejected the Gospel and pushed forward to present the Gospel to those who have not heard. His approach was presented in a famous book Missionary Method's, Saint Paul's or Ours by Roland Allen published in 2018. Allen maintained that the modern missionary movement has been bogged down with too many educational projects, too many social projects, and not enough evangelistic efforts. In the cities of America, many communities and ethnic groups exist not having heard the Gospel. Those places would be a perfect and convenient place to share the Gospel for the first time. Vincent Donovan, a Catholic missionary, adopted Paul's methods with the Maasai tribe in Africa. They were illiterate and had never heard the Gospel. With them, he followed Paul's pattern with astonishing results.[151] He had two problems: the local Catholic bishop did not approve of what he was doing, and he did not have the resources to deal with the response. What he experienced was that a village would either have a wholesale acceptance of the message or a wholesale rejection of the message. Donovan may not have known it, but he based his strategy on Isaiah 52:15 (LXX) just as Paul did.

> *"They who had no news of Him shall see, And they who have not heard shall understand."*

Seizing the opportunities to preach the Gospel kept Paul from coming to Rome, but that was somewhere he wanted to go. Another opportunity faced him and he shared that with the Roman Christians. He had a mission to fulfill in Jerusalem. An offering had been taken for the poor Christians in Judea, and Paul and his team were going to deliver the offering. What he had to say next was a perfect illustration of how the strong and the weak can be helpful. Northern and Southern Greece had collected such an offering. He explained the rationale for doing so.

> *Yes, they were pleased to do so, and they are indebted to them. For if the Gentiles have shared in their spiritual things, they are indebted to minister to them also in material things. (Romans 15:27 NAS)*

This project illustrated well what Paul had said in the previous five sections of chapters 14-15. Love and kindness should be expressed by the Gentile Christians (the strong) to the Jewish Christians (the weak). Ending this section, he requested the prayers of the saints in Rome that he would be protected from the unpersuaded, which is Paul's and Peter's term for unbelieving Jews, and that the mission would be successful. This was another attempt by Paul to sustain the unity of the church of Jews and Gentiles. The Book of Romans was one attempt and this offering was another. Then, in a very crisp ending of this section he wrote:

---

[150] Liddell and Scott, Lexicon, p. 1941. For the bad sense, see Roman numeral III on page 1941. Paul used the verb in Romans 15:20; 2 Corinthians 5:9; 1 Thessalonians 4:11.

[151] Vincent Donovan, Christianity Rediscovered (Orbis Books, 2003).

33 Now the God of peace be with you all. Amen. (15:33)

Paul's Use of Isaiah

It is worth our while to see Paul's use of Isaiah. His approach to that Book is similar to other writers in the New Testament. His presentation of the Gospel was frequently buttressed by the contents of Isaiah. In Romans 15:21, we have the last quote from Isaiah in Romans. Using that quote, he stated his goal was to preach where the Name of Christ has not been heard. We will also show the LXX quotes because Isaiah is what Paul largely quoted in Romans. If we look at an English translation of the Hebrew Bible, sometimes the quotes are significantly different. More often than not, the differences can be explained.

> *And thus I aspired to preach the gospel, not where Christ was already named, that I might not build upon another man's foundation; 21 but as it is written, "They who had no news of Him shall see, And they who have not heard shall understand."*

The full quote is:

> *Thus shall many nations wonder at him; and kings shall keep their mouths shut: for they to whom no report was brought concerning him, shall see; and they who have not heard, shall consider. (Isaiah 52:15 LXX)*

Paul did appear before Gentiles, Kings, and the people of Israel. When Ananias was commissioned to restore Paul's eyesight, he was told that Saul was a chosen instrument of God and he would proclaim the message of Christ before the three groups (Acts 9:15-16). The Isaiah quote was one of 14 in Romans, and in addition, Paul quoted the Old Testament in the Book 50 times. We will see how Paul used Isaiah to support the contents of Romans, especially in chapters 9-11. The Romans quote will be given first with the Septuagint quote following.

COMMENTARY ON ISAIAH AND ROMANS

A brief commentary will introduce the 14 sets of verses:

1. **First, he presented the failure of Israel in representing God correctly**

    *   *For the name of God on account of all of you is being blasphemed among the nations (Gentiles). (Romans 2:24)*

    *   *Thus saith the Lord, On account of you my name is continually blasphemed among the Gentiles. (Isaiah 52:5 LXX)[152]*

2. **He used Isaiah to underscore the sin of Israel and the world**

    *   *Quick are their feet to pour out (shed) blood. Destruction and misery are in their paths, and the way of peace they have not known. (Romans 3:15-16)*

    *   *And their feet run to wickedness, swift to shed blood; their thoughts also are thoughts of murder; destruction and misery are in their ways; and the way of peace they know not (Isaiah 59:7-8 LXX)*

3. **He used two quotes from Isaiah to support his belief that only a remnant will respond to the Gospel**

    *   *Moreover Isaiah proclaims concerning Israel, if the number of the sons of Israel should be as sand of the seashore, the remnant shall be saved. For the Lord shall make a word being accomplished and being cut short upon the land. And even as Isaiah said beforehand, if the Lord had not left us a seed, we would have become like Sodom, and like Gomorrah. (Romans 9:27-29)*

    *   *And though the people of Israel be as the sand of the sea, a remnant of them shall be saved. He will finish the work, and cut it short in righteousness: because the Lord will make a short work in all the world. (Isaiah 10:22-23 LXX)*

---

[152] The English Translation of The Septuagint Version of the Old Testament by Sir Lancelot C. L. Brenton, 1844, 1851, published by Samuel Bagster and Sons, London.

- *And if the Lord of Sabaoth had not left us a seed, we should have been as Sodom, and we should have been made like Gomorrha. (Isaiah 1:9 LXX)*

4. He again used two quotes to show that Israel will be offended with Christ, and yet the believing ones will not be ashamed

- *Even as it was written, behold I place in Zion a stumbling stone and a rock of scandal, and the one believing upon Him will not be ashamed. (Romans 9:33)*

- *And if thou shalt trust in him, he shall be to thee for a sanctuary; and ye shall not come against him as against <u>a stumbling-stone, neither as against the falling of a rock</u>: but the houses of Jacob are in a snare, and the dwellers in Jerusalem in a pit. (Isaiah 8:14 LXX)*

- *Therefore thus saith the Lord, even the Lord, Behold, I lay for the foundations of Sion a costly stone, a choice, a corner-stone, a precious stone, for its foundations; and <u>he that believes on him shall by no means be ashamed</u>. (Isaiah 28:16 LXX)*

5. Then, he repeated Isaiah again to emphasize the need to trust

- *For the Scripture says, everyone believing in him <u>shall not be ashamed</u>. (Romans 10:11)*

- *Therefore thus saith the Lord, even the Lord, Behold, I lay for the foundations of Sion a costly stone, a choice, a corner-stone, a precious stone, for its foundations; and <u>he that believes on him shall by no means be ashamed</u>. (Isaiah 28:16 LXX)*

6. Since Christ has come, Paul used Isaiah to emphasize the need for evangelism

- *How beautiful are the feet of the ones proclaiming good things. (Romans 10:15b)*

- *<u>as a season of beauty upon the mountains, as the feet of one preaching glad tidings of peace</u>, as one preaching good news: for I will publish thy salvation, saying, O Sion, thy God shall reign. (Isaiah 52:7 LXX)*

7. Again, Isaiah was used to show Israel's unbelief

- *Lord, who has believed our report? (Romans 10:16b)*

- *O Lord, who has believed our report? and to whom has the arm of the Lord been revealed? (Isaiah 53:1 LXX)*

8. He used the Old Testament Book to speak of the unbelief of Israel and the positive response of the Gentiles

- *Indeed, Isaiah is very daring and says, I was found by the ones not seeking me, I became visible to the ones not asking me. And he says to Israel, all the day I stretched out my hands to an unpersuaded and antagonistic people. (Romans 10:20-21)*

- *<u>I became manifest to them that asked not for me; I was found of them that sought me not</u>: I said, Behold, I am here, to a nation, who called not on my name. I have stretched forth my hands all day to a disobedient and gainsaying people, (Isaiah 65:1-2 LXX)*

9. Spiritually speaking, Paul said in Romans 11 that Israel was incapable of responding to the Gospel

- *Even as it is written, God has given to them a spirit of stupor, and eyes not being able to see, (Romans 11:8)*

- *<u>For the Lord has made you to drink a spirit of deep sleep; and he shall close their eyes</u>, and the eyes of their prophets and of their rulers, who see secret things. (Isaiah. 29:10 LXX)*

10. Eventually though all Israel will be saved. A future generation will respond

- *The rescuing one shall come out of Zion, he shall turn ungodliness from Jacob. And this is the covenant from me, whenever I should take away their sins. (Romans 11:26-27)*

- *And the deliverer shall come for Sion's sake, and shall turn away ungodliness from Jacob. And this shall be my covenant with them, said the Lord; (Isaiah 59:20-21 LXX)*

11.   **Paul marveled at how God had taken the unbelief of Israel and used it as a springboard to bless the Gentiles**

- *For who has known the mind of the Lord, or who has become his adviser? (Romans 11:34)*

- *Who has known the mind of the Lord? and who has been his counsellor, to instruct him? (Isaiah 40:13 LXX)*

12.   **In chapter 14, Paul wrote that both Gentile believers and Jewish believers will be judged by God**

- *For it is written, I am living, the Lord says, because to me every knee shall bow, and every tongue shall confess to God. (Romans 14:11)*

- *As I live, saith the Lord, (Isaiah 49:18 LXX)*

- *By myself I swear, righteousness shall surely proceed out of my mouth; my words shall not be frustrated; <u>that to me every knee shall bend, and every tongue shall swear by God</u>, (Isaiah 45:23 LXX)*

13.   **To give a clear picture of the Gentiles' place in the program of God to the Jewish Christians, he said Christ was the object of hope for the Gentiles**

- *And again Isaiah says, the root of Jesse shall be, and the one arising to rule the Gentiles, upon him nations (Gentiles) will be hoping. (Romans 15:12)*

- *And in that day there shall be a root of Jesse, and he that shall arise to rule over the Gentiles; in him shall the Gentiles trust, and his rest shall be glorious. (Isaiah 11:10 LXX)*

14.   **Finally, we return to where we began with Paul basing his missionary strategy on Isaiah**

- *But even as it is written, to whom it was not announced concerning him they shall see, and the ones not having heard, they shall understand. (Romans 15:21)*

- *Thus shall many nations wonder at him; and kings shall keep their mouths shut: for they to whom no report was brought concerning him, shall see; and they who have not heard, shall consider. (Isaiah 52:15 LXX)*

This is very important.

> **P**aul assumed that the mission to the Gentiles was based upon the Old Testament history and prophecies, plus the mysteries Christ revealed to him and the Apostles and prophets.

In constructing a Biblical Theology that is firmly fixed in Scripture, we must do what Paul did in taking the elements of the Old Testament especially concerning the future, and add to them the mysteries Christ revealed in Matthew 13 and the mysteries revealed to Paul. **A mystery was kept hidden and was only expressed when the proper agent appeared. The ultimate agent was the God-Man.** In turn, he revealed to Paul the mysteries such as our union with the Messiah (Colossians 1:27), the Gentiles as fellow-heirs as the Jewish believers (Ephesians 3:3), the relationship of Christ and the Church (Ephesians 5:32), the nature of godliness (the life of God in humanity, 2 Timothy 3:16), the rapture (1 Corinthians 15:51), the ingathering of Israel at the return of Christ (Romans 11:25), and the revelation of anti-Christ (2 Thessalonians 2:7-8). Putting together what Paul shared from Isaiah with the mysteries, we have a full picture encompassing the Old and the New Testament. In many ways Paul was a typical Jewish Rabbi who added to what he found by what he learned from the risen Christ. To him, the Old Testament was not something to be ignored, but to be taken seriously. The Apostle took the Old Testament very seriously unlike many Christians today.

16 GREETINGS & BLESSINGS

CHAPTER SUMMARY: In his **greeting** of believers at the end of Romans, his relationships and principles illustrated how believers should be honored, how genuine affection should be practiced, and how evil should be despised and avoided in the person of false teachers.

Back in chapter 12, Paul wrote of the motivational principles which would arise from a healthy Agape love for the brethren. In a very unique and crucial chapter in the Book of Romans, we have these principles displayed.

> *Love is without play acting or hypocrisy* [love must be genuine]. [Those who have it are] *Ones continually despising malicious evil, and continually joining themselves to what is beneficial, in relationship to affection of the brethren for each other having tender family affection, in relationship to honor giving preference to the others, (12:9-10)*

Three key qualities were present: love is beneficial and abhors evil, love is affectionate, and love honors the other. Such love results from the practice of the 7 skills. As we count ourselves continually alive to the Father (skill 1) through our Union with Christ (skill 2), while ignoring sin within (skill 3), we will experience the fruit of the Spirit (skill 4) and the perspective of the Spirit (skill 5). From that experience, we can participate in the transformation of our mind by consciously approving of the benefits coming from the Trinity (skill 6). This results in an other-centered Christianity (skill 7) as displayed in chapter 16. The skills (4 and 5) connected to responding to the Holy Spirit's leading and accepting his heavenly wisdom become the influence to practice other-centered love. Remember, it is so important to not be "command-centered" but to be Trinity-centered. Without focusing on the Father, living out of our Union with Christ, and responding to the Holy Spirit, meeting Christ's expectations of us is impossible. We will examine how those three qualities of honor, affection, and beneficiality (goodness) appeared in this final chapter.

Love Honors the Other

Let us now take a look at chapter 16. It abruptly starts in an interesting way. Up until this chapter, the only name mentioned at the beginning of his letter was Paul's own, but now we have listed 35 names and two references to unnamed individuals. Of further interest is that the first two names were that of women.

I recommend to you Phoebe our sister, who is a deaconess of the church in Cenchrea, in order that you would receive her worthily of the holy ones[153] *(the saints) and you should stand with her and help her in whatever matter she would have need of you. For also she has become a patroness of many and of myself. (16:1-2)*

Commentators assume that Phoebe carried the letter to Rome with her. Certainly, she had business in Rome requiring some help. Paul assumed the believers in Rome would want to help a sister who had been of significant help to Paul and others. The word **προστάτις prostatis** means a woman patroness. This would be a woman of resources who has "clients," people she helps.[154] The patron-client system was a major part of Greco-Roman culture. The wealthy would have allies called clients for whom they would do favors, and the clients would support them in any endeavors they were called upon to perform. Phoebe had used her resources to support Paul and many others. Her motivation certainly was not to procure influence with clients (otherwise Paul would not have recommended her). Using the phrase "receive her worthily of the holy ones or saints," Paul was not asking the Roman Christians to function like her clients, but to function as fellow members of the family of God.

The second person to be mentioned was Prisca, also called Priscilla. She and her husband Aquila, Paul called fellow-workers. More than that they risked their lives for Paul. Being well known among the churches, not only was Paul grateful for them but the churches of the Gentiles were grateful also. Three times the couple was mentioned in Acts, and three times in other books. The first time they appear, Aquila was mentioned first then Priscilla (Acts 18:2). The next two times, Priscilla came first. The second time she was mentioned first, the context is telling (Acts 18:18, 26). A certain Jew named Apollos was a dynamic proclaimer of Jesus as the Messiah. He did that accurately, but he only knew the baptism of John. Priscilla and Aquila took him aside[155] and taught him[156] even more accurately the things of Christ (Acts 18:24-28). Obviously, as a result, he must have received Christian immersion and was introduced to the mysteries that Christ shared with Paul. Apollos knew of the ministry of Christ and that Christ was the Lamb of God taking away the sins of the world. His knowledge was greatly expanded to include Christ's message for the Gentile world. The four out of six times in which Priscilla was mentioned first were in contexts of teaching the New Testament message (Acts 18:18, 26; Romans 16:3; 2 Tim. 4:19). His seemingly casual listing of two women first underscored a major part of what Paul learned from Christ: in Christ male and female are equally accepted, and their contributions should be honored.

Women were mentioned ten times in Romans 16. Two were mentioned first.[157] My thought is that this fits a pattern with Paul that was also noticeable with Peter. In other letters when husbands and wives were addressed, the wives were mentioned first. Note the order in Ephesians: wives are before husband, children before fathers, and slaves before masters. In each case, those who have the cultural authority are placed second and are told to treat well those who should be submissive to them. What we have in Ephesians, Colossians, and First Peter are called Haustafeln, a German word for "house tablet" meaning the rules as to how a

---

[153] The translation "saints" does not communicate the essence of the word **ἅγιος hagios**. This is due to religious confusion brought on by Catholicism, and misunderstandings of the meaning of holiness. Holy ones, a better translation, even though it sounds strange, means those who belong to God, who are uniquely his. "Just as the Israelites claimed for themselves the title **οἱ ἅγιοι**, because God selected them from the other nations to lead a life acceptable to him and rejoice in his favor and protection (Dan. 7:18,22; 2 Esdr. 8:28), so this appellation is very often in the N. T. transferred to Christians, as those whom God has selected **ἐκ τοῦ κόσμου** (John 17:14,16), . . ." Thayer, Lexicon, pp. 6-7. The term means believers are the property of God just as the Sanctuary in the Temple belonged to God and was holy, his property, and so are we.

[154] Thayer, Lexicon, p. 549, "a female guardian, protectress, patroness, caring for the affairs of others and aiding them with her resources."

[155] **προσλαμβάνω prolambano** "take aside, receive, take along" Thayer, Lexicon, p. 548. This is the same word used four times in Romans 14 and 15 where believers were told to receive one another the way God and Christ received them (Romans 14:1, 3; 15:7 two times).

[156] The same verb for an orderly presentation was used of Peter (Acts 11: 4), and Paul (Acts 28:23). Remember, Luke a very careful historian picked out this word describing what the three had done in communicating. Priscilla was obviously an unusually gifted woman.

[157] Our Executive Director, Gayle Encarnacion connected what we see here with the fact that Christ appeared first to a woman, Mary, and told her to tell the disciples what she had seen.

household should be led.[158] When compared to other lists of household rules outside of the Bible, what we have here is odd. All the other lists explain to the head of the house, a man, what his authority was and the roles of the other family members. Here in the Bible, the roles of those with little or no authority, wives, children, and slaves, were mentioned first. Most unusual of all is that these letters were meant to be read out loud in a mixed group of men, women, children, and slaves. As far as we know, this was the first time in Greco-Roman writings where a part of a speech was directly addressed to slaves while their masters were present. On top of that, the masters were commanded to treat their slaves as equals.

EPHESIANS 5-6
Wives addressed (5:22, 24, 33)
Husbands addressed (5:23, 25-31)
Children addressed (6:1-3)
Fathers addressed (6:4)
Slaves addressed (6:5-8)
Masters addressed (6:9)

Now notice Colossians: wives were before husband and the same exact pattern was followed.

COLOSSIANS 3
Wives addressed (3:18)
Husbands addressed (3:19)
Children addressed (3:20)
Fathers addressed (3:21)
Slaves addressed (3:22-25)
Masters addressed (4:1)

We see the same with 1 Peter 3. In a briefer list wives came first and the husband came second.

1 PETER 3
Slaves addressed (2:18-25)
Wives addressed (3:1-6)
Husbands addressed (3:7-11)

Therefore, Paul was not just making a theological point, he was just following his normal practice. Later, Paul mentioned Mary who worked hard for the Roman Christians (16:6). The Greek word for "worked hard" is **κοπιάω kopiao**. It means to work until one is weary.[159] What is interesting is that the word was not used for any of the 18 men mentioned, but it was used for Tryphaena and Tryphosa and also the beloved woman Persis (16:12). For Persis he noted, she has labored to exhaustion in many things. A favorite story of mine concerned Pastor Criswell, who was the Senior Pastor of First Baptist Church, Dallas, Texas, a huge church. He said when they hired a man, they had to give the man an office and significant pay. When they hired a woman, she got a smaller office, less pay, and she worked harder. Things may not have changed. The

[158] David E. Aune, The New Testament in its Literary Environment (Philadelphia: The Westminster Press, 1987), p. 196.
[159] Liddell and Scott, Lexicon, p. 978.

two couples he mentioned, Prisca and Aquila, and Andronicus and Junias, were well known in the churches. Particularly, the latter couple was well known among the Apostles. With the second couple, the man was mentioned first which again underscored how significant Prisca (Priscilla) was.

Paul honored these women. The Apostle was a very astute man. When he placed the emphasis on how hard-working these four women were, he knew of course that the same was not said for the men. Yet he did not hesitate to point out this virtue of the women. Nor did he hesitate to express his affection for Persis, and his affection for the unnamed mother of Rufus whom he also called his mother. Practicing this expression of Agape love, he honored those who were not often honored in Greco-Roman culture. What Paul wrote concerning these women was revolutionary in the Greco-Roman world. For example, the word "church," **ἐκκλησία ekklesia**, meaning an assembly, was used commonly in the Greek world. It was a deliberative body and no women could participate or serve in one. If women were found attending another type of assembly, the Olympic Games or the other games of Greece, they would be killed. Their lives were narrow and constrained. Paul did not use the term synagogue, another common Greek word for a gathering of women and men. If he did, this most likely would have implied Christians were just another Jewish sect. He chose a familiar term from the Greek world and filled it with new meaning as a place where women and men were equals in Christ.

Sarah Ruden wrote a remarkable book, <u>Paul Among the People: The Apostle Reinterpreted and Reimagined in His Own Time</u>. She is a scholar who specializes in ancient Greek and Roman literature. In part of it, she examined Paul's view of women and how he had women function in the church. His attitude was revolutionary towards women. Using women as fellow-workers and treating them as completely equal to men contrasted greatly with the culture. The culture treated slave women either as prostitutes or as persons to be practically worked to death if they were not pretty enough for men.[160] The Roman authors and poets viewed free women as over-sexed manipulators who should stay home while their husbands involved themselves with mistresses and orgies. Typically, Greco-Roman banquets did not have wives present, but prostitutes were and often food was offered to the idol or idols at the banquet. Contrastingly, Paul thought women were loved by God and worth dying for by the God-Man. When one considers how almost all of humanity is controlled by their culture and their family backgrounds, the changes Paul introduced to the Greco-Roman world were astounding. Sarah Ruden wrote, "I think Paul's rule [concerning women in church] aimed toward outrageous equality."[161]

Love Delights in the Other

Agape love, as we have mentioned over and over, was a word of profound affection. To make sure that was understood in the central passage of Romans 12:9-10, he wrote that Agape love expressed itself in "each other having tender family affection."[162]

This was present in chapter 16. Paul was a man of relationships and connections. He addressed 28 in the house churches of Rome and eight others were noted in the churches in Corinth. To those in Rome, he especially expressed affection. Epaenetus (16:5), Ampliatus (16:8), and Stachys (16:9) were called "beloved." Interestingly, as we noted, Persis was called "the beloved" (16:12). To an unnamed older woman, he referred to her as his mother (16:13). The term "love" in our modern evangelical churches appears to serve more like filler in an empty spot in a conversation or sermon, but what Paul practiced and preached had behind it an intensity of affection.

Love Pursues the Beneficial

Another element obviously present in chapter 16 was the pursuit of what is beneficial. Paul asked the Roman believers to be of benefit to Phoebe. Phoebe was a benefactress to many and to Paul. Aquila and

---

[160]   Sarah Ruden, <u>Paul Among the People: The Apostle Reinterpreted and Reimagined in His Own Time</u> (New York: Pantheon Books, 2010), pp. 72-118.

[161]   Ruden, <u>Paul Among the People</u>, p. 87. She wrote this in relationship to the practice of head coverings in the Corinthian Church. She interpreted the rules concerning head coverings as an example of the radical acceptance and equality of women.

[162]   See page 103.

Mastering the 7 Skills of Romans

Priscilla risked their lives for Paul, a sterling example of being beneficial. Another example was Andronicus and Junias (16:7). These were Jewish Christians and Paul called them his fellow prisoners. It is unclear as to when they were in prison, but imprisonment said something very important. Being glued to being beneficial (12:9), they were willing to risk life and limb for the benefit of the Gospel and Christians. Their reputation as Christian leaders made them of note among the Apostles. Prisca and Aquila (16:3), Aristobulis (16:10), Narcissus (16:11), Asyncritus (16:14), and Philologus (16:16) benefited others by having church groups in their homes.

This list of 28 Christians is impressive. They had been involved with Paul, and had been Christian leaders for a while. Possibly that was one reason why Paul sent them a profound and detailed presentation of what he had learned from Christ. They would understand and be able to explain it to their fellow Christians in Rome. With people of such depth in the churches of Rome, it underscored what Paul wrote in the previous chapter.

> And concerning you, my brethren, I myself also am convinced that you yourselves are full of goodness, filled with all knowledge, and able also to admonish one another. (Romans 15:14 NAS)

The word for "goodness" is **ἀγαθωσύνη agathosune**. It was derived from the word **ἀγαθός agathos** "good or honorable," with an emphasis on bringing benefit to others. That was the quality Christians were to be glued to in 12:9. The church people, Paul wrote, were filled with goodness; they were an other-directed people. With that being an inherent part of the definition of Agape love, he had reason to be confident that these good people could sort out the challenge of the weak and the strong in chapters 14-15. His confidence was more than a platitude.

Love Abhors Evil

The Christian who was to be dedicated to being beneficial also had to have an aversion to the maliciously evil (12:9). Paul assumed as we have stated before that Agape love has strong prejudices. Chapter 16 illustrated that with an abrupt change. False teachers pop up as Paul's next concern. This seems odd because so much space has been dedicated to the weak and strong question, yet the false teachers only get two verses. Before we look carefully at what Paul warned against, we must emphasize the fascinating part of the weak and strong issue. Paul stated bluntly:

> I know and am persuaded in the Lord Jesus that nothing is unclean in itself; but to him who reckons or assumes anything to be unclean, to him it is unclean. (14:14)

At the same time, he assumed that at the present time, the weaker brother was powerless to change. The end result was that the stronger would have to bear the debilitating weakness of the powerless (15:1). The first term, the weaker brother, meant a weakness or sickness that left the person often incapable of helping themselves, and the second term "powerless" was used of hopeless cripples. Even though the weaker brother did not actually believe what the Lord had said about nothing being unclean, the strong opinion of Paul the Apostle was to compassionately tolerate the divergent opinion. Yet he had no tolerance for truly divisive teaching resulting in spiritual damage.

> But I am beseeching you, brothers, to be watching those making divisions and stumbling blocks different from the teaching you have learned, and turn away from them. (16:17)

If those issues, the opinion about foods being unclean and certain days to be revered, were not handled wisely, they could easily cause divisiveness and damage people spiritually. With those issues, he trusted the Roman Christians to deal with them. With the false teachers, he wanted no dialogue, no compassion. Paul did not say exactly what these false teachers were saying, but what he appeared to be concerned about was not the content but the result. Two critical differences between him and them concerned Paul. The first was the results of the opinions and the second was the motive. The Apostle's toleration of confused belief almost seemed "infinite," but he had little patience for division-creating teachers of ill and pernicious motives. The strongest example of Paul's tolerance for confused beliefs, I believe, is 1 Corinthians 8. If Romans 14-15 are examined along with 1 Corinthians 8, we then will have an amazing picture of Paul's ability to have compassion towards and understanding of those who are religiously confused in the ranks of Christianity. We have looked at 1 Corinthians 8 previously.[163]

Now concerning things sacrificed to idols, we know that we all have knowledge. Knowledge makes arrogant, but love builds up. If anyone thinks he has learned, not yet he has really known, as it was necessary to have known. Yet if anyone would be presently loving God, this one has had a relationship with him and has been known by him. (1 Corinthians 8:1-3)

Paul made the profound comment that none of us have known spiritual truth as we ought to know, but if we are loving, we are personally known of God. This comment was made in relation to Gentile converts who, though they believed in God and Christ, still had a sense that the gods and goddesses of the Greco-Roman world had an existence, and idolatry was to be avoided at all costs. Paul accepted those with this peculiar admixture of Christian belief and pagan superstition as brothers (1 Corinthians 8:11-12). In 8:6-7 he made an acute psychological and spiritual comment on their condition.

Yet for us there is only one God, the Father, directly out of whom are all things, and we exist for him; and one Lord, Jesus Christ, through whom are all things, and we exist through Him. However not everyone has this as personal knowledge, but some until now have the cultural habit with reference to the idol that they are eating food sacrificed to an idol, and their conscience being weak is being defiled. (1 Corinthians 8:6-7)

These brothers were not completely certain that these lords and gods of heathenism did not exist (1 Corinthians 8:5). Yet the great Apostle of the Gentile mission was tolerant of them and considerate of them. No patience whatsoever existed within Paul for false teachers who misused truth to gain a following for their own benefit. He had no use for their motives.

For these men are of such a nature that they are not servants to our Lord Christ but their own belly, and through kindly sounding words and blessing they are seducing the hearts of the guileless. (16:18)

Extrapolating from the conduct and results of the false teachers, Paul directly went to motive. Their gracious sounding words and their habit of pronouncing people blessed meant nothing to him. The conduct was evil in a two-fold way: first, they would attempt to create their own party, a division, and secondly, the teaching they were presenting would set up those who chose to follow for a damaging fall, a stumbling. That means serious damage would be done to their Christian belief. Inevitably, the false teacher would lead the person away from the grace of the Trinity to some alternative. Any alternative to that glorious truth is only poison. Paul saw no virtue in selling poison to the naive. The simplest defense was to turn away.

Then, as he did earlier with the issue of the weak and the strong brother where he gave the differing parties a vote of confidence that they can treat each other well (15:14), he gave both of them another vote of confidence at this point.

For the report of your obedience has reached unto all, over which I therefore am rejoicing. I further desire all of you to be wise with reference to the good [beneficial], *and uncontaminated with reference to evil. (16:19)*

Such praise immediately followed his pointed attack against the motives of the false teachers. Presumably, the evil referenced in the verse was what the false ones were peddling. Then, he gave more encouragement that the God of peace will soon or speedily crush Satan under their feet. Usually, this verse has been taken two ways: the first is that it was talking about the return of Christ where he defeats Satan, and the second is that this verse addressed the problems within the church with false teachers. Paul was quite consistent in connecting false teachers with Satan: 2 Corinthians 2:11 where Satan might introduce an unforgiving attitude among believers; 2 Corinthians 11:13-14 where false teachers and Satan disguise themselves as angels of light; 1 Thessalonians 2:18 where Satan thwarts Paul's ministry; 1 Timothy 5:14 where Christian women were led to follow Satan. If this connection was correct, then Paul assumed that if the believers in Rome resisted the false teachers, Satan would "be crushed" in his efforts. This resisting harmonizes with James' comment,

---

163   See page 103.

141

Mastering the 7 Skills of Romans

" . . . immediately resist the devil and he will flee"(James 4:7). Satan is only a "confidence man" and when he is resisted, he knows the "jig is up." Picking up his "smoke and mirrors," he hurries on to another set of victims. I believe also that the reason Paul referred to Satan being crushed was to remind the Christians of Satan's certain, future defeat and to say at the same time that the false teachers will be defeated through Christian obedience. I do not believe an either/or choice needs to be made between a future crushing or a present defeat of Satan, the reference was to both.

Chapter 16 is a section of abrupt changes. Paul ended the section with a simple benediction: "The grace of our Lord Jesus be with you." Shortly, 16:25-27 has a longer benediction. Then, he proceeded to give greetings from what appeared to be his team. Timothy, Lucius, Jason, and Sosipater who were all Jewish Christians extended their greetings. Tertius, who wrote the text on behalf of Paul, joined in as well as Gaius, who would appear to be a Roman nobleman and Paul's host who was described as a man whose home was open to many.[164] Another prominent figure in Corinth, Erastus, the city treasurer, greeted those in Rome. And finally, a simple greeting was extended by Quartus, the brother.

Paul closed his warning about false teachers with a simple benediction asking the Lord's grace to be upon those in Rome. Then, he shared greetings from the co-workers in Corinth. Now, he ended the letter with a longer benediction. In this one, he appealed to the one who is fully capable of establishing them. With that, he used the common term for being solidly established as a Christian.[165] This establishing would be in harmony with three things:

1. Paul's Gospel. Interestingly, he put his name upon the Gospel that was extended to the Gentile world based upon specifically what Jesus Christ had told him.

2. The proclamation of Jesus Christ. This would not be preaching in church, but proclaiming to anyone about the message concerning the God-Man.

3. According to the mystery revealed by Paul. The mystery is the doctrinal truth not found in the Old Testament, but now revealed through the church. These truths, plus the message of the Old Testament, resulted in the unique Body of Christ which is not a synagogue, nor the nation of Israel, but a colony of Heaven on the earth, exhibiting the Culture of Heaven.

He extended the description of number 3 to say that this mystery has been manifested and made known through the writing of the prophets. This reflected Paul's great use of the Old Testament to buttress his proclamation of the Gospel. With this Gospel, we have the intended audience – all the world, the world of the non-Jews. Emphasizing the mystery that has been kept silent for long ages, Paul recognized this was not in the Old Testament and that his message came directly from the Messiah and not the books of the Old Testament. With the last verse he gloried in the intelligence and wisdom of God.

μόνῳ σοφῷ θεῷ, διὰ Ἰησοῦ Χριστοῦ, ᾧ ἡ δόξα εἰς τοὺς αἰῶνας, ἀμήν (*16:27*)

To the only wise God, through Jesus Christ, to whom the glory unto the ages, Amen!

With those words, we mere mortals must agree.

---

[164] Harvey, <u>Romans</u>, pp. 393-394.

[165] **στηρίζω steridso** "to establish or stand strong" Thayer, <u>Lexicon</u>, p. 588. Luke 22:32; Acts 18:23; Romans 1:11; 1 Thess. 3:2; 2 Thess. 3:3; 1 Peter 5:10 the word appears to be the common one for a maturing Christian.

17 | MASTERING THE 7 SKILLS OF ROMANS

CHAPTER SUMMARY: Paul described a series of seven problems and solutions within his book. These solutions, however, can only be addressed by Christians developing seven spiritual skills.

Paul described a series of seven problems and solutions within his book. These solutions, however, can only be addressed by Christians developing seven spiritual skills.

PROBLEMS ➡ SOLUTIONS ➡ SKILLS

We have subtitled this book, "A Problem-Solution Approach." We wrote this so the reader will have a sense of the structure and the flow of Paul's writing. In the process, we isolated seven problems with a solution for each of them. Many commentators, if not most, find the problems and are able to observe and note the solutions. Unfortunately, stopping it at that leaves the content stranded on the desert island of conceptional dry bones. Learning and understanding information about truth leaves out the ultimate goal which is the integration of the truth in the heart. Integration is when truth becomes the world our hearts inhabit, the emotional environment within, the thinking and perspectives we utilize, and the resulting relationships we sustain. Paul took what he offered as solutions and showed a seven-fold pathway to integration, the seven skills.

THE SEVEN PROBLEMS AND SOLUTIONS

PROBLEM	SOLUTION
1. Humanity turned over to its desires (1:24)	Believers given the capacity to manage desires and control them (6:11-14)
2. Humanity turned over to its dishonorable moods (1:26)	Believers given the capacity to deal with moods through the Holy Spirit (7:5-6)
3. Humanity turned over to a disapproved mind that failed the test (1:28)	The Solution is 7:23, 25. Believers have an approved mind that approves God's ways (12:1-2)
4. Humanity trapped by a chaotic culture exhibiting gross immorality (1:18-32)	The Solution is 8:3-13. Believers practicing the culture of Heaven (14:1, 4; 15:7)

	PROBLEM	SOLUTION
5.	The Jews adopted a performance based religion resulting in hypocrisy (2-3)	Believers living by the Law of the Spirit of life in Christ Jesus (8:2)
6.	Union with Adam resulting in sin within, death, condemnation, and status as a sinner (5:12-21)	Union with Christ resulting in death to sin, life in Christ, justification, and status as a righteous one (5:15-21; 6)
7.	The flesh given as the overarching problem resulting from God handing over humanity and the Fall of Adam (7:14, 18, 8:3-10)	Walking by means of the Spirit brings liberation from the power of sin within and the flesh (8:1-14)

LEARNING TO DRIVE

Why can we not leave it at the problem-solution stage? Let me tell you a story. A rich man in Shanghai who owned several businesses decided to start another business. With that in mind he had a factory built, and started hiring employees. Mr. Wong was the first hired. Many more were hired and Mr. Wong was one of the brightest and best. The rich man became richer. One day as he was being chauffer-driven to work, he saw Mr. Wong walking to work. The man thought, "Mr. Wong is my first employee and is hardworking and valuable. I know what I will do. I will give him a car as a reward for his service. I will tell everyone in the factory after I do it, and they will know that if they become like Mr. Wong, they might be rewarded too." Smiling to himself he thought it would make him look good and generous. In the evening of the next day, a car with its keys was delivered to the Wong's home. The deliverers told him that was his reward for his service, and the next day the factory owner was going to make an announcement about the reward.

In the morning, the rich man was in his chauffeur-driven car, and he saw Mr. Wong with his new car. Except Wong's twelve-year old son was at the steering wheel, and Mr. Wong and his wife were pushing the car along the street. Telling the chauffeur to pull the car over, the rich man got out of the car and yelled, "What are you doing?"

"We're pushing the car because my wife nor I know how to drive. If the car wasn't there when you made the big announcement, you would lose face."

Laughing the rich man said, "I will pay for your lessons, and I will drive your car and you and your family to work!" Smiling to himself, the rich man thought how humble he would appear.

Many Christians are like Mr. Wong. Loyal, hard-working, and appreciative of what the Bible said they received in Christ. Unlike the Chinese man, most likely, they know how to drive a car. When it comes to their spiritual lives however, they are car-pushers like Wong. Christians know logically they are very blessed with all spiritual blessings in Heavenly places. Not knowing how to access their blessings, they decide they don't want God looking bad. Putting in great effort, they imitate the fruit of the Spirit. Hiding their resentment of happier people, they serve. Feeling burdened, they keep busy. In fact, they feel more tired than when they were non-Christians. These poor souls end up pushing their spiritual cars down the streets of life, and they are exhausted.

We and they need to learn how to "spiritually drive."
That's what this chapter is, "A Manual on How to Manage the Spiritual Life."

Though Romans gave solutions for the problems of life, if we don't use the keys, the 7 skills, it won't help. Already you should have read about how to use them. Being spread throughout the commentary, and summarized in different places, now is the time to look at them in detail and start practicing them.

Now that we know their importance, let's examine those skills. About one-third of the way into Paul's writing, the first command in the Book of Romans occurred. Everything before developed the problem: humanity was handed over to the corruption of its own insides. Along with the problem, our resources for the solution, salvation, and our Union with Christ were presented by the Apostle. At 6:11, Paul commanded us to take the advantages of the resources, and with that, the first skill appeared. From there to chapter 12, a total of seven skills were presented. Paul gave more than seven commands in the Book, but these seven skills give the essence of the commands and carefully track the expectations God the Father has for the believer. In 6:11-14, the first three skills of the Book appear in a cluster of truth.

The Five Stages of Skill #1: Focusing on the Father and Staying in his Presence (6:10-11)

We will have to go through the following five stages to thoroughly enjoy our relationship with the Father.

1. Learning the truth that we have an affectionate Father in Heaven, who has compassion on our blindness and unbelief, who delights in who we are

2. Learning to assume we have a living and deep relationship with him (he knows us better than anyone else)

3. Going through the day assuming we have an accepting relationship with him no matter what is going on around us

4. Practicing sharing with him what is emotionally and relationally important to us

5. Enjoying the privilege

The first command in the entire Book of Romans told Christians to assume they are continually alive to God the Father the way the Son is alive this moment in Heaven.

> *10 For the death that He died, He died to sin, once for all; but the life that He lives, He lives to God. 11 Even so* [as he is alive] *consider yourselves to be dead to sin, but continually alive to God in Christ Jesus. (Romans 6:10-11)*[166]

As Christ is infinitely accepted by God the Father in a loving relationship, we are to accept that reality as our living relationship to God. Every barrier between us and God has been removed. Our guilt, shame, immaturity, sin, and anything else that is hindering us in our relationship to our Father God is gone. We are commanded (it is not a pious suggestion) to presently assume that as Christ is alive and accepted by the Father, so are we.

We must push our way through clouds of shame, guilt, and unbelief into the presence of the Father. Realizing we are continually alive to him and he to us, we must take advantage of living in his presence.

This assumption is supported by a scaffold of truth. The most basic truth is God the Father exists and is alive in Heaven. He is continually desiring to relate to us, and because we are in Union with Christ, no hindrance exists between him and us. So, we are commanded to assume such. You will find help and happiness in his presence. Scripture is wonderfully clear. We have been loved from the foundation of the world. As we enter the presence of the Father, he awaits with joy.

---

[166] See page 48.

My observation is that many Christians are leaning against a wall with their face pressed against the surface asking, "Where is God? Where is God?" Yet at the same time, the Father has his arm and hand on their shoulder trying to turn them to face him and relate to him. Our lack of relationship with God as a Christian is our choice and not his. What has to be rejected are the false beliefs that the Father does not like us and that we must earn his love.

Ask yourself this, are you preoccupied with what you have not done right, or are you preoccupied with sharing your weaknesses with him so as to receive wisdom and help? The goal is to more and more assume throughout our day we are living in the Father's presence.

SUMMARY OF THE FIVE STAGES TO EXPERIENCE FOR SKILL #1: FOCUSING ON THE FATHER

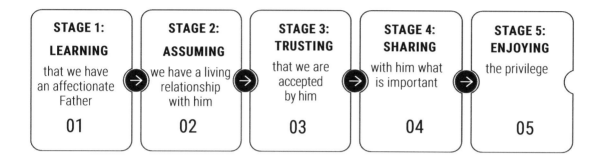

THE FOUR STAGES OF SKILL #2: ASSUMING OUR UNION WITH CHRIST (6:11)

We will have to go through the following four stages to have this as an assumption in our hearts.

1. Knowing the truth, we are joined to Christ

2. Believing and struggling with that as we pray

   a. We struggle because we are so used to defining our relationship with God based on our performance

   b. Recognizing such a struggle is normal for every Christian, we must persevere in assuming our Union with Christ

3. Feeling the emotional freedom as we choose to believe that is how the Father sees us

4. Anticipating the positive emotions from the fruit of the Spirit, as we go into the Father's presence based on our Union with Christ

With the previous command, an implicit assumption exists that this can only be done because we are in Union with Christ. We are joined to him, and he is joined to us.

> *Even so consider yourselves to be dead to sin, but <u>continually alive to God in Christ Jesus</u>.*
> *(Romans 6:11)*[167]

---

[167] See page 48.

Every second of our Christian existence and throughout eternity, we are accepted by the Father the way he accepts his Son. That is the practical definition and meaning of justification by faith. In our prayer life, we should always assume we are joined to Christ. God accepts us not on our own performance but on the perfections of his Son. As part of that acceptance, the central events of Christ's life have been counted to be our own: his suffering, death, burial, resurrection, ascension to Heaven, and his being seated at the Father's right hand. We have been joined to Christ for all eternity. As the Father looks at you on Earth, he sees you in Christ. When he looks at his Son at his right hand, he sees you. That is how you should see yourself.

Our Union with Christ does not cease when we sin. For remember the Father already sees us dying with Christ for all of our sin, past, present, and future. Do you realize that you are as secure as Christ is before the Father?

SUMMARY OF THE FOUR STAGES TO EXPERIENCE FOR SKILL #2: ASSUMING OUR UNION WITH CHRIST

THE FIVE STAGES OF SKILL #3: NOT LISTENING TO OUR APPETITES (6:12)

We will have to go through the following stages to sufficiently address the poison in our hearts.

1. Noticing we have desires that are not moral or right
2. Turning our attention away from them
   a. Turning our heart's attention to the Father
   b. Trusting him and sharing with him our concerns
3. Trusting him with the unmet desires we have chosen to ignore
4. Enjoying the freedom from strong desire, and the peace and self-control coming from the Spirit
5. Repeatedly practicing this as the need arises until it is an automatic response

The Christian has two sources of influence: the flesh and the Spirit. The Spirit's influence is unleashed as we enter into and stay in the Father's presence. We need to trust him as we are there. As for the flesh, we are to be like corpses and ignore its influence through our desires. As we pay attention to the Father, the Spirit pays attention to us. As we focus on the Father, the Spirit focuses on us.

Therefore do not let sin reign in your mortal body that you should obey its lusts, 13 and do not go on presenting the members of your body to sin as instruments of unrighteousness; but present yourselves to God as those alive from the dead, and your members as instruments of righteousness to God. 14 For sin shall not be master over you, for you are not under law, but under grace. (Romans 6:12-14 NAS)[168]

Liberation comes as we turn the focus of our hearts from our spiritually crippling, mismanaged desires within to focus on the Father. We have to retrain ourselves to seek the Father in Heaven, instead of seeking to satisfy the selfishness of our desires within us.

When we become Christians, we do not know how to manage them spiritually so they are often uncontrolled and misdirected. We have to practice ignoring them. Instead, we should go to the Father to find enablement from the Spirit so that the "self-control" or inner power we need is present. This initially will be completely counter-instinctual and seem impossible to us. Our inner desires and thoughts almost function like muscle memory. Like muscle memory which helps us to instinctively learn skills like swimming or bike riding, sinful habits within are so engrained they appear to be on auto-pilot and therefore uncontrollable.

The engrained habits seem so natural and innate that they appear to be unchangeable and unchallengeable. Radically turning our attention to God the Father and away from those desires and thoughts will result in a profoundly changed emotional and thought life. As we try it and discover it works, we will be encouraged to go on.

When we were in China at the largest Catholic training center in the country, one of our Chinese team members used the movie "A Beautiful Mind" as an illustration of what we are talking about. The movie was about a brilliant professor who became schizophrenic. Over a time period of years, a young girl, a college roommate, and a black-suited secret agent were talking to him. Even though he saw them, they did not exist. Only in his mind they did. Finally, he realized that he was schizophrenic and these persons were not real. The key clue was that the little girl never aged. Training himself to ignore them, he was able to have a successful career. In the same way, the Christian has to learn to ignore desires and thoughts from the flesh by turning our attention to God.

This so important to understand, so let me illustrate it another way. When I was 23 years old and in seminary, my friends and I went to a beautiful beach, aptly named Ocean Beach, in San Francisco that was almost directly under the Golden Gate Bridge. The day was lovely and we built a fire on the beach. After a while, I decided that I would walk into the surf because the water looked so inviting. I was used to Lake Erie near my home in New York State where the waters were calm and warm. Walking out, the water gradually came up over my knees, and I noticed a strange thing. As I stepped forward in the water, the sand felt like it was being vacuumed out from under my feet. Taking several more steps I thought this felt really odd. Then, I felt the water pulling me further into the surf. Suddenly I realized I was in a riptide current. It was strong. I needed to get out of there and back to the beach. Looking over my shoulder it got worse. Fog had come in and I could not see the beach! Recognizing the danger of being pulled out into the ocean, my thought was, "Whatever you do next, it better be smart." I decided that I would walk backwards and look over my shoulder. Making a false turn would be dangerous. A few months later, several teenagers from Utah were drowned by the same riptide. With every step, an inch or two of sand was pulled from under my feet so I carefully kept my balance. The water was cold and I was nervous. Through the fog, I saw the fire on the beach. I slowly turned around and headed toward the flames. At last, I was out of the water. My legs and shorts were still soaked and cold, but I was safe. Warming myself at the water, I did not mention to my friends what happened. The flesh is like the surf and the riptide. We have to avoid their pull and focus on the "fire" of the Father's presence so we do not lose our balance. Once out of the water, we will still feel soaked and cold, but around the fire and friends, we are safe. Drying out from the fire's heat, eventually we will feel comfortably warm. In the same way, as we present ourselves to the Father, the influence of the flesh through desires and thoughts will go away and the comfortable emotions through the Spirit will take over.

---

[168] See page 52.

The key spiritual lesson is that we are more than our desires
and our hearts belong to God.

Here is a good question to ask yourself: do you notice that you can just observe selfish desires and wrong thoughts and you do not have to respond to them? We need to use their appearance in our hearts as a reminder to go to the Father and ask for help in the time of need, trusting him as we do so. We have to persist in prayer and be in his presence until the Holy Spirit changes our unhealthy desire within to peace and self-control.

SUMMARY OF THE FIVE STAGES OF EXPERIENCING THE SKILL #3: NOT LISTENING TO OUR APPETITES

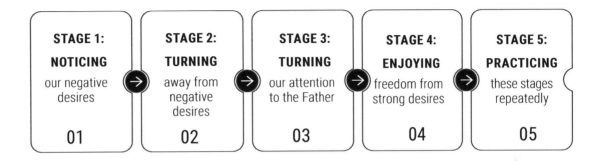

THE SIX STAGES OF SKILL #4: WALKING BY THE SPIRIT (7:6; 8:3-4)

The six stages in practicing this skill so as to be influenced by the Spirit are:

1. Knowing the truth that we are to allow the Holy Spirit to influence us in every area of our lives

2. Believing the Holy Spirit's influence will bring a beauty into our hearts, into our relationships, and the important issues of our lives

3. Sharing in prayer the issues of the heart, relationships, and life with God the Father

   a. Trusting him with the outcome

   b. Trusting him as we do what the Holy Spirit prompts us to do

4. Sensing the fruit of the Holy Spirit: love for others, peace in our hearts and lives, and joy in addressing issues versus dreading them

5. Sensing the Holy Spirit's wisdom or insights and following those in responding to the issues of life

6. Becoming expectant that through the day we will feel emotionally and sense cognitively how we should respond

As we experience the Spirit's influence, we must learn how to extend that influence into every area of our life.[169] Walking by the Spirit is the term for doing this in Romans. Romans 7:6 anticipated the new ability of walking by the Spirit in 8:3-4.

> *Then now being released from Law by dying to that in which we were being held, so that presently we can be serving in a newness from the Spirit, and not the oldness of the letter. (7:6)*

> *3 For the powerlessness of the Law in which it was weak on account of the flesh, God sending his own Son in the likeness of sinful flesh and for sin, he condemned sin in the flesh, 4 in order that the righteous requirement of the Law might be fulfilled among us, in the ones not walking according to the flesh, but according to Spirit. (8:3-4)*

God the Father and the Son sent the Spirit to be an ever-present help within us. We therefore have the opportunity to draw our entire life within the circle of his influence. The Greek term for "walking" involves the totality of our time and relationships. We have the privilege of not only having the Spirit's presence, but we also have his influence always available to us as we focus on the Father.

Paul the Apostle, Christ, and the rest of the New Testament writers assumed the Holy Spirit is continually with us. The term "walking" refers to how we live our lives. Walking does not refer to the individual step but the overall management of our emotions, activities, and relationships. We should continually be going to the Father and sharing our lives so that our thoughts, emotions, and relationships are influenced by the Spirit. The Spirit is ever-present in our lives to help us. As we respond to God the Father and rely on our Union with Christ, he responds to us.

The spiritual life is like driving a car. The car is our Union with Christ. We have to keep our eyes on the road and avoid looking continually off to the left or right so as to be distracted by the flesh. We have control of the steering wheel. It is our choice how we drive. As we drive the car, the Holy Spirit is in the passenger seat. He is there to help us drive correctly, but he will not control the steering wheel. We always have it under our control and choices. As we learn to follow the Holy Spirit's suggestions, we will find that the direction we drive the car is towards helping people.

Make no mistake, the Holy Spirit is not an intermittent presence. Christ sent him to be a permanent resident inside of us. He is there to help our emotional lives, our thinking, and our relationships. We do not have to be moral before the Holy Spirit will help us. He is there to help us to be moral.

SUMMARY OF THE SIX STAGES OF EXPERIENCING SKILL #4: WALKING BY THE SPIRIT

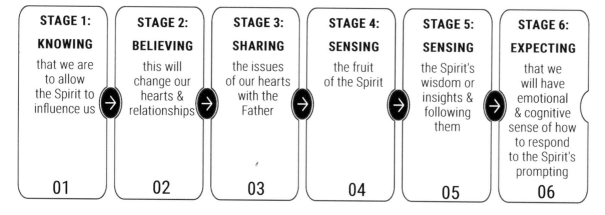

STAGE 1: KNOWING	STAGE 2: BELIEVING	STAGE 3: SHARING	STAGE 4: SENSING	STAGE 5: SENSING	STAGE 6: EXPECTING
that we are to allow the Spirit to influence us	this will change our hearts & relationships	the issues of our hearts with the Father	the fruit of the Spirit	the Spirit's wisdom or insights & following them	that we will have emotional & cognitive sense of how to respond to the Spirit's prompting
01	02	03	04	05	06

---

[169] See page 68.

The Five Stages of Skill #5: Having a Heavenly Perspective (8:5-6)

The stages in practicing this skill of having a spiritual perspective are:

1. Realizing that the Holy Spirit has a certain way of seeing things and thinking about things, Christ has a certain way of seeing things and thinking about things, and God the Father has a certain way of seeing and thinking about things

2. Recognizing that as the Holy Spirit shares Heavenly Wisdom, our responsibility is to choose to make that a part of our thinking

3. Sensing that we are building up a relational and analytical grid on how we approach life and relationships

4. Experiencing that working from a Holy Spirit perspective make us effective as a Christians

5. Living within that habitual way of thinking

Not only will our emotions and desires be motivated by the Spirit, he too will seek to create Heavenly perspectives within our minds.

> *For those who are according to the flesh set their perspectives on the things of the flesh, but those who are according to the Spirit, the things of the Spirit. 6 For the perspective set on the flesh is death, but the perspective set on the Spirit is life and peace, (Romans 8:5-6)*[170]

It is critically important to be able to discern the difference between a heavenly perspective and an earthly and fleshly one. Jesus Christ underscored how important it was to have a healthy perspective in one of his most creative and entertaining illustrations.

> *"And why do you look at the speck that is in your brother's eye, but do not notice the log that is in your own eye? 42 "Or how can you say to your brother, 'Brother, let me take out the speck that is in your eye,' when you yourself do not see the log that is in your own eye? You hypocrite, first take the log out of your own eye, and then you will see clearly to take out the speck that is in your brother's eye. (Luke 6:41-42 NAS)*

It is so easy to condemn another and give ourselves a free pass of grace. How do we avoid that? As stated, for the fourth skill, we always have the Spirit's presence to help us. Part of that help is to give us heavenly wisdom or a heavenly perspective. We experience this perspective as we pursue a relationship with the Father. We can tell that the perspective is from the Spirit because of the presence of peace, of practicality, and of power. The Holy Spirit has a perspective and that should become our own. He gives us that perspective through Heavenly Wisdom (James 3:17-18).

> *But the wisdom from above is first pure, then peaceable, gentle, reasonable, full of mercy and good fruits, unwavering, without hypocrisy. 18 And the seed whose fruit is righteousness is sown in peace by those who make peace.*

---

[170] See page 68.

Mastering the 7 Skills of Romans

We can recognize a perspective from the Spirit because it is wise, patient, and practical. It feels peacefully content. This perspective assumes our Union with Christ and the other biblical truths. As we see reality the way the Trinity does, we can effectively live this Christian life. Our view of God, ourselves, others, and the world can be in harmony with them and how they see things.

The perspective of the Spirit is shared by the Father and the Son. Can you imagine that you are in Heaven in the presence of the Trinity and the four of you are talking? Then, Jesus the Son of God says to you, "I am glad that we all see these things the same way." This thought attacks the lie that God the Father is thoroughly mysterious and unknowable. His wisdom is infinitely greater than ours, but the Bible assumes we can see things and think about things the way he does.

Are there areas of thinking and perspectives in your life that you know are out of harmony with the Bible and the Holy Spirit? Would not the joy, peace, and wisdom from God be a great replacement for those false thoughts and perspectives? We can participate in the life of the Trinity and share its joys and thinking. That is the promise of practicing the 7 skills.

Summary of the Five Stages of Experiencing Skill #5: Walking By the Spirit

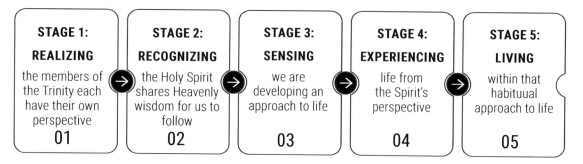

STAGE 1: REALIZING	STAGE 2: RECOGNIZING	STAGE 3: SENSING	STAGE 4: EXPERIENCING	STAGE 5: LIVING
the members of the Trinity each have their own perspective	the Holy Spirit shares Heavenly wisdom for us to follow	we are developing an approach to life	life from the Spirit's perspective	within that habituual approach to life
01	02	03	04	05

06

SKILL #6:

ALLOWING MY MIND TO BE RENEWED

THE SEVEN STAGES OF EXPERIENCING SKILL #6: ALLOWING OUR MINDS TO BE RENEWED (12:1-2)

The seven stages in practicing this skill of transformation are:

1. Committing ourselves to the purpose in life of being a living sacrifice and priest to God.

2. Believing that our minds need a complete internal transformation of how we see and think about everything.

3. Allowing ourselves to experience the fruit of the Spirit [Skill 4, 6]

4. Allowing ourselves to experience and accept as part of my thinking Heavenly Wisdom [Skill 5, 2]

5. Recognizing we have the privilege to evaluate if God's way through Christ is honestly acceptable!

6. Analyzing deeply with reflective thought as to whether:

    a. We believe this process and particular experience is beneficial for us

    b. We sense this process and particular experience is heart and life satisfying

    c. We sense this process and particular experience makes me a complete human being

7. Recommitting ourselves to continue in this path

The goal of the Skills in Romans is to have a thoroughly transformed mind which finds great satisfaction in God's ways.

I am beseeching all of you therefore, brethren, by the tender mercies of God, to present your bodies a living and holy sacrifice, acceptable to God, your reasonable service of worship. 2 And do not allow yourselves to be conformed to this age, but be thoroughly transformed by the renewing of your mind, that you may put to a process of approval what the will of God is, that which is beneficial and pleasing and complete. *(Romans 12:1-2)*[171]

As we practice Skills 1-5, we are told to calmly and regularly examine God's will for us as to whether it is beneficial, satisfying, and complete. As we do that, it will drive us further into deepening our relationship to the Trinity and our love and service to people. We participate in renewing our minds by continually practicing steps 1-5. As our mind is being renewed and we are experiencing the Christian life, we are to reflect on the ways of God. Does the experience we are having with the Trinity meet our thoughtful approval? That is critically important because it will supply the energy and enthusiasm to continue our walk with the Father and to deepen it.

Fascinating, it is just fascinating. In the beginning of chapter 1, humanity disapproved of the Creator God, and God disapproved of humanity (1:28). Now we have Christ through the Apostle asking us to examine God's will and his ways for our approval. What humility on God the Father's part! Of course, God has to approve me but dare I approve his ways! Our spiritual responsibility is to do that, to see if we approve of God's desires for us.

Having peace and affection from God, and thoughts and perspectives from him too is one thing. To have the heart and mind in true harmony with God's emotions and thinking is entirely a better thing. With that, we can enthusiastically throw ourselves into the spiritual life. The question to ask myself is: Do I have a positive desire to conform myself more and more to God's expectations because of the following pleasures: the pleasure of receiving spiritual benefit, the pleasure of finding it acceptable, and the pleasure of feeling whole as a human being?

Summary of the Seven Stages of Experiencing Skill #6: Allowing Our Minds to Be Renewed

STAGE 1: COMMITTING	STAGE 2: BELIEVING	STAGE 3: ALLOWING	STAGE 4: ACCEPTING	STAGE 5: RECOGNIZING	STAGE 6: ANALYZING	STAGE 7: RECOMMITING
to being a living sacrifice and priest to God	our minds need a complete transformation	ourselves to experience the fruit of the Spirit	Heavenly Wisdom	we can evaluate God's ways through Christ	God's ways deeply with reflective thought	ourselves to continue in this path
01	02	03	04	05	06	07

---

[171] See page 98.

THE EIGHT STAGES OF SKILL #7: LOVING, OTHER-CENTERED SERVING (12:4-6)

The stages in practicing this skill of an other-centered life are:

1. Isolating the particular ability God has given us to help other Christians and non-Christians

2. Rejecting the notion that we can do everything

3. Accepting the fact that we cannot do everything but we can do something in harmony with what God has given us as a gift of grace

4. Making sure our activity comes from Agape love (12:9-13)

   a. If not, practice Skills 1-6

   b. If so, proceed to practice our selected activity

5. Checking to make sure our emotions are connected to the emotional experience of those we are ministering to; we have compassion and affection.

6. Checking to make sure we have joy.

7. Allowing our joy to make this a repetitious habit.

8. Also enjoying the freedom that comes with happy service. The freedom we have is not co-dependency.

The six previous skills really emphasized what we were doing within our own mind and hearts. This last skill is all outwardly directed in the serving of others. More than anything else, the previous six skills emphasized the importance of the inward life while this seventh skill emphasized how this must flow into a significant ministry. As we practice the first six skills, we will have the love, gifting, and energy to benefit others. Not only benefitting them, we will also find great joy in doing so.

> *For just as we have many members in one body and all the members do not have the same function, 5 so we, who are many, are one body in Christ, and individually members one of another. 6 And since we have gifts that differ according to the grace given to us, let each exercise them accordingly: if prophecy, according to the proportion of his faith; (Romans 12:4-6 NAS)*

> *Love is without play acting or hypocrisy* [love must be genuine]. [Those who have it are] *Ones continually despising malicious evil, and continually joining themselves to what is beneficial, 10 in relationship to affection of the brethren for each other having tender family affection, in relationship to honor giving preference to the others, (Romans 12:9-10)*[172]

Through the powerful force of love and affection coming from our relationship to the Father and the work of the Spirit, we have the emotional energy and insight to happily serve others and glorify God. True biblical ministry should be driven by affection, a sense of serving within the gift the Holy Spirit has given and

---

[172] See page 102.

being involved in a significant work, all the time maintaining a positive dedication to serving and avoiding disputing and squabbling.

If we were members of a dance troop, a soccer team, or a baseball team, we would need to know our potential, the skills we have, the knowledge to develop those gifts, and the dance steps, or the plays, or the strategies of our team. Together we can be impressive and powerful, but much depends upon us being the best at our roles in the dance troop, soccer team, or football team. So it is with the spiritual life.

SUMMARY OF THE EIGHT STAGES OF EXPERIENCING SKILL #7: LOVING, OTHER-CENTERED SERVING

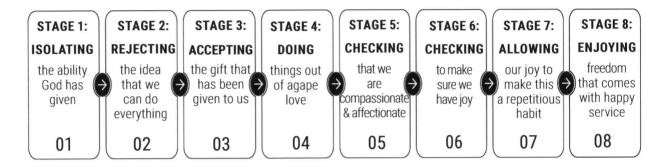

Entering the Life of the Blessed

What we have described is a lifelong practice. Attempting the healthy management of the heart is a deep and serious commitment. Moralism says if we do the right thing, we will be blessed. Scripture says blessing is a gift already given. Grace allows us to sustain a healthy relationship with God the Father, to live our Christian life out of Union with Christ, and to be empowered by the Spirit. Our responsibility is to enter the life of the blessed. Such a life flows from these 7 Skills of Romans.

7 SKILLS OF ROMANS

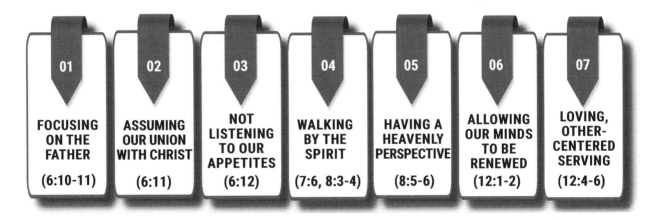

EI | EXCURSUS I: THE LAW & THE RITUAL

WHAT IS THE LAW?: If you cannot explain the relationship of the Church, the Body of Christ, and its relationship to the **Law** of Israel, possibly you may function well as a Christian, but more likely you will not function well and you may well be susceptible to performance-based Christianity and legalism. Understanding of this area is quite important. So, we are going to investigate in detail the relationship of Israel, particularly its **Law**, and the Church.

The Law of the Old Testament often was described three different ways. First, it was used to refer to the contents of the whole Old Testament. Second, it was used for the teaching and the rules of the first five Books of Moses. The Hebrew word for "Law," **Torah,** not only meant "Law," but also "teaching" in the Hebrew language. Third, Law was used for the 613 commandments of the Law of Moses as given in those first five Books. Paul the Apostle typically referred to the third use when he wrote about the Law in Romans and his other writings. When the Book of Romans is examined and the place of Law in that book is studied, a strange mutation appears. The glorious Law of the Old Testament has become a source of hypocrisy in the New and a dangerous enabler of sin. Let us begin the study of that peculiar mutation by going to the beginning and examining the Law in its formative beginnings and its original content before Paul the Apostle addressed it.

On the deeper level what was the Law? Or let me ask this a different way. If you wanted to take a group of inter-related tribes, a very large crowd of people, and make a nation out of them, what would you do? This crowd of tribal persons also was semi-pagan. Indeed, Yahweh was a semi-obscure person from their past tribal lore. Nor did they have a country, a land to call their own. You would have to give them a land, common laws, and a religion to be taken seriously. The intended result is the real goal of creating a culture. Referring to the laws, would they be just good advice or would they have teeth? Law without penalty would likely just be good advice.

If you were God, and many of those laws involved you and the worship of your person, how serious should the penalties be? For two challenges exist, to create a religion, and to create a culture.

Answering these questions probably could take many directions. But in the Old Testament, the Law was the answer to taking disparate tribes and making them a unified people with a common culture and practicing a common religion.

Yahweh's approach to creating a culture and forming a nation was illustrated at Mount Sinai. In Exodus 20 the Ten Commandments were given.

> *And all the people perceived the thunder and the lightning flashes and the sound of the trumpet and the mountain smoking; and when the people saw it, they trembled and stood at a distance. 19 Then they said to Moses, "Speak to us yourself and we will listen; but let not God speak to us, lest we die." 20 And Moses said to the people, "Do not be afraid; for God has come in order to test you, and in order that the fear of Him may remain with you, so that you may not sin." (Exodus 20:18-20 NAS)*

The method he used to create the Nation was fear and the Law.

Wanting to impress upon them the seriousness of the enterprise, he used "special effects" and a voice that made the people think doom was impending. And the Law was as fearsome as the voice, for within it was repeated threats of execution by God and a legal system often requiring death for religious and legal infractions.

The Rabbis attempt to turn the scene at Mount Sinai into a moral lesson with spiritual application, but no matter how much it was spiritualized, the scene was intended to terrify. Rabbi Soloveitchik softened Sinai in a comment on Exodus 19:13.

> *"The purpose of reading the Torah aloud in the synagogue is not solely to teach the congregation, but also to arrange an encounter with God, as experienced by our ancestors at Mount Sinai. Every act of reading from the Torah is a new giving of the Torah, a revival of the wondrous stand at the foot of the flaming mountain. The reading of the Torah is a 'staging' of the giving of the Torah and a renewal of the awesome, sublime experience." He quotes a maxim in the Talmud: "Just as at [Mount] Horeb there was dread and awe, trembling and fear, so too here [with respect to the study of Torah] it must be done with dread and awe, trembling and fear." Man strives to become God's partner in creation, but does so in profound awareness of his mortality and the fragility of his existence.*[173]

Even though the words of Exodus were quoted, one cannot help but have the impression that the force of what actually happened at Mount Sinai was softened. If Rabbi Soloveitchik was correct that the Synagogue attenders should be recapitulating the experience at the Mount, then the older ones would be having heart attacks, and the younger ones would be traumatized. The listeners would not be meditating on the wonder of the revelation. Instead they would be hiding underneath the pews! Exodus 16:19 said the people trembled with fear.[174] A major purpose of the Law was to intimidate the people. Yahweh said he would provide an unforgettable experience at the Mount that would be remembered forever (Exodus 19:9).

The Law also contained an entire detailed system on how to approach Yahweh in a clean state so that he might be addressed in the Tabernacle.[175] Two lessons were obvious, the Law was stringent, and God was unapproachable except through a system of cleansing or Atonement. Atonement in the Old Testament directly addressed the issue of human unacceptability or uncleanness and indirectly addressed the issue of human sin. As we proceed with this section, we will also see a strange and startling contrast that was a shock to the Israelite and a surprise to us: Yahweh of the Old Testament often acted very differently than the frightening impression the Law gave. In one sense, Yahweh was the greatest lawbreaker in the Old Testament! For now

---

[173] Chumash Mesoras HaRav: The Pentateuch Annotated with the Writings of Rabbi Joseph B. Soloveitchik from "the Insider's Guide to the Hebrew Bible," by David P. Goldman in The Claremont Review of Books, Vol. 19, no. 1 " . . . he was the first Orthodox Jewish presentation of the Pentateuch likely to interest a broad audience. Rabbi Joseph Soloveitchik (1903–1993) was a unique figure in the religious world."

[174] חָרַד (**Gharad** "tremble, be terrified") as a verb means "to be terrified," as an adjective "trembling," and as a feminine noun "trembling, fear, anxiety." Brown, Driver, and Briggs, A Hebrew and English Lexicon of the Old Testament (Oxford: Clarendon Press, 1906), p. 353.

[175] In Hebrews 12:18-24 the author contrasted Mount Sinai with the giving of the Law, and the future home of Christians. The contrast was immense. With Sinai the people were filled with fear. With the Heavenly Jerusalem we can be filled with joyful expectancy.

though let us examine the Law.

Judaism has found 613 laws in the Books of Moses, and that list can be confidently used to describe the Torah meaning the Law.[176] I divided the Law into two parts: 370 commands deal with what I call "worship," and the remaining commandments I call "other."

613 LAWS IN THE BOOK OF MOSES	
370 Commands On Worship	**343 Other Commands**
Those commands placed under worship dealt with:	The remaining laws we call other because they did not directly involve Yahweh and his worship but deal more so with civil affairs. They total just 243. They deal with:
1. Holy days and Festivals	1. Love and Brotherhood
2. Dietary Laws	2. The Poor and Unfortunate
3. Sacrifices for the Temple/Tabernacle	3. Treatment of Gentiles
4. Purity or being clean before God	4. Marriage and Family
5. Temple and Tabernacle	5. Sexual Relations
6. Tithes	6. Business Practices
7. Roles and Rules for Priests	7. Employees and Slaves
8. Idolatry	8. Vows and Oaths
9. Sabbath Rules	9. Judicial Matters
10. God and how to respond to him	10. Injuries and Damages
11. Signs and Symbols such as circumcision	11. Property and Land
12. Nazirite Rules	12. Criminal Laws
13. How to treat Torah	13. Punishment and Restitution
	14. Prophecy
Note how much is taken up with a proper response religiously.	15. Agriculture
	16. Clothing
	17. Leprosy
	18. The king

Many of these laws can be found in the laws and customs of other ancient Near Eastern lands. Often the laws dealing with civil affairs were fairer than what the surrounding nations had. Yet it is obvious that the preponderance of the laws dealt with religion or how to be religiously pure or clean so as to enter the presence of Yahweh in the Temple.

GREATNESS OF LAW

The Old Testament presented the Law as something marvelous and great. For example, note Deuteronomy 4:6-8.

---

[176] A good place to examine those commandments is on the website: https://www.jewfaq.org.

"So keep and do them, for that is your wisdom and your understanding in the sight of the peoples who will hear all these statutes and say, 'Surely this great nation is a wise and understanding people.' 7 "For what great nation is there that has a god so near to it as is the LORD our God whenever we call on Him? 8 "Or what great nation is there that has statutes and judgments as righteous as this whole law which I am setting before you today? (Deuteronomy 4:6-8 NAS)

Furthermore, the Law can have a beneficent effect on the Israelite.

The Law of the LORD is perfect, restoring the soul; The testimony of the LORD is sure, making wise the simple. (Psalm 19:7 NAS)

These positive effects did not exist apart from a relationship to Yahweh and a seeking of him. Yahweh had to empower Law. In that sense the Law was powerless to help without the active engagement of God. A most telling example of this was Psalm 119. In order for the Law to be effective and change an Israelite's life, Yahweh had to help. Note verses 18 and 34.

Open my eyes, that I may behold Wonderful things from Thy Law. (Psalm 119:18 NAS)

Give me understanding, that I may observe Thy Law, And keep it with all my heart. (Psalm 119:34 NAS)

Psalm 119 ended in the most remarkable way. The Psalmist asked Yahweh to seek him because he was like a sheep who wandered off and was perishing. The reason given for this seeking was that the Psalmist had not forgotten Yahweh's commandments.

I have gone astray like a lost sheep; seek Thy servant, For I do not forget Thy commandments. (Psalm 119:176 NAS)

This was in counter point to the very beginning of the Psalm where he wrote:

How blessed are those who observe his testimonies, Who seek Him with all their heart. (Psalm 119:2 NAS)

Without the seeking of Yahweh for the lost sheep, no possible seeking of Yahweh would occur. To understand the Law and legal system of the Old Testament, we will use illustrations: the first is the donut and the second is Chernobyl. The Law is a very peculiar system and the closer it is examined the more strange and also fascinating it becomes. The donut will be used to explain how the Law functioned in the Old Testament, and Chernobyl will be used to explain the relationship of the Old and the New Testament. Firstly, we will look at three distinct parts of the offering or sacrifices of the Old Testament: the five Levitical offerings, the Day of Atonement, and the sacrifice of the Red heifer.

Levitical Offerings – the Limitations

There are five categories of sacrifices described in Leviticus. A close examination may surprise those who just assumed sacrifices took care of the sins of Israel. It was far from that. The five sacrifices were divided into two sets: those that were voluntary and those that were required for wrongdoing.

The Old Testament sacrificial system is very different than the impressions that Christians sometimes have. It was quite limited in scope. In a sense, as we said, it was like a donut with a large hole in the center.

Voluntary Offerings

The nature of the sacrifices has to be examined because they can be grouped in to two kinds. We will use Rabbinic sources as explanation.

With very few exceptions (Lev. V, 1, 20-26) [Lev. 6:1-5 NASV], deliberate sins are excluded from the sphere of sacrifice: but in all cases, whether the sin be deliberate or involuntary, repentance and restitution of the wrong must precede the sacrificial act.[177]

---

[177] J. H. Hertz (Chief Rabbi), <u>Leviticus: The Pentateuch and Haftorahs</u> (London: Oxford University Press, 1932), p. 2.

In a commentary on the opening chapters of the Book of Leviticus, a distinction is made that is very important.

> *1.1-3.17: Gift offerings. Chs 1-3 [in Leviticus] are a single, uninterrupted divine speech. The theme is "gift offerings," . . . used in each ch to characterize the offering prescribed (see 1.9 n.). Gift offerings are distinct from expiatory sacrifices (treated in chs 4-5), express the worshipper's desire to present something to the LORD as a token of love and reverence. The Rabbis referred to them as "nedavah," "voluntary," since they could be made at will – in fulfillment of vows, at private visits to the sanctuary, in supplication at times of distress, in gratitude for deliverance from danger or harm, or simply in a spontaneous urge to pay homage to God.*[178]

The expiatory offerings, which were sin offerings, and the guilt offerings addressed specific wrongdoing, but the first was for acts of ignorance. "Both sacrifices applied only to sins 'through ignorance' in opposition to those done 'presumptuously' (or 'with a high hand'). **For the latter the law provided no atonement** [emphasis mine], . . ."[179]

Obligatory Offerings

This is the extent of wrongdoing requiring sacrifice; in other words, a sin offering. It dealt with mistakes and hesitations to do right, and thoughtless oaths.

> *'Now if a person sins, after he hears a public adjuration to testify, when he is a witness, whether he has seen or otherwise known, if he does not tell it, then he will bear his guilt. 2 'Or if a person touches any unclean thing, whether a carcass of an unclean beast, or the carcass of unclean cattle, or a carcass of unclean swarming things, though it is hidden from him, and he is unclean, then he will be guilty. 3 'Or if he touches human uncleanness, of whatever sort his uncleanness may be with which he becomes unclean, and it is hidden from him, and then he comes to know it, he will be guilty. 4 'Or if a person swears thoughtlessly with his lips to do evil or to do good, in whatever matter a man may speak thoughtlessly with an oath, and it is hidden from him, and then he comes to know it, he will be guilty in one of these. (Leviticus 5:1-4 NAS)*

The fifth one was a **Asham** אָשָׁם "guilt offering" dealing with deliberate wrongdoing. Of the five offerings this was the only one that addressed willful wrongdoing, but the wrong doing was very limited and sometimes almost inconsequential. Note how limited it was, and note the underlined text.

> *Then the LORD spoke to Moses, saying, 2 "When a person sins and acts unfaithfully against the LORD, and*
>
> *deceives his companion in regard to a deposit or a security entrusted to **him**, or through robbery,*
>
> *or if he has extorted [Hebrew: oppressive behavior] from his companion,*
>
> *3 or has found what was lost and lied about it and sworn falsely, so that he sins in regard to any one of the things a man may do;*
>
> *4 then it shall be, when he sins and becomes guilty, that he shall restore what he took by robbery, or what he got by extortion, or the deposit which was entrusted to him, or the lost thing which he found, 5 or anything about which he swore falsely; he shall make restitution for it in full, and add to it one-fifth more. He shall give it to the one to whom it belongs on the day he presents his guilt offering. 6 "Then he shall bring to the priest his guilt offering to the LORD, a ram without defect from the flock, according to your valuation, for a guilt offering, 7 and the priest shall make atonement for him before the LORD; and he shall be forgiven for any one of the things which he may have done to incur guilt."*
> *(Leviticus 6:1-7 NAS) [Hebrew Bible 5:20-26]*

---

[178] Baruch J. Schwartz, The Jewish Study Bible Berlin, Adele, and Brettler, Marc Zvi, Editors, (Oxford University Press, New York: 2004), p. 208.

[179] Alfred Edersheim, The Temple: Its Ministry and Services (Grand Rapids, Michigan: Wm. B. Erdmans, 1960), p. 128.

What is crucial to notice was how limited the offerings were: they only applied to lesser infractions of the Law. Two things have to be noted about the two last offerings, the sin offering and guilt offering. They were limited in the level of the infraction, and secondly, it appeared that Yahweh himself would take justice into his own hand and cut off the more serious offender from the people. The forgiveness of the serious offender obviously was in the hands of Yahweh alone. This we can see by a few examples among many.

Limitations of the Sacrificial System: Death to the Offender of Ritual

First, Yahweh cut off those who did not participate correctly in the clean/unclean, pure/impure sacrificial system.

> *And any man from the house of Israel, or from the aliens who sojourn among them, who eats any blood, I will set My face against that person who eats blood, and will cut him off from among his people.*
> *(Leviticus 17:10 NAS)*

> *"Neither shall you do any work on this same day, for it is a day of atonement, to make atonement on your behalf before the LORD your God. 29 "If there is any person who will not humble himself on this same day, he shall be cut off from his people. 30 "As for any person who does any work on this same day, that person I will destroy from among his people. (Leviticus 23:28-30 NAS)*

Then, there were more serious infractions such as infanticide in offering children to Molech.

> *'I will also set My face against that man and will cut him off from among his people, because he has given some of his offspring to Molech, so as to defile My sanctuary and to profane My holy name.*
> *(Leviticus 20:3 NAS; see also Leviticus 18:29-30; 20:5)*

Also involving oneself in the supernatural world of the spiritists and mediums led to the same result.

> *'As for the person who turns to mediums and to spiritists, to play the harlot after them, I will also set My face against that person and will cut him off from among his people. (Leviticus 20:6 NAS)*

The phrase to "cut off" was used most of the time without directly stating it was Yahweh who was the agent. Both the Old Testament and the New Testament used what is called the "divine passive." In some ways, it was like a Rabbinic device to indirectly refer to God out of reverence. The following examples most likely referred to Yahweh cutting off people and not necessarily laying down an expectation that the people of Israel should do the action. Almost all of these examples deal with ritual impurity. Here are two examples among many.

> *But the person who eats the flesh of the sacrifice of peace offerings which belong to the LORD, in his uncleanness, that person shall be cut off from his people. (Leviticus 7:20 NAS)*

> *'Seven days you shall eat unleavened bread, but on the first day you shall remove leaven from your houses; for whoever eats anything leavened from the first day until the seventh day, that person shall be cut off from Israel. (Exodus 12:15 NAS)* [Exodus 12:19, 30:33, 30:38; Leviticus 7:20-21, 25-27, 17:4,14, 19:8, 22:3; Numbers 9:13, 15:30-31, 19:13, 20]

Notice the following where being put to death and cutting off were the same thing.

> *'Therefore you are to observe the sabbath, for it is holy to you. Everyone who profanes it shall surely be **put to death**; for whoever does any work on it, that person shall be cut off from among his people.*
> *(Exodus 31:14 NAS)*

This language was also used for social relationships interestingly enough involving blood.

If there is a man who takes his sister, his father's daughter or his mother's daughter, so that he sees her nakedness and she sees his nakedness, it is a disgrace; and they shall be cut off in the sight of the sons of their people. He has uncovered his sister's nakedness; he bears his guilt. 18 'If there is a man who lies with a menstruous woman and uncovers her nakedness, he has laid bare her flow, and she has exposed the flow of her blood; thus both of them shall be cut off from among their people. (Leviticus 20:17-18 NAS)

Death to the Criminal

It is very important to realize how limited the sacrificial system was: only two types of cases demanded a sacrifice from the people: sins of omission (the discovery of inadvertent wrongdoing), and sins of commission (involving non-serious offenses). Otherwise, the person fell under the criminal law of the Torah and faced serious penalties. The principle was Lex Talionis, or the principle that retribution should be equal to the offense.

"But if there is any further injury, then you shall appoint as a penalty life for life, 24 eye for eye, tooth for tooth, hand for hand, foot for foot, 25 burn for burn, wound for wound, bruise for bruise. (Exodus 21:23-25 NAS)

The death penalty was a very normal part of the Law.

'If there is anyone who curses his father or his mother, he shall surely be put to death; he has cursed his father or his mother, his bloodguiltiness is upon him. 10 'If there is a man who commits adultery with another man's wife, one who commits adultery with his friend's wife, the adulterer and the adulteress shall surely be put to death. 11 'If there is a man who lies with his father's wife, he has uncovered his father's nakedness; both of them shall surely be put to death, their bloodguiltiness is upon them. 12 'If there is a man who lies with his daughter-in-law, both of them shall surely be put to death; they have committed incest, their bloodguiltiness is upon them. 13 'If there is a man who lies with a male as those who lie with a woman, both of them have committed a detestable act; they shall surely be put to death. Their bloodguiltiness is upon them. (Leviticus 20:9-13 NAS)

So outside of the sacrificial system was a very stringent Law that was to be enforced by Yahweh or the people. The sacrificial system again and again was connected to avoiding ritual impurity. The system of ritual was so detailed, and the people were so imperfect that the Tabernacle and the Temple could not help but become polluted. To deal with that, we come to the annual event of the Day of Atonement.

The Day of Atonement – Cleansing the Priesthood, the Temple, and the People

A common mistake when it involved the sacrificial system was believing it existed to take away sins, but the real goal was to take away the pollution and uncleanness resulting from the sins of criminal behavior and the sins of not maintaining ritual purity. The latter would almost automatically create multitudes of acts of impurity. Scholars agree that the Day of Atonement existed to deal with the impurities of the people. The Hebrew word for "atonement" is **kifper** or כִּפֶּר and academics maintain that it is derived from "rubbing clean."[180] Note in verse 16:16 the emphasis was on uncleanness at the beginning of the verse and at the end. Leviticus said that clearly.

*"And he shall make atonement for the holy place, **because of the impurities** of the sons of Israel, and because of their transgressions, in regard to all their sins; and thus he shall do for the tent of meeting which abides with them in the **midst of their impurities**. (Leviticus 16:16 NAS)*

---

[180] Robert Alter, The Hebrew Bible: A Translation with Commentary (New York: W. W. Norton, 2019), Vol. 1, p. 421. Alter quoted Jacob Milgrom who is considered one of the greatest scholars on the Book of Leviticus who described atonement as being directed at uncleanness.

"So the priest who is anointed and ordained to serve as priest in his father's place shall make atonement: he shall thus put on the linen garments, the holy garments, 33 and make atonement for the <u>holy sanctuary</u>; and he shall make atonement for <u>the tent of meeting and for the altar.</u> He shall also make atonement <u>for the priests</u> and <u>for all the people of the assembly.</u> 34 "Now you shall have this as a permanent statute, to make atonement for the sons of Israel for all their sins once every year." And just as the LORD had commanded Moses, so he did. (Leviticus 16:32-34 NAS)

The Day of Atonement and its purpose was neatly summarized by Professor Robert Alter in his commentary and translation of the Hebrew Bible. He commented on Leviticus 16:16.

> *16. **he shall atone over the sacred zone**. This clause is the conceptual heart of the entire atonement ritual. During the year, the accumulated sins, transgressions, physical pathologies, and inadvertencies of the Israelites had built up a kind of smog of pollution that threatened the sanctity of the Tent of Meeting and the Holy of Holies within it – by implication for later times, the sanctity of the Temple. This elaborate rite of purgation scrubbed everything clean of impurity, making the sacred zone cultically viable for another year. Again, evidence abounds of annual rites for cleansing the temple in Mesopotamian culture that may have served as precedent for what we have here.[181]*

In verses 18-19 we can see what atonement did: it cleansed away impurity and it made something holy, or the property of Yahweh, which meant it had to be clean.

> *"Then he shall go out to the altar that is before the LORD and **make atonement** for it, and shall take some of the blood of the bull and of the blood of the goat, and put it on the horns of the altar on all sides. 19 "And with his finger he shall sprinkle some of the blood on it seven times, and cleanse it, and from the impurities of the sons of Israel **consecrate** [Hebrew: make it holy] it. (Leviticus 16:18-19 NAS)*

This then ensured that Yahweh would remain with the people of Israel for another year. This event did not judicially take away sin. Instead it cleansed the Temple from the impurity of sin. True forgiveness was always in the hands of Yahweh and not a part of the sacrificial system.

The Red Heifer Sacrifice – the Mysterious Numbers 19:1-22

We have looked at the Levitical sacrificial system and we have examined the Day of Atonement. What remains to look at is the Sacrifice of the Red Heifer. The Red Heifer sacrifice occurred away from the Tabernacle or Temple and the High priest was there. The Heifer was slaughtered and then burned to ashes. The blood of the animal was sprinkled toward the entrance of the Tabernacle.

> *'Next Eleazar the priest shall take some of its blood with his finger, and sprinkle some of its blood toward the front of the tent of meeting seven times. (Numbers 19:4 NAS)*

Ashes were then added to water and they were used to cleanse the person who touched a corpse. A story I read years ago (and I cannot remember where) underscores the strangeness of this rite. The story was that a Rabbi died and went to Heaven and saw God seated on his throne and Yahweh was studying Numbers 19:1-22. He then asked the Rabbi what the significance of that rite was! What was so strange was that this cleansing act was apart from the physical presence of the Tabernacle, and it dealt with cleansing from death. It operated outside of the Temple system. I have mentioned the Red Heifer sacrifice because it was similar to what Christ did. Apart from being physically present at the Temple, Jesus enacted the great cleansing from the impurity and guilt of sin. He was the ultimate Red Heifer.

---

[181] Alter, <u>The Hebrew Bible</u>, Vol. 1, p. 422. We must remember that Israel was firmly set between the cultures of the Ancient Near East and Christianity. To appreciate the Old Testament one must look at the Ancient Near Eastern background to understand what the Israelite and the people around him would understand, and also understand how that formed the background of the Church. More on that later.

Therefore Jesus also, that he might sanctify the people through his own blood, suffered outside the gate. 13 Hence, let us go out to Him outside the camp, bearing his reproach. (Hebrew 13:12-13 NAS)

The Character of Yahweh

We come to a very strange thing. If we simply analyzed the Law and then looked at the portions of the Law that described how Yahweh would cut off, that is kill, those who disobeyed him, we would think Yahweh is a dangerous, punitive God. Yet if we enter the Tabernacle or the Temple and seek this God, we would experience someone profoundly different. We would experience what Moses did when he asked to see Yahweh's face. In that event he met a different kind of God who had just passed judgment on idolatrous Israelites, resulting in over 3000 deaths (Exodus 32:28). Yahweh appeared to Moses and said:

Then Yahweh passed by in front of him and proclaimed, "Yahweh, Yahweh, compassionate and gracious, slow to anger, and rich in loyal love and reliability; 7 who keeps loyal love for thousands [of generations], who continually forgives iniquity, transgression and sin; yet he will by no means leave the guilty unpunished, visiting the iniquity of fathers on the children and on the grandchildren to the third and fourth generations." (Exodus 34:6-7)

Described above was the God of the Book of Psalms who inhabited the Temple. He was a distinctly different person than the impression that would be so easily created by the Law. The Rabbis considered Exodus 34:6 the central description of God in the Old Testament.

Let us describe these characteristics.

CHARACTERISTIC	DESCRIPTION
Compassionate	This comes from the Hebrew word for "womb." When used of a male, it meant "compassion." In Psalm 103 which was a meditation on Exodus 34:6, the Psalmist described how a father has compassion on his children so Yahweh has compassion on those who respect him, who seek him (Psalm 103:13-14).
Gracious	The word first occurred in the Hebrew Bible in Exodus 22:26 describing how an Israelite should return a fellow Hebrew's cloak so that he could sleep warmly at night. If the man did not get his cloak, he could cry out to Yahweh and God would hear because he was gracious. The word might be more accurately translated as tenderly gracious.[182] This word has its most occurrences in the Psalms describing the God of the Temple (Psalm 86:15, 103:8, 111:4, 112:4, 116:5,148:5).
Slow to Anger	Literally in Hebrew "Long of anger" meaning it took a great deal of time for Yahweh to become angry. This was what angered Jonah so, because Yahweh ceased his planned destruction of Nineveh (Jonah 4:2; ironically, he quoted Exodus 34:6 in his complaint). Psalm 34:6 said Yahweh's anger was but for a moment but his pleasure forever.
Rich in Loyal Love	**Chesed** חֶסֶד "loyal love" is one of the great terms of the Old Testament. Occurring in context after context, it emphasized God's loyalty and affection for his own. In Psalm 23, the Shepherd Psalm, David said (translating literally from Hebrew), "Only goodness and loyal love pursued or persecuted me all the days of my life." Instead of using "pursued" or "persecuted" of Saul, David used it of Yahweh who only displayed kindness toward him.

---

[182] Which is how the Jerusalem Bible translated the word ". . . at least with me he will find compassion (Exodus 22:26)." For Exodus 34:6 the Jerusalem Bible translated gracious as "compassionate," and the first word compassionate as "tenderness." Found in Bible Works, 9th edition.

CHARACTERISTIC	DESCRIPTION
Reliable	This is often translated as "truth," but in Hebrew it also had the element of "reliability" attached to it. Psalm 57:10 stated that his truth or constancy was to the clouds. If it were merely "truth" as we understand the term, it would be strange, but as "constancy" it made sense. The <u>Jerusalem Bible</u>, a fine translation by Catholic scholars, translate it as "constancy." The word occurred numerous times in Psalms describing Yahweh.

These were the characteristics of the God of the Temple. Looking carefully at the Law one would be hard pressed to end up with this character description. Instead, the law would give the impression that this God was completely preoccupied with ceremonial cleanliness and the death penalty awaited those who were not. Further, the death penalty was a major part of the legal system, showing up frequently in criminal law. As an example, the scorning of parents was to be answered by the death penalty (Leviticus 20:9). Also, Yahweh frequently stated that those who displeased him would be cut off completely from the people. If we were to isolate those realities from the rest of the Old Testament, particularly from the Book of Psalms, we would have a very different picture of God than what is found in the rest of the Old and New Testament.

Grace Transcends the Criminal Law

One of the observations and conclusions of Wellhausen, the formulator of the documentary hypothesis, was that there was very little evidence in the Old Testament that Israel practiced the Law. Therefore, he concluded that the Law in its detail was created after the Captivity. I believe his conclusion is quite wrong for many reasons.[183] But he was right that Judah and Israel (the Northern Kingdom) did not really practice the Law. They rebelled against it and eventually Baal was installed in the Temple in Jerusalem. But there was also something even stranger: Yahweh did not practice the Law! A relationship of trust with him would take the Israelite out of the black and white sphere of the Law and would place him in a gracious and loyally affectionate relationship with Yahweh. The best known example was King David who arranged the killing of Uriah the Hittite and who committed adultery with the man's wife. Both should have led to his execution by the people or cutting off by Yahweh.

> Yet Yahweh contradicted his own Law so as to have mercy upon David.
> He was not enslaved by the Law: the Law was his slave. The moral Law of Israel was the creation of Yahweh. His righteousness was not bound by it.

But Yahweh of the Temple and Tabernacle had a freedom in forgiveness, a superiority to the criminal code, and his grace and love were unlimited. His resources were not only his ability to forgive, but his resources went far beyond what was within the Law. Note the various descriptions of his character and his forgiveness.

For you yourself, Oh Lord, are good, and forgiving, and rich in loyal affection to all who call upon you. (Psalm 86:5)

Note there was no reliance on the Temple system for that forgiveness. It was a sovereign right of he who gave that system in the first place. In Psalm 86:5 forgiveness was placed between his beneficiality and his loyal affection. It really was the character of God from which forgiveness and grace flowed. The sacrificial system had other purposes. As we said, King David arranged the murder of Uriah the Hittite so that he could take his wife and cover up her pregnancy. After being confronted by Nathan, David repented. He recognized no sacrifice would suffice for what he did.[184]

---

[183] Julius Wellhausen, <u>Prolegomena to the History of Israel</u> tr. J. Sutherland Black and Allan Menzies, (Edinburg: Adams & Charles Black, 1885).

[184] Uriah means "Yahweh is my Light." Uriah took a Hebrew name and left his Hittite culture and converted. Uriah was a fine man who had many characteristics David displayed in his earlier years. One could say in murdering Uriah, he murdered his younger self (2 Samuel 11:8-15).

For you are not delighting in sacrifice that I might give it. You are not pleased with burnt offering. 17 The sacrifices of God are a shattered spirit. O God, you will not despise a shattered and a crushed heart. (Psalm 51:15-17)

What we have in the Temple relationship with Yahweh was the reality of a transparent and trusting relationship between God and the Israelite. That has to be separate from the legal system because the legal system simply did not address the desperately evil situations human beings became captured within. The Law simply condemned and executed. Yet Yahweh would push his Law aside in order to show mercy and grace. Such pushing aside was not capricious, but was realistically based on a sinning Israelite's willingness to seek his face.

In Psalm 32, a reflective Psalm of David, he rejoiced over the process of confession resulting in forgiveness. Describing the joy of forgiveness at the beginning and in the middle of the Psalm, he emphasized what Yahweh did for him (verse 5). Towards the end of the Psalm, he mentioned the crucial element, faith or trust. So apart from the limited system of sacrifice was the relational reality existing between the trusting Israelite and the reliable God.

A Psalm of David. A Maskil . Oh the joys of the one whose transgression is being lifted away, the one whose sin is being <u>covered</u>! 2 Oh the joys of the man to whom Yahweh is not imputing iniquity, and in whose spirit no deceit! (Psalm 32:1-2)

My sin I made known to you, and my iniquity I did not <u>cover</u>; I said, "I will confess for myself my transgressions to Yahweh;" and you yourself took away the guilt of my sin. Selah. (Psalm 32:5) [185]

Many are the pains of the wicked; but he who trusts in the Yahweh, loyal love is surrounding him. (Psalm 32:10)

Psalm 130 was another meditation on forgiveness. In verse 3, the Psalmist said no one would be able to stand before Yahweh if God kept a record of iniquities. Then, he made the comment that Yahweh reserved the right of true forgiveness so that he would be respected or feared.

For with you forgiveness that you are respected. (Psalm 130:4)

In the arrangement of the sacrificial system, true forgiveness was left in the hands of Yahweh. A minimal amount of offenses were directly addressed through animal sacrifices, but a whole catalogue of sin, transgression, and iniquity were under the judgment and the gracious forgiveness of Yahweh.

Grace Transcends the Ceremonial Law

The majority of the Law dealt with acceptability with Yahweh and the problem of impurity or uncleanness. In the same way serious sin was under the rule of God and so was the system of ritual purity. At any time seemingly Yahweh could set aside his own laws. The opening chapters of Zechariah contain a series of visions that address the issues of the Captivity of Judah and its return to the Land. Chapter 3 dealt with the priesthood. Right before the capture of Jerusalem and the captivity to Babylon, the priesthood was involved with the worship of idols and other gods in the Temple (Ezekiel 8). Now that they were back in Judah, what would God do with this polluted and guilty priesthood? The vision of Zechariah 3 answered that question.

In the vision were three personages: Joshua the High Priest, Satan or more exactly "the Opponent or Accuser" because that was what the Hebrew word "Satan" meant, and the Messenger of Yahweh.

Then he (the Messenger who accompanied Zechariah in the visions) showed me Joshua the Great High Priest standing before the Messenger of Yahweh, and the Accuser (Satan) standing to his right accusing him (to satan him). (Zechariah 3:1)

---

[185] Note the use of the same Hebrew word for "cover" in verse 1 and verse 5. This use of repeated words is a common literary practice of Hebrew writers.

As Zechariah watched, he heard the Messenger of Yahweh rebuke the Accuser.

> *Then Yahweh said to the Accuser (Satan), "Let Yahweh rebuke you Accuser, and so let Yahweh rebuke you the one choosing Jerusalem. Is this not a burning branch being rescued from the fire?"*[186] *(Zechariah 3:2)*

Then, the condition of Joshua the Great Priest or High Priest was described. His garments were covered with filth. The Hebrew word meant typically human excrement or very disgusting vomit or both. What this said very plainly was the Accuser certainly had a case against Joshua and the priesthood: they were as guilty as sin. At the very beginning of the priesthood, Nadab and Abihu, two sons of Aaron, were killed by Yahweh because they used the wrong incense (Leviticus 10:1-2). So much more, the priesthood now led by Joshua was a complete failure and apostate. If any group transgressed all the rules of the priesthood, it was these sons of Aaron. Ordering the attendants standing by, the Messenger of Yahweh had the filthy clothing removed, and the festival priestly clothing placed on him. Then, he told Joshua that he caused his iniquity (עון **Achwon**, "outrageous guilt, punishment") to pass away. This Messenger calmly ignored the Law, neglected to mete out deserved punishment, and graciously rescued the High Priest.

> Yahweh contradicted the Law and acted in grace.
> His laws and his justice were subservient to the compassion and grace of his heart.

The criminal law as well as the ceremonial were under Yahweh's sway. Now we will turn our attention to the nations around the people of God. We will see again that those fully deserving judgment escaped the doom that Yahweh had pronounced upon them.

Grace Transcends the Sins of the Nations (Nineveh)

The pattern of Yahweh's interaction with Israel and the Gentile world was not determined by the 613 commandments of the Old Testament Torah. Instead, God's character determined his interaction. Therefore, the judgments inherent in that Law were easily pushed aside by the compassionate character of the God of Israel. A striking example was God's forgiveness of the Ninevites described in the Book of Jonah. If any nation deserved judgment, Nineveh did. The nation set the standard for viciousness for the ancient world. Yet with a minimal amount of repentance on the Ninevites' part, Yahweh repented of his decree to destroy the nation. This led Jonah the prophet to contrast the expected judgment with the character of God as described in Exodus 34:6.

> *Then he prayed to Yahweh and said, "Ah! Yahweh, was not this what I thought while I was still in my land? Therefore, in order to stop this I fled towards Tarshish, for I personally knew that you are a gracious and compassionate God, slow to anger and abundant in loyal love, and one who continually <u>feels bad and repents</u> concerning calamitous judgment. (Jonah 4:2)*

This word I translated as "feel bad and repents" was directly connected to Exodus 34:6. Even though it did not appear in Exodus 34, Jonah knew it appeared two chapters earlier so he included it in his complaint. Two chapters earlier, Yahweh repented (Exodus 32:14, same word) from destroying the entire Nation. Angered over the Golden Calf apostasy and intending the people's destruction, Yahweh changed his mind when Moses interceded and talked God out of annihilating the Nation. In the 33rd and 34th chapters, Moses requested to see Yahweh's face and in 34:6 God stated the qualities that resulted in the repentance of 32:14. So, repenting on God's part was truly the background to Exodus 34:6!

---

[186] This may seem strange but we have Yahweh referring to seemingly another Yahweh. This was similar to Exodus 3:1-7 where Moses met the Messenger of Yahweh, and he was identified as Elohim or God. I think we can safely assume this Messenger was the preincarnate Son of God. This trio in Zechariah, the Messenger, the Accuser, and Joshua may have had something in common. Satan, as far as I am concerned was the Anointed Cherub who acted as a screen between Yahweh and his angelic order in Heaven (like a High Priest, described in Ezekiel 28:11-16), Christ became a Heavenly High Priest, and Joshua was an earthly one. Ironically Satan saw Joshua reinstated to an earthly High Priesthood while he was thoroughly condemned and never will be reinstated.

The qualities "gracious and compassionate God, slow to anger and abundant in loyal love" from Exodus 34:6 show up throughout the Old Testament. Besides Jonah 4, Yahweh's repenting from his intention to judge was mentioned in Joel 2:13. Repenting showed the tension between the moral Law and God's true character. Law did not control Yahweh. Yahweh had the Law in servitude to himself. Jonah was so upset over the contradiction between the well-deserved destruction of Nineveh and God's very poor habit of repenting of his judgments that he asked Yahweh to take his life. In the face of that request, Yahweh tried to teach his prophet to be compassionate. Compassion transcended the Law; the Law did not determine Yahweh's grace and character, Yahweh's heart did.

Grace Provided Help

Not only would Yahweh treat the believing Israelite with grace and tender favor in spite of the Law, he made other resources available to the believing Israelites and also the Nation as a whole.

In the first place as we already stated, he provided spiritual help to meet the expectations of the Law. This was illustrated by Psalm 119 that repeatedly requested Yahweh's help so that the Psalmist would keep the Law. Note these requests.

> *Open my eyes, that I may behold Wonderful things from Thy Law. (Psalm 119:18 NAS)*

> *Give me understanding, that I may observe Thy Law, And keep it with all __my__ heart.*
> *(Psalm 119:34 NAS)*

Help was provided. The Nation was also given the help of the Holy Spirit. Isaiah mentioned the Spirit's presence among the people as they came out of Egypt. An equipping and helping presence was there.

> *Then his people remembered the days of old, of Moses. Where is he who brought them up out of the sea with the shepherds of his flock? Where is he who put his Holy Spirit in the midst of them,*
> *(Isaiah 63:11 NAS)*

The Help of the Spirit

Further, the Psalmist assumed the Spirit was available to help him.

> *Disciple me to do your pleasure, for you are my God; let your good Spirit lead me on into an upright land. (Psalm 143:10)*[187]

Each member of the Trinity was available to help Israel and the individual of the Nation. The Holy Spirit was available and active. The Messenger or Angel of Yahweh appeared and helped Israel. Yahweh, God of Highest heaven, was there to help. The Spirit empowered the prophets to lead, comfort, and confront the leaders and people. In Nehemiah 9:5-38, the Levites prayed to Yahweh and in the prayer they did a commentary on God's grace to the Nation. The Nation did not deserve grace because of its failures and rebellion. A careful reading would reveal that in contradiction to the Law, Yahweh and his Spirit blessed and worked with the people for their good.

> *"However, you extended yourself for them for many years, and you warned them by your Spirit through your prophets, yet they would not listen. Therefore you gave them into the hand of the peoples of the lands. (Nehemiah 9:30)*

The Help of the Prophets

The prophets were another gift of grace to Israel just as they were to the early church (Ephesians 2:19-20).

---

[187] The Old Greek (LXX) text of Psalm 143:10 has the same word **ὁδηγέω hodegao** for "lead" that the Gospel of John (16:13) had when it stated the Spirit would guide or lead into all truth.

The Old Testament prophets were to present a vision of Yahweh's truth so as to stabilize the Nation.

> *Where there is no prophetic vision, the people become out of control; happy is he who continually keeps the Law. (Proverbs 29:18)*

The Prophets were partners with Yahweh in trying to help the people.

> *"And you will say to them, 'Thus says the LORD, "If you will not listen to Me, to walk in My Law, which I have set before you, 5 to listen to the words of My servants the prophets, whom I have been sending to you again and again, but you have not listened; (Jeremiah 26:4-5 NAS)*

THE TEMPLE, THE PROPER WORSHIP AND SEEKING OF YAHWEH

The Hole Within the Law

We have seen that the sacrificial system was preoccupied with ritual cleansing and it did not at all deal with serious sins. Instead, serious sins were left in the hands of the people of Israel to enforce the Law and also Yahweh stated that he personally would deal with those who failed. The Law was like a donut.

> The Law with its 613 commands was to be obeyed, but a large part of the Old Testament was separate from it. Obviously, what was not included was the person of Yahweh, his relationship to Israel, and the nation's history.

As it was being kept holy and was cleansed year by year, the Temple was the abiding place of Yahweh. But the compassion, grace, and mercy operated within a relationship to Yahweh and was not based on the Law itself. Yahweh made the Law an operative system. It must never be forgotten that it was not the legal system that brought help and grace. Yahweh's heart was the source.

To underscore what I am saying, I will describe a Hebrew word **Darash** דָּרַשׁ, meaning "to seek." This verb meant to seek a relationship, or to seek with diligence. It emphasized seeking with care and concern.[188] The sacrificial system supplied a substructure, but the heart of the Temple was the deity within it. The power behind the Law was Yahweh. To access this gracious person, the Israelite had to seek him.

> *But you shall <u>seek</u> the Lord at the place which the LORD your God shall choose from all your tribes, to establish his name there for his dwelling, and there you shall come. (Deuteronomy 12:5 NAS)*

He was to be sought at the Temple (Psalm 9:11; 10:4; 14:2; 22:27; 24:6; 34:4, 10; 53:2; 69:32; 77:2; 78:34; 105:4; 119:2, 10). As an example, King Hezekiah was one of the great rulers of Judah. He was faithful to the Law. Note at the heart and soul of what he was doing was seeking Yahweh.

> *And thus Hezekiah did throughout all Judah; and he did what was good, right, and true before the LORD his God. 21 And every work which he began in the service of the house of God in law and in commandment, seeking [דָּרַשׁ] his God, he did with all his heart and prospered.*
> *(2 Chronicles 31:20-21 NAS)*

This was also true in the process of making the Law of Yahweh effectual in the life. A relationship with Yahweh is the critical center of the Old Testament, and the critical center of the Law.

> *How blessed are those who observe his testimonies, Who seek [דָּרַשׁ] Him with all their heart.*
> *(Psalm 119:2 NAS)*

---

[188] Brown, Driver, and Briggs, <u>Lexicon</u>, p. 205. A synonym for דָּרַשׁ **darash** "seeking" is בָּקַשׁ **bakesh**, which emphasized seeking the favor of a King or God. The first emphasized the seeking of the relationship, and the second emphasized gaining favor. One should note Judges 6:29 where they did the first **darash** in order to do the second **bakesh.**

Seeking Yahweh Was a Matter of the Heart

In the great speech of Moses to Israel in preparation of their entrance into the promised land, he reviewed the Law Yahweh had given. In the face of the daunting demands of the Law, he gave the secret of keeping this Law. The secret was to have a vital relationship to Yahweh, a heart's relationship. Deuteronomy 27-30 was the final exhortation of Moses and the elders to the people. He encouraged them by saying it was not an impossible task to keep the Law. Obedience was not to be too wonderful for them to accomplish nor was it too far away from them. It was as close as their hearts and their mouths. What was necessary was to turn or repent with all their hearts and souls.

> *when you listen to the voice of Yahweh your God to keep his commandments and his statutes which are written in this book of the Law, when you turn to Yahweh your God with all your heart and soul. 11 "For this commandment which I command you today is not too wonderful for you, nor is it far away. 12 "It is not in heaven, that you should say, 'Who will go up to heaven for us to get it for us and make us hear it that we may do it?' 13 "Nor is it beyond the sea, that you should say, 'Who will cross the sea for us to get it for us so that we hear it, that we may do it?' 14 "But the word is exceedingly close to you, in your mouth and in your heart, that you may do it. (Deuteronomy 30:10-14)*

In Romans, Paul recognized the importance of this passage in the Deuteronomic speeches. This concluding statement by Moses was taken by him and he applied it to believing the Gospel (Romans 10:6-10). He recognized that Moses was giving the heart of the matter and what mattered was the human heart. Earlier in this section we spoke of how God would work with the Law so that the believing Israelite would understand it and could practice it.

Law and Grace – Summary Principles

A strange sensation arose in the contrast between the Law of God and the character of God in the Old Testament. The sensation was dissonance and intellectual curiosity and some confusion. Naturally this leads to the question, why? Why did Yahweh encircle himself within Israel with a very limited sacrificial system that did not address high-handed sin or even significant wrong-doing? Why did Yahweh give a legal system that frequently inflicted death, and even more frequently, why did he say he would cut off those who displeased him? When the character of Yahweh and his actual actions were examined, they consistently contradicted the rigors of the Law. I believe several reasons exist.

THE RATIONALE BEHIND THE LAW	THE RATIONALE BEHIND HIS GRACIOUS ACTIONS
1. The legal system and sacrificial system would be readily understood by all the neighbors of Israel because a similarity existed between the religious systems of those nations and Israel. The emphasis on purity and being religiously clean, and the sacrifices were common. As we look at the complete Bible, the Old and New Testament, the culture of Israel was actually placed between the countries of the Ancient Near East and the future church. It was a bridge.[189]	1. In setting aside the Law and acting graciously, Yahweh was simply being true to himself. On the one hand, he had certain righteous expectations of how he should be viewed and treated, and on the other hand, his character practiced leniency and grace. As a result, the greater the guilt and the more serious the penalty, the greater the grace!
2. The sacrificial system and the ceremonial Law impressed upon the Israelite how important it was to be religiously acceptable to Yahweh. Acceptance through purity, not created by self, was actualized by the priests and animal blood. The sacrifices were not intended to pay for sin and absolutely not for serious sin. They were intended to make Israel religiously acceptable so they could enter the presence of God and find grace and help in a time of need.	2. This contradiction between the expectations of the Law and his character as displayed in the Old Testament would create a proper understanding of the Cross. It would be where righteousness and compassion would meet and be merged by Christ.

---

[189] See Eckman, Head to Heart, p. 79.

THE RATIONALE BEHIND THE LAW	THE RATIONALE BEHIND HIS GRACIOUS ACTIONS
3. The death penalty and the threats of being cut off communicated how seriously Yahweh was about his expectations. A death penalty applied for incorrectly mixing the incense for the Temple seems extreme, but it did underscore that Yahweh was real and should be taken seriously. In this way, as Paul was going to repeatedly say, Israel and we would know what sin was and what the expectations of God were.	3. The Old Testament Law and history and writings would create the proper backdrop for the coming of the Messiah and the introduction of the institution of grace, the Church. As such, the Old would create the concepts and vocabulary to explain what God was doing in the New Testament.

In the same way the religious practices of Israel and the Temple itself could be understood against the backdrop of the Ancient Near East, the Church similarly could be understood against the backdrop of Israel.

Grace is grace only when it is a life and death matter.
After we are surprised by our own impoverished character and shocked by our sinfulness,
God's compassion is recognized as grace greater than our sin.

The Greatest Shock of the Old Testament (The Transition to Romans)

As the Old Testament is examined, the dissonance we can see becomes almost a consistent pattern between the Law of God with its sacrificial system and cleanliness rules, and the compassion and grace of God. The very predictability of such dissonance was what made Jonah's complaint in Jonah 4 a summary statement of how God acted in the Old Testament. If one became truly familiar with God's Law and God's compassion, then what we will examine next should be a shock. An unfortunate thing is that consistent reading and listening to the text we will look at deadens the effect it had on the original hearers. The text is highly original and very different from the rest of the Old Testament. Now we will look at how Isaiah's Song of the Suffering Servant was in sharp contrast to the Law and a shocking contrast to the rest of the Old Testament.

Most everyone agrees Isaiah contained the greatest concentration of prophecies and many of the most sublime passages in the Old Testament. If the sacrificial system of the Hebrew is carefully understood, and the severity of the Law and of Yahweh's threats are appreciated, the Servant Song at the end of chapter 52 and all of chapter 53 has a most shocking poetic contrast to them.

The Song of Isaiah 52-53 was one of four Servant Songs in the latter part of Isaiah (Isaiah 42:1-4, 49:1-6, 50:4-7, 52:13-53:12). The fifteen verses between 52:13-53:1-12 can be divided into five three-verse sections.

1. The Servant's Exalted Reward (52:13-15)

2. The Servant's Suffering (53:1-3)

3. The Servant's Suffering for Us (53:4-6)

4. The Servant's Suffering (53:7-9)

5. The Servant's Reward (53:10-12)

It exhibits a very clear chiastic order with the key thought being placed in the center. What the Servant did, he did for us. The most obvious element was the suffering of the Servant. Such suffering was immediately connected to benefiting others. In fact, it was for others.

SERVANT'S SUFFERING
1. A man of pains and being known of sickness (53:3)[190]
2. Our sicknesses he carried and our pains he bore[191] (53:4) carried in (53:12) bore in (53:11)
3. He was being pierced because of our transgressions (53:5)
4. He was being crushed because of our iniquities (53:5) crushed by Yahweh (53:10)
5. The discipline of our well-being (Shalom) was on him (53:5)
6. And by his wound was a healing for us (53:5)
7. And Yahweh caused to meet (פגע) our iniquity upon him (53:6) meet or interceded (53:12)
8. For he was cut off from the land of the living because of the transgression of my people a stroke for them (53:8)
9. He was given a grave with evil men, and with a rich one in his deaths (53:9)
10. And Yahweh was delighted to crush him, he made (him) sick, if his soul was put as a guilt offering (53:10)
11. From the pain of his soul he shall see, he shall be satisfied (53:11)
12. And their iniquities he will bear (53:11)
13. And with the transgressors he was counted (53:12)
14. And he carried the sin of many (53:12)
15. And for the transgressors he (פגע) interceded (53:12)

This suffering for others with reference to the sinfulness of others and the removing of their sins is shocking. Such a concept was found nowhere else in the Old Testament. Animals were always involved in dealing with uncleanness and sin.

Abraham tried to sacrifice his son and was eventually stopped (Genesis 22:8-13). David wished he had died for Absalom his rebellious son; it was a useless wish (2 Samuel 18:33). Moses volunteered to die for the people and he was turned down (Exodus 32:32).[192] The Canaanites and some Israelites sacrificed their children to Molech and were condemned by Yahweh (2 Kings 23:10). In fact, Yahweh said no such thing ever entered his heart (Jeremiah 32:35). Yet in Isaiah 53, over and over again, this Servant was a substitute for the people so as to remove sin, iniquities, and transgressions. Strikingly, the reason for animal sacrifice was to remove the impurity and uncleanness of the people's sin, yet uncleanness was never mentioned in the Servant's Song.

A major motif in the song goes unnoticed by the commentators, and that is the "Motif of Sickness and Health." The motif was obscured by translators due to their difficulty in translating the word חֱלִי **ghelie** "sickness." It was the most common Hebrew word for sickness used in the Hebrew Bible. Even though the translators certainly knew the meaning of the word, they apparently did not grasp the motif being created. The King James Version has "griefs" understanding the affliction as being emotional; the LXX (Septuagint) has "sins"; the New American Standard has "griefs"; one of my favorite translations the New Jerusalem Bible has is

---

[190] "Pains" in 53:4 and 5 may be directly connected to sickness as is done in Job 33:19 where the pains appear to be those of the sick-bed. In Jeremiah 34:15 the pain is incurable because of the multitude of iniquity. Pain seems to be the lot of the sinner.

[191] These are all my original translations.

[192] Gordon P. Hugenberger, "The Servant of the Lord in the 'Servant Songs' of Isaiah," in The Lord's Anointed (Grand Rapids, Michigan: Eerdmans,1995), pp. 137-138. This contains the important point that Moses offered his life and interceded for the people, but Moses offer of dying for the people was rejected. The Servant's offer was not!

"sufferings." All the translations were struggling with interpreting a very straightforward Hebrew word because they did not grasp the motif. The motif started with the word "sickness" in 53:3, "sickness," and "sicknesses" in 53:4. The question naturally is: what kind of sickness was this? The answer was implied by the words that followed: "transgression" and "transgressors" found in verses 5, 8, and 12; "iniquity" found in verses 5, 7, and 11; "sin" just found in verse 12. The sickness may well have something to do with sin.

The center of a chiastic often would have the key idea; the central idea was in the center of this chiastic poem. With 15 verses, the center is the eighth line which is verse 53:5. The second half of the verse said, " . . . the discipline of our well-being (Shalom) was on him, by his wound was a healing for us (53:5)." The Hebrew word Shalom means a state of peace and well-being, health, and his wound brought us healing. The wound most likely referred back to the beginning of the verse that said the Servant was being pierced for our transgressions and was being crushed for our iniquities. That discipline and that wounding (the references in the second half of the verse) brought health and healing. From what? Obviously sin. Sin was being represented by sickness and lack of health. Why? The Song is about the rescuing of the people of Israel by the suffering of the Servant. The motif of sickness carried the idea that the people had a curable condition but it would take the suffering of another to alleviate the illness.

Two striking things among a number are in this Song. The first was the suffering of one human being to take away the sin of others. The suffering of one human being for others was evident, but the second reality was evident due to its absence! The second was the absence of cleansing or making acceptable. Animal sacrifices normally took care of uncleanness, resulting in purity and cleanness. Not a word is said about cleansing the people. Instead, the message was the healing of the people. What was the central goal of the substitution of the Servant for the people? The chiastic center stated it, healing. Not physical healing but spiritual healing of the illness of sin. It is striking that the central three verses go from the third person to the first person. In the other verses, the Servant was suffering for them, but in the central three verses it was for we and us. It was as if the sinners were speaking and telling the purpose.

The Song naturally divides into five three-verse sections. The third section, the middle one, introduced the Servant's suffering for the transgression and iniquities of others. After that, the next three-verse section spoke of the Servant's death. In verse 8, he was cut out of the land of the living and in verse 9, he was with the wicked and with a rich man in his grave. That section should be noticed carefully because after it, Isaiah introduced a new topic. The vocabulary of the middle three-verse section: "sickness," "carried," "bore," "crushing," "transgression," "iniquity," and "meeting," was repeated in the last section following the statements of the Servant's death. In the midst of the repeated vocabulary, seven benefits resulting from the Servant's suffering and death were stated. The difference to be noticed was that the benefits of the substitution were in the middle three verses, but the rewards of the Servant was in the last section as it utilized the same vocabulary set. These benefits were what justified the horrible treatment of the Servant from Yahweh's perspective.

Seven benefits came from the Servant's suffering. The first benefit was that he would have seed. זֶרַע **zerach** "seed" could refer to actual offspring or to a people.[193] If his soul or life was given or placed as a Guilt Offering (**Asham**[194]אָשָׁם "guilt offering"), he will see offspring or a people or both. If asked who the seed were, the only intelligent answer would be found with the people he substituted for and the people who were justified, the many.

THE SEVEN REWARDS FOR THE SERVANT AND YAHWEH WERE:
1. He will see a seed. The seed could not help but be connected to the people who have had the Servant as their substitute.
2. He will prolong his days. This was after the mention of his death and burial (53:9). Obviously this more than implied life after death.

---

[193] Brown, Driver, and Briggs, Lexicon, pp. 282-283, 4.a. and b.

[194] See page 160 to see that an Asham was the only sacrifice for deliberate wrongdoing and also required adding a fifth to the value of the reparations. So in picking Asham Isaiah emphasized the Servant died for deliberate sin, and also paid more than what the infraction actually cost. In the case of Christ the payment was infinite.

	THE SEVEN REWARDS FOR THE SERVANT AND YAHWEH WERE:
3.	The delight of Yahweh will prosper in his hand. Fascinatingly at the beginning of verse 10 it said Yahweh was delighted (a verb) to crush him, and now Yahweh's delight (same word as a noun) is prospering in his hand.
4.	The Servant will be satisfied. In how he lived and how he died, and for whom he died for, the Servant was satisfied. In an earlier Servant Song (49:4-6) the Servant complained to Yahweh that his efforts were for nothing. But in chapter 53 he was restored to life and he was satisfied.[195]
5.	The Servant will justify the many.[196] An amazing statement because those who were guilty of iniquities, transgressions, and sin through the Servant's suffering and death were justified. Immediately afterward the text said, " . . . and their iniquities he was bearing." The set of substitutionary language from before the Servant's death were now joined to the Servant's rewards. Isaiah 53:1 asked the question who believed the report concerning the Servant, and here at the end of the poem the reward of those who have believed was given – justification by faith.
6.	Yahweh will grant him a portion with the many. A portion typically referred to dividing abundance, such as a field, or silver, or inheritance, or a division among thieves, or a division of people and groups.[197] Portion was closely connected to inheritance in both the Old and New Testament. Note that Yahweh was the source of what the Servant received.
7.	The Servant will allot booty with the strong. Note that after the Servant was granted his portion, he shared it with the strong. The many and the strong were used to describe the Nation of Israel and also other strong and numerous nations. Those familiar with the language of the Old Testament would recognize Isaiah was speaking of this Seed becoming a great and strong people (Exodus 1:9; Numbers 14:12; Deuteronomy 9:14; Deuteronomy 28:5). The word booty implied that the Servant in some sense has defeated enemies and won such a victory that all that is left of the enemies was the booty laying around for the taking (Exodus 15:9 "spoil," and Isaiah 9:3 "apportion").

Who exactly were these ones who have become his seed? The answer is in the Song. They were the ones who believed the report (53:1). They were the ones who said by his wound they were healed (53:5). They were the believing and confessing remnant. The reason for calling it a remnant is based on the assumption that most rejected the Servant who saw him (53:2, 3, 4, 6, 8, 9), but the remnant looked beyond the terrible suffering of the Servant to see a Redeemer.

Transition to Paul

The Theology of Paul in Romans is quite a shock in that it is so different from the Old Testament and at times much different than the Gospels. Such shock it has in common with the Song of the Servant of Isaiah 52-53. Romans is a transition from the Jews of the Gospels to the Gentiles of the Epistles, and the Song of the Servant was a transition from the Old Testament to the New. Elements in the Song harmonize with elements in Romans and the New Testament. With the Songs of the Servant we have an anchor in the Old Testament for the substantial changes of the New. At the same, time we have insights from the Song that may explain what happened in the strange transformation of the Law of the Old Testament from a blessing to a spiritually dangerous entity.

What were the seemingly shared characteristics of the Song with the Theology of Paul? First, two things were unmentioned in Paul and the Song.

1. The first astonishing reality was that the purity and cleanliness issue was unmentioned. The majority of the Old Testament Law was ignored. In the same way, the issue of uncleanness was largely

---

[195] Eckman, Head to Heart, Session 8.

[196] 'Deutero-Isaiah and Trito-Isaiah' 342. "F. Crusemann considers that this verse offers the earliest clear expression of the concept of justification." Comment made by Hugenberger, "The Servant of the Lord," in The Lord's Anointed (Grand Rapids, Michigan: Eerdmans, 1995), p. 137, f.n. 93.

[197] Ernst Jenni and Claus Westermann, tr. Mark E. Biddle, Theological Lexicon of the Old Testament (Peabody, Massachusetts: Hendrickson, 1997), Vol. 1, p. 431.

unmentioned by Paul except when Paul addressed it as false teaching by those in error. The 370 Laws of the cleanliness and purity system were not mentioned in the Song of the Servant and they were rejected by Paul as non-applicable in the Dispensation of Grace.

2. Animal sacrifices were unmentioned, but the language of sacrifice was. The language began in 52:15 with the Servant sprinkling many nations or Gentiles. The word "to sprinkle" occurred time after time in Leviticus for sprinkling the blood of animals upon the objects of the Tabernacle. The three major words for human sin, "iniquity," "transgression," and "sin," were all connected to the Servant's suffering. These were the words repeatedly used with the five sacrifices and also the Day of Atonement. In the Song, no imaginable way exists to not connect them to sacrifice. In 53:4, 12 the Servant lifted up the sicknesses and the sin of the people. "Lift up" was a very common term for taking away sin, and was used for the Scapegoat (Leviticus 16:22; see also Leviticus 10:17). The Guilt Offering (the Asham) was directly related to the Servant's suffering (53:10).

THE RESULTS FOR GOD AND THE SERVANT COMPARED TO ROMANS[198]

1. The Father Found Great Joy In the Servant's Suffering

To make sense of this, one has to take in the totality of the Servant's Song. From God's viewpoint, he was seeing the multitudes of humanity joined to the Servant's suffering. He was not seeing the Servant alone, but he was seeing all the children of God joined to the person and the event. More than that, he was watching all of his children being rescued from transgression, iniquity, and sin. The Father's view of the Cross was definitively developed in Romans 6. Believers have been immersed with Christ into his death (Romans 6:3); we have been joined to him in his resurrection (Romans 6:4-5); indeed, our connection to Adam has been severed through him (Romans 6:6). In Isaiah 52:15 the nations were sprinkled by the Servant. A strange usage, but the verb "to sprinkle" in the Hebrew Hiphil form was used repeatedly with the cleansing of Aaron and many others from impurity (Exodus 29:21; Leviticus 4:6, 17; 5:9 and many more). One would assume the Servant was sprinkling them with his own blood. It is a metaphor of course, but it implied the world-changing nature of what the Servant did. Romans 5 stated that all men received a justification for life from what Christ had done; all the world was affected by the Cross (Romans 5:18). Not only did the Father see many joined or connected to the suffering, he also saw healing flowing from it.

> *But he was pierced through for our transgressions, he was crushed for our iniquities; The chastening for our well-being fell upon Him, And by his scourging we are healed. (Isaiah 53:5 NAS)*

2. The Servant and Yahweh Have Rescued the Children, the Seed, and the Father Found Joy in the Son's Triumph.

God will see his delight increase through the Servant (53:10). The Hebrew word translated "delight" was found in the Greek Old Testament in numerous ways: as a divine determination and a divine desire. Those Greek terms did not find their way into Romans, but certainly an aspect of "delight" did: it is called love. The verb "to delight" was found in man to woman, and man to man relationships in the Old Testament (Genesis 34:19; Deuteronomy 21:14; 25:7, 8; Ruth 3:13 Ruth and Boaz; 1 Samuel 18:22 love and delight; 1 Samuel 19:1 David and Jonathan). We can assume that delight and love were linked in the Old and New Testament: you cannot have one without the other. Paul did not mention love near the beginning of the Book but in chapters 5 and 8, God and Christ's love for their own was expressed (Romans 5:5, 8; 8:35, 37, 39). Probably the best commentary on Yahweh's delight was Romans 8:32.

> *He indeed who did not spare his own Son, but handed him over for us all, how will he not also with Him graciously give us all things?*

The intensity of the Father's love and delight has as its only adequate illustration, the giving of the Son. A

---

[198] Eckman, Head to Heart, pp.80-81.

reader might not recognize the implicit ignoring of the Son's suffering in Romans 8:32-39, but it was hardly avoidable in Isaiah 53:10 in the statement, God was delighted to crush the Servant. What the two sections have in common was the joy of the rescue and deliverance of the people. To have such joy existing within two members of the Trinity underscores how deeply we are loved.

3. The Rewards of the Servant

Now we will examine the rewards of the Servant. If the Servant made his soul an offering, he would see seed. In Romans, Paul made the Gentile and Jewish believers the true seed of Abraham and inheritors of the promise. The seed in Isaiah 53 were seemingly those who believed in the Servant (53:1). In Paul the true seed were those who believed the Gospel of the Servant (Romans 4:13, 16, 18; 9:8). Paul spoke of the offspring or children (τέκνον teknon "child," Romans 8:16, 17, 21) of God, and he equated that to the seed (Romans 9:7, 8). Paul also used the Greek term for a mature son (υἱός huios "son"). This occurred in Romans where the mature sons of God would be revealed with the coming of the Son of God (Romans 8:19), and it was also the sons who respond to the leading of the Holy Spirit and continually and loudly recognize God as their Abba Father (Romans 8:15).

4. The Servant Will Make His Days Longer

In the context of the Song it spoke of the resurrection of the Servant. This resurrection was central to Paul who said that Jesus was designated the Son of God through the resurrection from the dead (Romans 1:4).[199] Since we are the seed, this resurrection, because of our Union with Christ, was also ours (Romans 6:5). This resurrection from the dead was central to Paul's Gospel (Romans 4:24; 6:4, 9; 7:4; 8:11; 10:7-9; 14:9), and also central to the Christian life because we partake of that resurrection now. The Servant's life after death was the basis of his rewards and for Paul, Jesus' resurrection, the Ultimate Servant of God, was central to the Son's ministry and our relationship to him.

5. The Servant Will See and Be Satisfied (Isaiah 53:11)

The seeing related to his resurrection from the dead. He will see the results of his suffering. The Hebrew word for "satisfied" meant to be richly satisfied with food or richly satisfied with an abundance. The results of the Servant's sufferings were described in detail in the Book of Romans: the Son will be the first-born among many brethren (Romans 8:29).

6. The Servant Will Justify the Many

Justification was connected to faith in Isaiah 53:1 and to the Servant's suffering and resurrection. That was a unique combination of truths in the Old Testament. But in Romans, it envelops the entire theology of the Book. "To be justified" was found in Romans 2:13; 3:25, 28, 30; 4:5; 5:1, 9; 6:7; 8:30, 33. Justification was introduced with Abraham (Genesis 15:6) when righteousness was reckoned to him or counted to him. In Isaiah, the Servant "caused to justify" the many. The verb form was a Hiphil meaning "the Servant caused the justification of many." The word "many" was repeated by Paul in his central sections on justification and the work of Christ. Many died through Adam's choice and many will receive the gift of grace (Romans 5:15). Through Christ the many will be made righteous (5:19). Interestingly the phrase "the many" was used to describe the Body of Christ as the members were called to serve one another (Romans 12:5).

7. He Will Divide a Portion With the Many

Typically in the Old Testament, dividing a portion referred to the giving of an inheritance. Romans 8:17 stated that we were not only heirs but fellow-heirs with Christ. With our Union with Christ we were called not only to be joined to Christ's suffering but to inherit with him.

---

[199] Excellent comments are found in Harris, <u>Prepositions</u>, pp. 111-112.

8. He Will Divide the Booty With the Strong

The booty referred to that which belongs to the victor. Such implied that somehow a victory occurred through the suffering and death of the Servant. The most obvious victory was the one over sin, transgression and iniquity. That was the same victory that Paul celebrated. But Paul extended that beyond just the conquest of sin. In Romans 8:37 we were triumphantly victorious through the one having loved us.[200]

Did Paul consciously have Isaiah 52-53 in his mind as he wrote Romans? The answer is certainly, because Paul referenced the contents of Isaiah as he wrote.

> *Paul cites Isaiah sixteen times in Romans, and eleven of these occur in Romans 9-11 where fifteen different verses from Isaiah are used (Isa. 29:16 only counted once). Moreover, chapters 9-11 contain a total of thirty citations from the OT, so the use of Isaiah constitutes more than one-third of the total, and far outweighs the use of any other single OT book in this section of Romans (Gen--3 citations [4 vv.]; Exod--2 citations; Hos--2 citations; Joel--1 citation; Pss--3 citations [4 vv.]; Mal--1 citation [2 vv.]; Deut--3 citations [7 vv.]; 1 Kgs--2 citations [3 vv.]; 1 Sam--1 citation; Job-1 citation). Here we find a striking, concentrated use of the OT, and chiefly of Isaiah, in a critical argument concerning the Jew-Gentile-in-Christ issue.*[201]

Isaiah 53:1 was quoted by Paul in Romans 10:16. Yet the truths of Isaiah 52-53 were explicit all through Paul's Book. What makes the Servant Song so important was its reality as the major stepping stone from the Old to the New Testament. Without Isaiah, the human sacrifice of Christ would only be connected to the attempted sacrifice of Isaac by Abraham. But with Isaiah, we have the wondrous truth of the substitutionary atonement of the God-Man and its concomitant truth of justification by faith.

In Paul, we have the clear transmutation of the Law and in the Servant's Song, we have the transmutation of the Law implied. As we stated at the beginning, the Law addressed a wide range of issues. As we observe Paul's use of the Law, it is obvious that much of it was considered by him as abrogated by the ministry of the Messiah and his death, resurrection, and ascension to Heaven. The immediate impact can be seen with the nullification of the Laws involving worship and purity.

370 commands dealt with what I call "worship," and the remaining commandments I call "other."

Those commands placed under worship dealt with:

1. Holy days and Festivals
2. Dietary Laws
3. Sacrifices for the Temple/Tabernacle
4. Purity or being clean before God
5. Temple and Tabernacle
6. Tithes
7. Roles and Rules for priests
8. Idolatry
9. Sabbath Rules
10. God and how to respond to him
11. Signs and Symbols such as circumcision
12. Nazirite Rules
13. How to treat Torah

---

[200] Gustaf Aulen, <u>Christus Victor</u> (London: Spck Publishing, 1970). It is considered the great statement on the early church's belief that Christ's work on the Cross and his resurrection was a victory and the taking of booty or spoils. In his work Christ conquered sin, the devil, death, guilt, and the Law. It is well worth reading.

[201] Douglas A. Oss, "A Note on Paul's Use of Isaiah," in <u>Bulletin for Biblical Research</u> (2, 1992), p. 106.

Mastering the 7 Skills of Romans

As we look at the list, the signs and symbols disappear, including circumcision from Paul's teaching. With that, nine commands are negated. Events and days were also set aside by Paul (another 36 commands). Along with that, the laws of the Sabbath and the Jubilee years would then be ignored, another 17 laws. Paul did comment on respecting a day, and his observation showed significant indifference.

> *One man regards one day above another, another regards every day **alike**. Let each man be fully convinced in his own mind. 6 He who observes the day, observes it for the Lord, and he who eats, does so for the Lord, for he gives thanks to God; and he who eats not, for the Lord he does not eat, and gives thanks to God.*
> *(Romans 14:5-6 NAS)*

Paul's comment was antithetical to the Law: the Law did not give options. We can see these Laws were brushed aside. Dietary laws were given the same treatment. The principle was the practice of love and not the rule.

> *Therefore let us not judge one another anymore, but rather determine this-- not to put an obstacle or a stumbling block in a brother's way. 14 I know and am convinced in the Lord Jesus that nothing is unclean in itself; but to him who thinks anything to be unclean, to him it is unclean. 15 For if because of food your brother is hurt, you are no longer walking according to love. Do not destroy with your food him for whom Christ died. 16 Therefore do not let what is for you a good thing be spoken of as evil;*
> *(Romans 14:13-16 NAS)*

With Paul's approach, another 27 laws were set aside. What replaced them was love and consideration for others. This was in harmony with Christ's teaching (Mark 7:14-23; Matthew 15:8-20) where Jesus declared all foods clean, and in the Matthew passage, in addition he also negated ceremonial washings.[202] Notice that clean and unclean did not appear in the Songs of the Servant. Those rules were set aside by Christ, and Paul instead elevated the principle of consideration and love of the fellow Christian.

With the priesthood of the believers, and of more significance, the fact that believers were now the Inner Sanctuary of God because the Trinity was present within the church, the rules concerning the Jewish priesthood were all set aside. Paul stated unequivocally that believers were the Inner Sanctuary of God. He used the Greek term for the dwelling place of God (**ναός Naos** "Inner Sanctuary where God dwells" 1 Corinthians 3:16 and 6:19). The same term was used by Christ when he compared his own body to the inner sanctuary of the Temple in Jerusalem (John 2:19-21). Paul did not use that term in Romans but the critical, central reality was there.

> ### The members of the Trinity were inhabiting the members of the Body of Christ with the implied result of us becoming the Temple of God.

It must be realized that in the imagery of the Temple and the priesthood that it was more significant to be the Holy of Holies than a mere priest who could only enter the Holy of Holies once a year. Another 30 rules from the Law were set aside and obviously another 33 rules concerning serving in the Temple became irrelevant.

If the Temple in Jerusalem was now irrelevant, even more so should the sacrificial system be. The Suffering Servant Song negated animal sacrifice and the magnificent work of Christ abolished the Levitical system of sacrifice. A total of 102 rules became obsolete. Since purity and impurity were related to the Temple, the 16 laws of impurity and purity lose their meaning because of the infinite acceptance in Christ. The priesthood and Levites collected tithes and taxes, so of course that would disappear too (another 24 laws). Connected to that were the laws of the firstborn; they too were abrogated (4 laws).

The remaining laws can leave us with these possible approaches: they too can be dropped as irrelevant to Christianity, or in principle they can be connected to New Testament spirituality, or by analogy or "spiritualizing," can be connected to Christianity. Let us see what approach Paul took. In the list of commands

---

[202] This same truth was subtly communicated when the waters of ceremonial cleansing at the Wedding in Cana were changed into wine (John 2:6-10). No longer was there a need for ceremonial cleansing. Instead the real need was to rejoice in the presence of the Messiah for he was the true Bridegroom!

isolated by the Rabbis, 10 laws were directly related to God. If Yahweh was blasphemed, the death penalty was to be applied (Leviticus 24:11-16). On the one hand, the death penalty was abrogated in the life of the church.[203] On the other hand, the New Testament applied the blasphemy charge to defaming the Holy Spirit and by extension to Christ (Matthew 12:31-34). For the church, it **would not** have been a simple thing to take the Law of the Old Testament wholesale into its life. It would have been impossibly difficult. To believe that Yahweh is one and also not to have any other gods beside Yahweh was Old Testament law (Exodus 20:3; Deuteronomy 6:4). Yet these laws take on a completely new meaning as the Trinity was integrated into their understanding. In the same way the death penalty was dropped in Christianity for idolatry, and yet the refusal to be involved in idolatry or any form of superstition was kept (46 laws applied in Torah).

In the Old Testament Law, a reverence for the Torah was demanded (Deuteronomy 6:7; 13:1). Of course, this lost its efficacy with the revelations of the New Testament. With the full revelation of the Trinity, and with that, the invitation for the Christian believer to enter fully into the life of the Trinity, the importance of the Law and its connection to the cultus (the Temple worship) declined to the point of irrelevance. Another six laws became non-applicable. Instead the believer was called to be continually alive to the Father (Romans 6:11), through Union with Christ (Romans 6:1-11), as sustained by the Spirit of God (Romans 7:4-6 note the contrast with the Law).

A similar sort of challenge was involved with the rules concerning the prophets in the Law. Three laws applied to the prophets and one demanded the death for the false prophet (Deuteronomy 18:22). That of course was not applicable to the church; however the church could shun and exclude false teachers (Romans 16:17-19). The obvious problem with the Law was that with the changed conditions of the church, its application becomes largely impossible. For example, because of the passage of history and the transition to Christianity, three institutions were abrogated: four laws for lepers and leprosy, seven for the Kingship, and ten for the Nazirites. Further, the rules of warfare have no meaning for the church (another 26). Since Israel was a true nation-state, the Law contained ordinances involving agriculture and husbandry. The church is not such, so those seven laws are irrelevant. Of more consequence but of equal irrelevancy were the laws concerning judges, punishment, and restitution. The church was not intended to be a nation with a land to call its own, but instead it was to look forward eagerly to a new transformed universe and world (Romans 8:18-23). Now these laws in principle might be helpful to a national legal system, and certainly at times Old Testament laws were used to create a legal system, but that was for countries and not the church, the Body of Christ. Another 24 laws became irrelevant along with the 36 laws dealing with a court. Property and property rights were also applicable to a land, but not to a church so another 11 laws were set aside.

Rules concerning clothing would not apply. For example, the Law forbade wearing garments made of wool and linen together (Deuteronomy 22:11). The remaining two laws dealt with men and women not wearing each others' clothing (Deuteronomy 22:5). That of course would apply to the church so as to respect common decency within the culture. This leads to a segue. Often a distinction is made between the ceremonial law of the Old Testament and the moral law of the Old Testament. Using the illustration of the ordinances concerning clothing, the garment created of a mixture of wool and linen might be called ceremonial law, while not wearing the clothing of the opposite gender might be called moral law. This would be because of the need for a respect for common decency in a culture. There is a whole set of laws in the Old Testament, albeit fewer in number than the ceremonial laws, that would fall into the category of moral law. A simple example is the law against murder (Exodus 20:13). On the face of it, that law is as applicable to the church as it was to Israel.

But the fundamental difference between the two institutions was that for the church, moral principle was completely divorced from the Temple system and sacrificial system.

---

[203] Matthew 18:15-20 gave excommunication, and not death, as the greatest punishment the church could apply. It is very important to notice Christ's call for two or more others to participate be noticed because that was the Old Testament requirement for witnesses in a case involving the death penalty. In effect, what Christ also did in the Matthew 18 passage was to abrogate the death penalty for the church.

Mastering the 7 Skills of Romans

As Paul in Romans stated, the Law in its moral applications told us what is sinful (Romans 3:20; 7:7), but it lacked any capacity to help us to be moral. This was because the Yahweh of the Old Testament ceased empowering the Law. Instead, empowerment comes through participation in the life of the Trinity (Romans 8:1-4). Those moral laws are met through the power of the Holy Spirit in a living relationship to God the Father.

One of the delightful aspects of Old Testament Law was the emphasis on compassion and fairness. No penalties were prescribed for not showing compassion (unless it fell under the reparation command of the Guilt Offering (**Asham**)). These laws of compassion included the law of love for those within the Covenant of Yahweh (Leviticus 19:18). Also, taking revenge, holding a grudge, gossiping, cursing, and humiliating others was forbidden. Helping a neighbor to unload a heavy burden from a beast was commanded (Exodus 23:5; Deuteronomy 22:4). Widows and orphans were to be protected and not oppressed (Exodus 22:24; Deuteronomy 24:6, 10, 12, 17). The poor man was to be taken care of kindly (Deuteronomy 15:7, 11). These positive laws would of course be reflected in the ethics and principles of the church.

The Old Testament was similar to other Ancient Near Eastern legal systems because they addressed concrete legal and moral issues (we call that case law: law dealing with particular actions). Also the Israelite rules protected the employees, servants, and slaves. Wages, for example, should not be delayed in payment (Leviticus 19:13). Nor should slaves be abused (Leviticus 25:43; 25:53; Deuteronomy 23:17).

To divide the Law into two parts, as I do, is artificial because Jesus, Paul, and James viewed it as a complete unit.[204] This is very important. The Law was an entire system that had the gracious God Yahweh at its center. Yahweh provided help in keeping the Law and also protection and care. With the rejection of Christ, the edifice of Israel as represented in Jewish institutions in Galilee and Judah was still there, however, Yahweh, the Messenger of Yahweh, and the Holy Spirit had abandoned Israel and entered the life of the church. An individual Israelite who believed in Jesus the Messiah was of course the exception. That Israelite would be given the privilege of participating in the Trinitarian family. The edifice of Israel was still there, but it was empty of the divine presence. What must be remembered was that the edifice was the legal system of purity laws and moral laws.

In contrast to that, the Body of Christ was to function by participation in the life of the Trinity by faith. It is very similar to Habakkuk's situation when the temple was burned. The city of Jerusalem was captured, and the people were sent into captivity. The edifice of Israel did not exist. What was his answer?

> "Behold, as for the proud one [referring to the Babylonians], his soul is not right within him; But the righteous will live by his faith. (Habakkuk 2:4 NAS)

Paul took the phrase " . . . the righteous will live by his faith" as the key to participating in Trinitarian life. That which was left of Israel's edifice that was of value to the church was not the ceremonial law but instead the moral rules that informed the Christian as to what was right or wrong. That was all that was left of the legal system to be carried into the church.

Paul said it this way:

> There is therefore now no condemnation for those who are in Christ Jesus. 2 For the Law of the Spirit of life in Christ Jesus has set you free from the Law of sin and of death. 3 For what the Law could not do, weak as it was through the flesh, God did: sending his own Son in the likeness of sinful flesh and as an offering for sin, he condemned sin in the flesh, 4 in order that the requirement of the Law might be fulfilled in us, who do not walk according to the flesh, but according to the Spirit. (Romans 8:1-4 NAS)

We must remember that **νόμος Nomos** "law" the Greek word for Law was also the Greek word that was used to translate תּוֹרָה **Torah** "Law." We Westerners have the peculiar problem that when we hear the word Law we think of a legal system. In the case of Paul's use of Law, we first must think of the entire Old Testament system, then we have to make the decision: was he describing an aspect or the entirety? In verse 8:2 Paul stated that the Old Testament legal system, the Torah resulting in failure and condemnation, has been replaced by a new Torah (Law) of the Spirit of life in Christ Jesus. Then in verse 3 he explained that the

---

[204] Jesus, Matthew 5:13-22; James, James 2:10-12.

weakness of the Law was that it was dependent on human effort, the flesh. Under the reign of the Spirit, the moral requirement of the Law (not the ceremonial because that was completely replaced by the Person and work of Christ) would be met by believers who organize their life by the Spirit.

SUMMARY: WHY WAS THE LAW SO WEAK?

The four reactors at the Chernobyl Plant were created to supply massive amounts of light and electricity for Ukraine. Indeed they did so until everything went wrong. The fourth reactor had a design flaw and with human mishandling of an emergency at the plant, disaster occurred. On April 26, 1986, a sudden surge of power during a reactor systems test destroyed Unit 4 of the nuclear power station. The accident and the fire that followed released massive amounts of radioactive material into the environment. A number died and close to one-third of a million people had to move out of danger. The plant was created to provide benefit. An inherent design feature caused a failure, and then human mismanagement made it worse. Now the radiation lingers and Chernobyl is uninhabited. Ironically the empty city is described as a paradise of nature where wild animals roam freely. One can use Chernobyl as an illustration of the Old Testament Law. In the same way as Chernobyl, the Old Testament Law is lovely as long as no human beings are involved with it. Let us see why.

LAW – A GREAT GIFT

The Law was Given by God through Moses as a Gift to Israel

> *The Law of the LORD is perfect, turning the soul; the testimony of the LORD is sure, making wise the simple. 8 The precepts of the LORD are right, rejoicing the heart; the commandment of the LORD is pure, enlightening the eyes. 9 The fear of the LORD is clean, enduring forever; the judgments of the LORD are true; they are righteous altogether. 10 They are more desirable than gold, yes, than much fine gold; sweeter also than honey and the drippings of the honeycomb. 11 Moreover, by them Thy servant is warned; in keeping them there is great reward. (Psalm 19:7-11 NAS)*

This wonderful gift had the ability to profoundly bless a person. This blessing was dependent upon two realities: human cooperation with the expectations of the Law, and more importantly and secondly, the reality of Yahweh's empowerment so the Israelite could perform the Law. Like the Nuclear Reactor, the Law provided light and blessing for the people of Israel. But healthy human cooperation was needed and without it the Law became dangerous. The need for cooperation was expressed in the Blessings and Cursings of Deuteronomy.

> *"Now it shall be, if you will diligently obey the LORD your God, being careful to do all his commandments which I command you today, the LORD your God will set you high above all the nations of the earth.2 "And all these blessings shall come upon you and overtake you, if you will obey the LORD your God. (Deuteronomy 28:1-2 NAS)*

This human cooperation was dependent upon spiritual help from God. Psalm 119, the longest Psalm in the Bible, recognized the need for divine help to effectively live the Law.

> *Deal bountifully with Thy servant, That I may live and keep Thy word. 18 Open my eyes, that I may behold Wonderful things from Thy Law. (Psalm 119:17-18 NAS)*

Three things had to come together: the Law, divine enablement, and human cooperation. The key element of course is divine enablement. Without God's help, the Law is inert, and we shall soon see, even dangerous.

The Great and Dangerous Change in the Law

A grand transition occurred with the coming of the Messiah, Jesus. As Jesus was entering the city of Jerusalem and soon to be rejected by his people, he uttered these words.

Mastering the 7 Skills of Romans

"O Jerusalem, Jerusalem, who kills the prophets and stones those who are sent to her! How often I wanted to gather your children together, the way a hen gathers her chicks under her wings, and you were unwilling. 38 "Behold, your house is being left to you desolate! (Matthew 23:37-38 NAS)

The Greek word for "desolate" is **ἔρημος eramos** "a desert." The house, meaning the Temple, became not only empty of God's presence; it in fact became a desert. No spiritual provision was present, no benefit, no help. The Messiah had been rejected and killed. As the Spirit left Saul to inhabit King David, so the Holy Spirit and God abandoned Israel to inhabit and empower the life of the Church. The Law was left behind with Israel! No empowerment was present and so keeping the Law was now impossible.

What the Church, the new people of God, was given was a Father and Son relationship with God, Union with Christ, and the permanent presence and empowerment of the Holy Spirit. Law was left in the dust at the foot of the Cross. The Church was not given the Law. Paul repeatedly proclaimed such.

For sin shall not be master over you, for you are not under Law, but under grace. (Romans 6:14 NAS)

Therefore, my brethren, you also were made to die to the Law through the body of Christ, that you might be joined to another, to Him who was raised from the dead, that we might bear fruit for God. (Romans 7:4 NAS)

Magnificently, the Body of Christ now had life within the Trinity and not life within the confines of the Law. Where did that leave the Law of the Old Testament? Like Chernobyl, it went from being a source of light and help to becoming dangerous. Law became dangerously radioactive. With the withdrawal of the life of God from Israel, with the departure of Jesus the Messiah to become the Head of His Body, the Church, and without the empowerment of the Holy Spirit, the Law was left barren, powerless, and dangerous in the hands of sin.

Remember, without divine empowerment and human cooperation with that power, Law is lifeless: more than lifeless, dangerous. As a result, Paul the Apostle, the Apostle to the Gentiles, pointed out profoundly and powerfully the problem of the Law. Without divine empowerment, all the Law could do according to Paul was to frustrate and show the power of sin in people's lives.

The sting of death is sin, and the power of sin is the Law; 57 but thanks be to God, who gives us the victory through our Lord Jesus Christ. (1 Corinthians 15:56-57 NAS)

Paul said that the Law is not given power from the Holy Spirit (He is not available anymore to help the Law), but Law empowers sin! What a change. The word for "power" is **δύναμις dunamis**. We get dynamo from that Greek word. Law is now sin's dynamo! Law now frustrates people, Christian or non-Christian, and dramatically shows how powerless we are without divine help and how strong sin is. As more and more rules and laws are stuffed into the maw or mouth of sin, the stronger it gets. Paul affirmed this in Romans. In describing how we need the Holy Spirit's help, he emphasized several times that since Law has no empowerment, all it can do is stir up guilt, shame, worthlessness, and strong desires. Note carefully these following three verses from Romans 7 where Paul dedicated an entire chapter to teach non-reliance on the Law and complete reliance on the help of the Trinity.

*But sin, taking opportunity through the commandment, produced in me coveting of every kind; for apart from the Law sin is dead. 9 And I was once alive apart from the Law; but when the commandment came, sin became alive **again**, and I died; (Romans 7:8-9)*

For while we were in the flesh, the sinful passions, which were by the Law, were at work in the members of our body to bear fruit for death. (Romans 7:5 NAS)

Sin is like the "Invisible Man" in the movies. Unseen he could walk unobserved anywhere. But when the Invisible Man had a reason to be seen, he would put on clothes and wrap his face in bandages, and he would be seen and he would communicate. In the same way, Law gives visible form to invisible sin: it gives definition. Also it revealed to human beings how really weak they are and how powerful sin within is.

Life is Within the Trinity

In a different Book, Philippians, Paul stated again the futility of relying on Law. In one of most shocking and thought provoking statements, Paul first described his life as a Pharisee. He said he was blameless in his practice of the Law. He kept the rules, gave the proper sacrifices, and killed Christians (which is murder, but the Law made him legally blind).

> *as to zeal, a persecutor of the church; as to the righteousness which is in the Law, found blameless.* (Philippians 3:6)

After being confronted by Christ and believing in the Gospel, he made this shocking and astounding statement on his life as a Pharisee.

> *More than that, I count all things* [that is the things of the Law and Israel] *to be loss in view of the surpassing value of experiencing Christ Jesus my Lord, for whom I have suffered the loss of all things, and count them but dung in order that I may gain Christ,* (Philippians 3:8)

The word "dung" in Greek is **σκύβαλον skubalon**. What it meant in ancient Greek was animal dung, animal dung that was discarded and not used as manure. Modern translations often have "rubbish" which is less shocking but not as accurate. Life as a Pharisee in the Law Paul described as being as useless as animal dung soon to be thrown out. For Paul, the Law became overtly useless and dangerous. In the Old Testament it had the empowerment of God. When it was disobeyed though, as Old Testament history showed, it only brought curses, wrath, and judgment. In the New Testament, without any such empowerment, it brought guilt, shame, and humiliation upon people, and power and dynamic strength to sin. Sin could display how strong it was because it could turn the Old Testament Law of God into a cudgel or club against the heart and soul of the non-believer and the believer. But the ultimate reason is that no Law, no rules, no legal expectations could match what became available through Christ and the Holy Spirit. Paul's life goal was to participate in the life of Christ, and not build his life on the Law.

> *and may be found in Him, not having a righteousness of my own derived from the Law, but that which is through faith in Christ, the righteousness which comes from God on the basis of faith, 10 that I may know Him, and the power of his resurrection and the fellowship of his sufferings, being conformed to his death;* (Philippians 3:9-10 NAS)

At one time, Chernobyl brought light to millions in the Ukraine. The people considered it a blessing. Through poor human planning and errors, it lost its ability to bring good. Now it brought radiation, sickness, and death. So too with the Law, Law which brought light and good was changed through a monumental event. Now it spawned pain and death. The monumental event was the coming of Christ and the subsequent gift of the Holy Spirit. Such realities rendered the Law useless. Without spiritual empowerment, Law had no strength to withstand the control of sin. Tragically it actually became an enabler of sin!

What we are left with is the great need to live within the family of the Trinity. With God as our Father, with Christ as our identity before God, and the Holy Spirit as our enabler, we must focus on them and not the Law.

EII | EXCURSUS II: SOVEREIGNTY & GOD'S RIGHTEOUS & LOVING FREEDOM

Our approach to understanding the Book of Romans is a "problem-solution" analysis. Paul would broach a problem with the human condition and within the text of Romans he would give a solution. The problem would be compounded because with the problem, a judgment from God negatively affecting humanity would be present too.[205] As these problems and solutions were examined, the issue arose – are we observing a display of God's sovereignty or of his righteous and loving freedom? Our belief is that the issue and answer to sovereignty and God's righteous and loving freedom is directly connected to the "problem-solution" nature of the Book of Romans.

As we continue on in this vein, we must define what we mean by sovereignty. Sovereignty means first of all that God as Creator has the right to rule his creation and determine its fate. Based on the claim to being the Creator and the absolute power of such a person, we can say he is the unchallengeable sovereign or ruler. This seems reasonable and biblical. Sovereignty also appears to mean to some that his will determines ultimately or controls the will of creatures, angelic, and human. In other words, he knows the future of his creatures because he has absolutely determined it. Romans appears at times to be used by many to buttress this picture of God as the sovereign controller and decider of everything, particularly in chapters 9-11.

A number of portions are used to support this view of God as the sovereign decider.

1. God decided the fate of Esau and Jacob before they were born. Further, he placed his love upon Jacob, and his hatred upon Esau in a seemingly sovereign way. (9:10-14)

2. God hardened the heart of Pharaoh as he wished. (9:17)

3. God is a potter and humanity is the clay. A potter can do anything he wants with the clay. (9:21-24)

4. God seemingly elected the members of the Body of Christ according to his sovereign grace. (8:33; 11:5-7)

5. God's mind and activity are mysterious beyond our understanding and implies therefore a corresponding mysterious sovereignty that humans find impossible to understand. (11:33-36)

---

[205] **κρίμα, ατος, τό krima** Judgment usually used of a negative judgment, and also used of judicial decrees in general. Of particular significance this was used of God's judgment on Adam's Fall in Romans 5:16, . . . **τὸ μὲν γὰρ κρίμα ἐξ ἑνὸς εἰς κατάκριμα**, "On the one hand, the judgment out of the one man was unto condemnation . . .". Arndt and Gingrich, Lexicon, p. 451.

As we have supplied commentary on Romans, we have addressed four of the five issues on the list except for number four dealing with election. For the other four, we have argued that the major issue being addressed was the shocking setting-aside of Israel for the Church. The goal of Romans 9-11 was not to elevate God's sovereignty, but to justify the radical decision of God favoring the Church over the nation. What Paul was doing was defending God's righteous and loving freedom in setting aside the nation. I believe we have sufficiently answered the issues behind the four points. Now we want to turn to the issue of sovereignty and examine it.

Sovereignty in the way it seems to be normally understood is somewhat akin to determinism. Two types of determinism are normally discussed, materialistic determinism and idealistic determinism. The first revolves around the physical constraints of the universe and assumes free will is an illusion. Free will is typically presented as simply having evolutionary value, but is so constrained by physical reality that it is meaningless. The other, idealistic determinism, assumes an all-knowing mind has predetermined everything that exists and also determined or controlled what human beings do. In both cases free will is illusionary. Idealistic determinism, at the very least, needs to be reexamined because of the way the doctrine of the Trinity was presented in Romans 8. In Romans 8 we find the Trinity in dialogue.

> *And likewise also the Spirit helps us (**συναντιλαμβάνομαι sunantilambanomai** "joins in helping") with our particular weakness, we do not understand how it is necessary to pray, but the Spirit itself intercedes [for us] (**ὑπερεντυγχάνω huperentunkano** "intercede for another") with voiceless groanings. And the one continually searching the hearts understands what the perspective of the Spirit is because he intercedes (**ἐντυγχάνει entunkanei** "intercedes") on behalf of the holy ones [the saints]. (8:26-27)*

Each of the Spirit's actions on our behalf is in the present tense. The intercession is so intense it does not come out, but remains within him as voiceless groanings. God the Father is reduced to searching the perspective of the Spirit to ascertain the Spirit's request. The Son does the same and here also we find the use of the present tense.

> *who is the one condemning? Christ Jesus is the one having died, and rather the one being raised, who is also at the right hand of God, who also is presently interceding (**ἐντυγχάνει entunkanei** "intercedes") for us. (8:34)*

What is obviously not there is the impression of determinism. Instead we have the three members of the Trinity dynamically interacting for our good. Decisions are being made in time, not in eternity past. The Holy Spirit was helping with our weakness, our inability to pray correctly. Christ Jesus and his intercession was placed right before the section describing all the threats and difficulties of living on this Earth. Both were speaking to the Father for our benefit and protection (Romans 8:28). Fascinatingly enough, the emphasis on the interaction in intercession was placed right next to the description of God's purpose (8:28), his foreknowing (8:29), his predestination to being conformed to Christ (8:29-30), his calling (8:30), his justification (8:30), and his glorification (8:30). That which was from the foundation of the earth found itself culminated in the present interaction of the Trinity for our benefit. Those elements were the backdrop of the Heavenly discussion, but they apparently did not control the intercession or the resulting decisions.

The Father, Son, and Holy Spirit are interacting in intercession as free agents for our benefit. The text is rich with the implication that a "discussion of sorts" is going on within the Trinity on our behalf. What it implies of course is the opposite of strict determinism: it implies free present-time interaction with human life and activity.

To be made in the Image of God means to be granted the human freedom of choice. Why do we have it? It is because of the relational freedom of the Trinity as they fellowship in other-centered love. Since we were made in the Image of God, the capacity for relational freedom was granted to us, and then lost by us, and will be restored to us. With the Fall, our freedom was mutated into the slavery to sin. With faith in Christ, true freedom is restored and our slavery is ended as we learn to participate in the life of the Trinity (John 8:32, 36). Such participation is based on an invitation to share in the love, other-centeredness, righteousness, and freedom granted by Christ.

Philosophically, determinism does not take into account three interactive persons. Normally, determinism if it involved a mind, is presented as singular in nature. A singular mind completely controls a singular result. A one-to-one relationship exists between what is in the mind which then is determined by the will so that it is manifested fully in time. That is not in Romans 8. What we see in Romans 8 is a Heavenly conversation and not blatant determinism. One might argue that it matters not if the decision is made by one or three. Whatever the three determine is sovereign. Two problems exist with that. First, the intercession is obviously in the present; it was not determined in the past. What we have is the appearance of a lively, divine dialogue, and not a singular monologue. Second, the contents of Romans 11 in the illustration of the Olive Tree militate also against determinism.

The Implications of the Olive Tree Illustration

What was interesting about Romans 9-11 was that it was an argument for the righteous and loving freedom of God, and not seemingly an argument for determinism. Further, Romans 9-11 significantly implied that we have true freedom also, the freedom to obey or disobey. Such obedience or disobedience will determine the reaction of God. The Olive Tree illustration and the mystery of the fullness of Israel being placed back in the Olive Tree needs to be examined. In the illustration, the wild Olive branch of the Gentiles was placed in the native stock of the Olive Tree. The Olive Tree represented a place of blessing stretching back to the Patriarchs. The Gentile Christians needed to be careful so that what happened to Israel, being taken out, did not occur to them.

> *It is quite true they were broken off due to unbelief, and you are standing by faith. Do not have a proud perspective, but fear. For if it is true God did not spare the natural branches, neither shall he spare you. (Romans 11:20-21)*

Certainly Paul assumed some relationship between the humble obedience of free choice and the timing of the salvation and restoration of Israel. This was much more dynamic than what a truly deterministic theology could accept. To accept determinism, one must assume that the Trinity itself was then controlled by an overarching determinism, and not a plan accepted by all three of them that granted true freedom to creatures in present time.

Finally in this short reflection on the freedom of the Trinity and the freedom of creatures, a philosophic observation should be made. Classical philosophy, particularly Aristotelianism, is based on binary thought. A cannot equal B. If determinism exists, then freedom by necessity cannot exist. If freedom exists, then determinism cannot. We may understand that logic, but I do not think that ultimately this is a logical problem. It is more of a problem of process or mechanism. The reality of the interaction among humanity and the Spirit, the Son, or the Father is not understood or may not ever be understood by us. It is like what Jesus said to Nicodemus.

> *The Spirit (wind) blows where he desires and the sound of him you are hearing, but you never know where he is coming and where he is going. So it is with everyone being begotten out of the Spirit. (John 3:8)*

Not only in relationship to the wind and the Spirit, but endlessly in life we see the effects but we do not understand the causation. That appears to be what Jesus said to Nicodemus. The interaction between the Spirit and a person we do not understand, but we certainly see the effects. We certainly also see the effects within the Bible of the interaction between God's choices and human choices, but as to how they ultimately relate, we cannot explain. But several things appear obvious.

First, Paul always assumed an ethical basis to any of God's activity; his actions are motivated by righteousness and love. That was why Paul wrote:

> *Absolutely not! But let God be true and every person a liar, even as it has been written, in order that you should be justified in your words and you shall be victorious in your judging. And if our unrighteousness recommends the righteousness of God, what shall we say? Is God unrighteous bringing the wrath (I am speaking the way a man speaks)? Absolutely not! Since how shall God judge the world? (Romans 3:4-6)*

God's relationship to the world was not based on sovereignty but ethics. An ethic so driven by love that sending his Son to the Cross did not seem unreasonable to him. In fact, he delighted in it (Isaiah 53:10). Second, Paul assumed that God can creatively, with love and righteousness, radically respond to what humanity does. He can be unpredictable. As a sovereign he can do what he wants, but as an ethical being his power is constrained by his nature and his grant of freedom to humanity. Freedom exists because we are made in the Image and likeness of God. Third, human choice and freedom does affect what deity did, and as our freedom to love and relate is restored, so the experience of God's blessing grows and so does our sense of participating in the Father's plan.

Now let us examine God's choice of the elect before the foundation of the world. Binary logic leaves us with a choice, is humanity's response determined by God, or is God merely responding to seeing humanity believing the Gospel? Fortunately, other numerical systems exist! Our numerical system is based on ten digits and not two. We can have such systems based on three factors or thousands. A binary system is based on zero and one. A trinary system is based on minus one, zero, and one. In a sense, everything is a trinary system. The relationships between the Three determine reality. The love and freedom of the Three become the basis of the Image and likeness of humanity. We were given true freedom and relationship in the Garden, and now through Christ, freedom and relationship were restored. Something much deeper than determinism is going on. What that is, we presently do not know. We may never know. But what we do know is that God sent the Son of God to do the dying on our behalf and the dead and resurrected God-Man is a sufficient answer for any question.

Does determinism exist in Romans 9-11? No, but something deeper and more mysterious exists. What exists is the interaction of the Three with humans made in the Image of the Father and the Son. At present, the boundaries of that interaction are impossible to describe.

EIII | EXCURSUS III: SEVEN DISPENSATIONS IN THE BOOK OF ROMANS

Mastering the 7 Skills of Romans presupposes a Trinitarian, a Personalist,[206] and Dispensational Theology.[207] These three elements are interwoven in the text of the book. Probably the least obvious to spot are the dispensational elements. Yet it is striking how well Romans fits the dispensational outline of biblical history and prophecy.

1. Dispensation of Innocence - Adam and Eve (Genesis 1-3)

This of course was implied by Romans 5 as it described the Fall of the first man. This first dispensation ended in human failure, and the judgment was the profound change in human nature and the expulsion from the Garden (Genesis 3; Romans 5:15-19). Humanity joined Satan's rebellion and began its presence on Earth in failure.

2. Dispensation of the Spirit (Genesis 4-11)

Typically this dispensation has been named "Conscience."[208] The time period is probably misnamed because within the contents of Genesis 4-11, God was working through his appearances, and further, the Holy Spirit was presented in the context of Genesis 6 as working with all of humanity. I believe that Romans 1 described the historic event of humanity rejecting the personal presence of God as he appeared to individuals in Genesis 4-11 and humanity's embracing idolatry. Further, the ministry of the Holy Spirit was rejected as "he acted as a judge" with humanity (Genesis 6:3). לֹא־יָדוֹן רוּחִי בָאָדָם לְעֹלָם **lo-yadon ruachy badam lolam** "my Spirit shall not act as a judge forever . . . his days shall be a hundred and twenty years."

---

[206] A Personalist Philosophy and Theology assumes that ultimate reality is not a monad, a singular (an individual in isolation), but instead is relational. Ultimate reality is a relationship. In the case of Christianity, it is the relationships among the Father, Son, and the Holy Spirit. The relationships among the Three are then expressed in the creation of the relational realities of spirits and humanity. Seemingly, radical sovereignty requires a monad or singular to be perfectly expressed while Personalism requires Persons in relationships to be expressed. Personalism fits Trinitarian Theology and reality far better.

[207] Over the years I have studied in Oxford University and been the recipient of a Masters of Divinity, a Masters of Theology, and a Doctorate in Philosophy. My conclusion is that Dispensationalism addresses the challenges of much of liberal theology and reformed theology in surprisingly creative ways. From the strange twists and turns of the documentary hypothesis to the even stranger logic of classic reformed theology, dispensationalism has something profoundly thoughtful to say.

[208] Alfred Thompson Eade, The Expanded Panorama Bible Study Course (Westwood, New Jersey: Fleming H. Revell, 1961), pp. 54-69.

דין **din** is the Hebrew word for "acting as a judge." דון **don** is a Hapax Legomena (only occurs once in Old Testament Hebrew), so the better possibility is "to act as a judge."[209] I do not believe that this may be referring to an internal or transformational ministry, but more of a withholding ministry that is akin to 2 Thessalonians 2:7

> *The mystery of iniquity is already working, until the one who is continually holding back should be taken out of the midst. (2 Thessalonians 2:7)*

The events of Genesis 4-11 involve all of humanity and therefore, it described humanity's refusal to know God and to respond correctly to him. Yahweh appeared personally (Genesis 4:2-13; 5:24; 6:13; 9:8) and yet the people pursued idolatry and polytheism.

The end of the dispensation was the judgment at the Tower of Babel on the human effort to establish a name or an identity apart from God (Genesis 11:4). Specifically, the judgment was the multiplication of languages, and the scattering of humanity across the Earth.

3. Dispensation of Promise (Genesis 12-50)

From working with all of humanity as illustrated by the Flood and Babel story, Yahweh changed his strategy and selected one man, Abram, and his family to be the recipient of promises that eventually would change the course of human history (Romans 4). Apart from the Law, Abraham was justified and his family was granted grace apart from their character. He was justified as the father of faith for both the Gentiles and Israel. The judgment on the increasingly dysfunctional family of Jacob was the expulsion from the land of promise, and the sojourn in Egypt.

4. Dispensation of Law (Old Testament)

Having been given the Law at Mount Sinai, Israel proceeded to break it, ignore it, turn to idolatry, and finally according to Paul, attempt their own justification by keeping its commands (Romans 2-3, 7, 9-11). The judgment was the desertion of God's House where it was left a spiritual desert (Matthew 23:38). The Greek word for desolate is ἔρημος **eramos** "a desert." The House, meaning the Temple, became not only empty of God's presence; but in fact, it also became a desert. No spiritual provision was present, no benefit, no help. The Messiah has been rejected and killed. Yet at the center of this seven-fold scheme was the death of the God-Man for human sin.

5. Dispensation of Grace (John-Jude)

A distinct time period appeared to be allotted by Paul for the time period of the Dispensation of Grace. It will last until the fullness of the Gentiles enter into the Body of Christ (Romans 11:25). Then, the dispensation of grace ends with the Rapture and the judgment of the believers' works (1 Corinthians 3:11-15). Those works will reveal whether the dispensation has been a failure or not, and the timing of Israel being placed back into the Olive Tree will also indicate the success or failure of the Church (Romans 11:22, 25).

6. Dispensation of Tribulation (Revelation 4-19)

The references of Paul to "the wrath" such as in Romans 5:9; 12:19 certainly referred to the devastating display of God's anger. Typically the Greek language has the article "the" when it referred to this divine future world-wide intervention. Otherwise it was without the article "the" such as in the references to where in God's anger, he handed humanity over to its desires, emotions, and limited thinking (Romans 1:24, 26, 28). World wide judgment will fall because of humanity's choice of the Wild Animal, the Beast, instead of the slain lamb of God.

---

[209] Brown, Driver, and Briggs, Lexicon, p. 189. It suggested that the Hapax is dubious and gave דין **din** "judge" as the alternative. The implication was that the Holy Spirit was acting like an Old Testament judge relative to humanity.

7. Dispensation of the Millennium (Revelation 20:4-6)

With the appearance of the rescuer or Redeemer in Romans 11:25-27 **ὁ ῥυόμενος ha ruomenos** "the rescuing one" it seems that the Kingdom promises to Abraham and Israel will be kept. Revelation 20:7-10 described the failure of humanity at end of the Millennium when Satan was released from the Abyss, and he led the nations into a rebellion against the Holy City. Following that is the ultimate judgment of the Great White Throne wherein he who has died for all of humanity judged the unsaved dead (Revelation 20:11-15). The temptation in the Garden and the temptation at the end of the Millennium creates an inclusio or "book ends" for the story of humanity. Whether humanity had paradisiacal conditions in the Garden or the perfect conditions of Christ's reign over the earth, humanity fails.

ETERNAL STATE

It is interesting that neither Hell (Hades) nor the Lake of Fire or Heaven are explicitly mentioned in Romans. This may underscore what Paul was doing in the writing of Romans. He wanted the Church to be the answer to the Cultural Collapse of chapters 1-3. He wanted to create an alternative culture based on the Trinitarian Family. Chapters 1-3 and 12-16 also create an inclusio or "book ends" for Romans.

The eternal state is the ultimate answer to the human failure of the Seven Dispensations. Only the work of Christ and the reign of grace is sufficient to rescue failed humanity. Those Dispensations are the ultimate failing display of human character and the glorious display of God's character to the watching Universe of spirit beings. As God said to Satan, "Have you placed your heart upon my servant Job?"[210] In the same way, God apparently has proposed the same question to the watching universe, "Have you placed your heart upon God's ways with humanity, and the wondrous grace of the redemption wrought by the Son of God?" One of the great purposes of humanity and the Church is to be an object lesson to the Heavens.

and to bring to light what is the administration of the mystery which for ages has been hidden in God, who created all things; 10 in order that the manifold wisdom of God might now be made known through the church to the rulers and the authorities in the heavenly places. (Ephesians 3:9-10 NAS)[211]

---

[210] Job 2:3 My translation from Hebrew. What often is omitted in English is the direct translation of the Hebrew word לֵב "heart." God was giving Satan an example in Job to place his heart upon.

[211] **οἰκονομία, ας, ἡ** management of a household, administration, office Lk 16:2–4; Col 1:25; *commission* 1 Cor 9:17; stewardship Eph 3:2. Plan of salvation 1:10; 3:9. Training in the way of salvation 1 Ti 1:4, * [economy] [pg 137] Gingrich, Lexicon, Bible Works 10. Note that Dispensation essentially means a "stewardship."

BECOME A BWGI CERTIFIED TRAINER

Do you want to be **trained** and **equipped** to teach life-changing, powerful, and high-impact material by Dr. David Eckman? Or do you want to be trained on how to facilitate a group? Or do you want to lead a small group through a book by Dr. Eckman? If so, visit our website to be trained today!

TAKE A CLOSER LOOK AT THE 5-COURSE DISCIPLESHIP CONCENTRATION:

BC101- Foundations of the Spiritual Life is a discipleship process that leads the student to live within the life of the Trinity so as to experience God as an Abba Father, Jesus as our Identity, and the Holy Spirit as our Helper. The expected outcomes are deeply experiential and relational. These outcomes are such to mark the participant the rest of her or his life.

BC102- Theology of Romans course was designed to give Christians confidence to live their lives out of Trinitarian Theology. Romans is the theological backbone of Head to Heart.

BC103- Head-to-Heart: Experiencing the Father's Affection. The Head-to-Heart: Experiencing the Father's Affectionate Acceptance small group experience may well be the most effective and most thoughtful group experience presently being practiced in the United States. It is truly transformational with long term positive results in the lives of the participants. The expected outcomes are various, but the most common one is a deepening experience of God the Father's love.

BC104- Theology of Emotions surveys the Old and New Testament's description of the source, function, and management of emotions. The purpose is to create a true biblical psychology for the benefit of pastoral counselors, Christian counselors, disciplers, and Bible teachers. As part of this, we will examine the place of suffering and how Scripture powerfully addresses the pain of life.

BC105- Skills for Living is a secular version of a Christian mental health program that follows the pattern of Head to Heart. It was designed to train counselors in the 60 mental health centers of the universities of Beijing. Skills For Living serves as an introduction to mental health principles, and second, to create a bridge for sharing the Gospel. In this course, parallel Christian books will be used to present the Christian context of the contents.

For more resources scan the QR Code
or visit us at

WHATGODINTENDED.ORG

WHAT'S NEXT?

We hope that you have enjoyed the <u>Mastering the 7 Skills of Romans</u> book. We invite you to read through one of Dr. Eckman's other books on a variety of topics.

BECOMING WHO GOD INTENDED

"I strongly urge you to get Becoming Who God Intended and put it to work in your life."
—Josh McDowell

How Do You See Yourself? How Do You See God?

Whether you realize it or not, your imagination is filled with pictures of reality. The Bible indicates these pictures reveal your true "heart beliefs"—the beliefs that actually shape your everyday feelings and reactions to family, friends, and others, to life's circumstances, and to God. Maybe You're Getting the Wrong Picture. Perhaps you're. . .

· struggling with anxiety, guilt, or habitual sins
· frustrated because your experience doesn't seem to match what the Bible talks about
· wondering if your emotions and feelings fit into the Christian life at all

If so, you may be working from the wrong set of pictures. Becoming Who God Intended shows you how you can allow God's Spirit to build new, biblical pictures in your heart and imagination.

God Has a Great New Picture for You! Getting the true pictures in your mind—grasping reality from God's perspective—will help bring your thoughts and emotions under control. It will lead you to a life filled with the positive emotions of love, joy, and peace. And you will finally be able to live out the richness of true Christianity . . . the life God the Father has always intended for you.

KNOWING THE HEART OF THE FATHER

You're stuffed full of Christian information. But where is God in all of it?

Maybe You're Thirsting for a felt experience of the Bible's truth. Perhaps Christianity seems irrelevant to where your heart is really at. What if you could . . .

1. have an all-encompassing sense that you have a loving heavenly Dad
2. have a sense of being enjoyed and delighted in by Him?
3. recognize that He sees you differently than you see yourself?
4. realize that who you are is more important to Him than what you do?

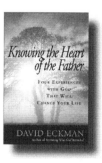

These four experiences are integral to Biblical Christianity. Discover what often stands in the way of them, and how you can begin to know the heart of the Father in a deeper way as He works these realities into your life.

OTHER BOOKS BY DR. DAVID ECKMAN

Becoming What God Intended
A Study for Spiritual Life Formation

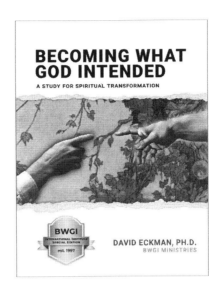

This book is designed to help the Christian become what God always intended. Working through this book will result in a deeply happy and loving relationship with God the Father through the work of Christ. You will discover how the disarming acceptance of God creates character within the Christian's heart, and how the character is sustained by deep gratitude. Through those characteristics we have the basis to become WHAT GOD INTENDED.

There is a Small Group Facilitator Guide at the end of the Becoming What God Intended workbook. It contains twelve small group sessions that address the chapters of the workbook. Further, it has other resources that should make the small group experience a rich feast.

Tens of thousands of people around the globe have been impacted by this workbook. They have also listened and watched Dr. Eckman speak on each chapter. The CD, DVD's and On-line videos have been used together with the workbook for even richer group study experience.

www.WhatGodIntended.org

HEAD TO HEART
SMALL GROUP DISCIPLESHIP PROGRAM

Head to Heart is unlike any other small group material or discipleship program in a number of special ways. This life-changing journey is not simply about learning the truth of the Bible but integrating the truth into the heart. You will discover a new way of seeing that will change everything because, "how you see, is how you live."™

The Head to Heart program has three key elements:

1. Focused Biblical teaching

2. Identification of your False Pictures & Beliefs

3. A design of teaching and small groups that help you to integrate God's truth

Experience the life of the Trinity:

- Discover the Father heart of God

- Experience the empowerment of the Holy Spirit

- Live out your Union with Christ

Many have gone through the exciting transition of knowing something of God to experiencing what God intended. We are delighted to welcome and invite you to the Head to Heart journey!

If you have any questions or would like to talk to someone about next steps, email us at Head2Heart@bwgi.org or contact us at 925.846.6264.

WWW.HEAD2HEART.ORG